9051560

DATE DUE

JUN 2 2 1994

A History of Jewellery
1100—1870

PLATE I
Gold brooch, enamelled and set with a ruby, diamond and pearls.
Middle of the fifteenth century

JOAN EVANS

A History of
JEWELLERY
1100—1870

DOVER PUBLICATIONS, INC.
New York

IMPORTANT NOTE: The illustrations in the present edition have been reduced by 5–15 percent, but the text has not been modified. This should be taken into account wherever size is indicated or referred to in a caption, list of illustrations, etc.

Published in Canada by General Publishing Company, Ltd., 30 Lesmill Road, Don Mills, Toronto, Ontario.
Published in the United Kingdom by Constable and Company, Ltd., 10 Orange Street, London WC2H 7EG.

This Dover edition, first published in 1989, is an unabridged republication of the work published in 1970 by Faber & Faber, London, England, and Boston Book and Art, Boston, Mass., as the second revised edition of the work originally published by Faber & Faber in 1953. In the interest of saving space, some of the illustrations have been moved from their original locations. The Roman-numbered plates were in color in the 1970 edition.

Manufactured in the United States of America
Dover Publications, Inc., 31 East 2nd Street, Mineola, N.Y. 11501

Library of Congress Cataloging-in-Publication Data

Evans, Joan, 1893–
    A history of jewellery, 1100–1870 / Joan Evans.
       p.   cm.
    "Unabridged republication of the work published in 1970 by Faber & Faber, London, England and Boston Book and Art Shop, Boston, Mass."
    Bibliography: p.
    Includes index.
    ISBN 0-486-26122-0
    1. Jewelry—History.   I. Title.
NK7306.E8   1989
739.27'09—dc20

89-11885
CIP

To

GEORGE RAVENSWORTH HUGHES

Clerk to the Worshipful Company of Goldsmiths

Preface

Our knowledge of jewels is primarily derived from jewels themselves; nothing can take the place of the experience derived not only from observing them but also from handling them. For this reason the concentration of collections of antique jewels in Museums increases our knowledge of them less than it might, for once they are in a Museum show-case they can no longer be handled except by a privileged few. Similarly their very beauty is diminished, for jewels are designed to be worn, and only in wear can their essential fitness be demonstrated and their essential beauties be displayed.

The jewels of the seven and a half centuries included in this book are nearly all known to us not, as are those of earlier periods, by their having been buried with their possessors, but by their survival as personal possessions that pure chance, family sentiment or a recognition of their beauty have caused to be preserved. Of these most of the important examples up to about 1700 are now in Museums or in private collections of repute. Of those after that date many are still in the jewel-boxes of royal and private families and are not easy to discover: but they are still alive in so far as their owners wear them on suitable occasions.

A second source of our knowledge of jewels is the evidence of portraits. It begins to be valid in the second half of the fifteenth century, for jewels are rarely shown in any great detail on mediaeval funereal effigies and monumental brasses,[1] though they are depicted with infinite care alike by the painters of the late Middle Ages and the Early Renaissance, and indeed by portrait painters of every kind from about 1470 until about 1910.

Thirdly, much may be learned from the study of the surviving designs for jewels. Few of these survive from the Middle Ages but those that are painted in the margins of the fifteenth-century Books of Hours, but a significant number of drawings of the sixteenth century and a very large number of engraved designs dating from the end of the fifteenth century to the end of the nineteenth are known. Only recently have they been supplanted in their diffusive influence by the half-tone plates published at Paris[2] that now circulate among the members of the Trade.

[1] It is said, however, that a goldsmith was employed for a month on the collar of the effigy of Ferdinand of Portugal at Innsbruck. V. Oberhammer, *Die Bronzestandbilden des M. Grabmal zu Innsbruck*, 1935, p. 152.
[2] Notably *L'Officiel de la Bijouterie*.

PREFACE

A source of information, no less exact but a good deal less vivid, is documentary: the bills for jewels, inventories of them,[1] advertisements of them and literary references to them, that in one form or another cover the whole of our period.

Political considerations have almost automatically set the geographical limits of this book. Except for notes made and photographs secured long before the War I have been unable to include anything from behind the Iron Curtain. On this side of it I have received endless kindness, both from officials and from private collectors. In France I would wish particularly to thank Mademoiselle l'Attachée Commerciale at the Archives Photographiques, Monsieur Jean Prinet of the Bibliothèque Nationale, Monsieur Pierre Verlet of the Musée du Louvre and the Musée de Cluny, the director of the Musée de Versailles, the Keeper of the Musée Condé at Chantilly, and the Keeper of the Musée des Arts Décoratifs at Paris, and my friend Mlle. Marguérite Prinet; in Italy Mr. Jocelyn Ward Perkins, Director of the British School at Rome; the Keeper of the Museo Civico of Turin; the Director of the Uffizi Gallery at Florence; in Belgium the Secretary of the A.C.L., Brussels; in Switzerland Monsieur W. W. Guyan, Directeur du Musée de Tous-les-Saints, at Schaffhausen; in Scandinavia the Director of the National Historical Museum, Stockholm; Dr. Victor Hermansen of the National Museum of Copenhagen, and the Very Revd. the Dean of Upsala; in Germany Mr. Christopher Norris, formerly of the Monuments and Fine Arts Section of the Control Commission; the Marburg Institute; Count Wolff Metternich; Dom Vikar Dr. Erich Stephany of Aachen; Dr. Delbrueck of Bonn, the Director of the Hessisches Landesmuseum of Darmstadt and the authorities of the Landesbildstelle Sachsen; in Austria Dr. Buschbeck, Director of the Kunsthistorisches Museum, Vienna; and in the United States the Director of the Metropolitan Museum of New York, and the Director of the Cleveland Museum of Art, Cleveland, Ohio.

In my own country, certain of the pieces here illustrated by gracious permission are drawn from the royal collection at Windsor Castle. A detail from the Van der Goes altarpiece at Holyrood House is also reproduced by gracious permission. I have been generously helped by Mr. R. L. S. Bruce Mitford of the British Museum; Mr. John Summerson of Sir John Soane's Museum; Sir Owen Morshead, the Queen's Librarian; Sir James Mann, Keeper of the Wallace Collection and his assistants Mr. Francis Watson and Mr. Robert Cecil; Dr. Margaret Whinney and Professor Wilde of the Courtauld Institute; Dr. Charles Parker and Mr. John Woodward of the Ashmolean Museum; Dr. Carl Winter and Mr. Goodison of the Fitzwilliam Museum; Mr. Robert Stevenson, Keeper of the National Museum of Scotland; the Keeper of the Museum of the Society of Antiquaries of Newcastle-upon-Tyne; the Duke of Portland; Mr. H. Clifford Smith;

[1] An invaluable bibliography is the *Bibliographie des Inventaires imprimés* published by F. de Mély and E. Bishop in 1892.

PREFACE

Mrs. Talbot Rice; Miss Olive Lloyd Baker; Sir Malcolm MacGregor of MacGregor; the Warden of New College, Oxford; the Keeper of the National Gallery; the Director of the Victoria and Albert Museum; Mr. Lawrence Tanner, Keeper of the Monuments at Westminster Abbey; Mr. George Zarnecki of the Conway Library, Courtauld Institute of Art; the Librarian, Guildhall Library; Dr. L. D. Ettlinger of the Warburg Institute; Lady Lucas; the Revd. Father Chadwick, S. J., of Stonyhurst College; the Librarian of the Record Office; the Keeper of the Walker Art Gallery, Liverpool; Mr. Norton of Messrs. S. J. Phillips and Mr. Nyburg of the Antique Art Galleries.

My old friend Mr. C. C. Oman has not only allowed me to have many things specially photographed, but has also very kindly read the manuscript of this book and given me the benefit of his learning, criticism and advice.

WOTTON-UNDER-EDGE, 1951   J. E.

Preface to Second Edition

A number of minor alterations and corrections have been made in this new edition. The most important of these will be found on p. 95, where Dr. Steingräber's recent convincing identification as German of a group of enamels previously described as Spanish has been accepted and the text modified accordingly. The original list of illustrations has been brought up to date by indicating changes of ownership which have occurred since the book was first published. In one or two cases, where pieces illustrated were in 1953 in the hands of the trade, it has not proved possible to identify present owners, and I would ask them to accept my apologies if their names are omitted. The bibliography has been much enlarged and brought up to date as far as August 1968: about a hundred and fifty new titles have been added.

A word about the new illustrations. Two new colour plates have been added as nos. II and III;[*] and sixteen pages of new black and white plates have been incorporated among the rest in chronological sequence (plates 6, 7, 26, 27, 53, 57, 76, 78, 101, 102, 168, 173, 188, 189, 190 and 192). Most of the plate numbering has been changed. In plate 41a another early sixteenth-century jewel has been substituted for that previously reproduced. On looking through the original plates in the course of planning this new edition I came to the conclusion that in spite of the many difficulties I experienced in obtaining photographs during the years after the War, all the important types and periods of European jewellery up to the beginning of the nineteenth century were already satisfactorily represented. Consequently only a few pieces from this period have been added, either because of their unique interest and importance, like the gold brooch of circa

*In black and white in the Dover edition.   II

PREFACE

1300 set with mediaeval cameos, found in 1968 at Oxwich Castle, Glamorganshire, the Islamic crystal mounted as a pendant circa 1300, recently acquired by the Victoria and Albert Museum, and the Swan Badge of circa 1450 found at Dunstable and now in the British Museum; or because nothing of the type was already illustrated, as in the case of the Nuremberg head-dress of gold and pearls of circa 1600. Through the kindness of Dr. Mihalik, of the Hungarian National Museum, I have also been able to add a few splendid pieces of mediaeval jewellery from Hungary, a country with a long and lively tradition in the jeweller's art, but not represented in the first edition.

Since this book came out, interest in nineteenth-century jewellery has rapidly increased, and important pieces have begun to find their way from private jewel-cases into museum collections. In the first edition the historical styles of the nineteenth century were only scantily represented, and I decided to add to this new edition examples of jewellery designed by Pugin and Castellani, as well as a selection of other pieces from less well-known hands. Though the representation of nineteenth-century jewellery is inevitably less comprehensive than it might be, certain important aspects of the art during this period are in this edition duly emphasised.

Although jewels can and do give delight as works of art in their own right, a history must emphasise their relation to costume and to the changes of fashion which have determined so often their popularity and their disappearance. A number of reproductions of works of art and portraits which illustrate what jewels were worn and the manner of wearing them at different periods figured in the first edition. I have decided to increase that number, for not only do pictures and sculptures teach us much about what survives, but they tell us much about jewellery which we only know from documents and other literary sources. The strangely Gothic arrangement of Caterina Cornaro's ornaments shows a fashion of wearing jewellery not otherwise recorded. The contrast between the orderly spaciousness of High Renaissance splendour, as shown in the portraits of Henry VIII and Princess Mary, and the bejewelled dresses of Dorothée de Croy and Maria Capponi from the first decades of the seventeenth century states a transformation of social values more eloquently than any words. Katharina Barbara, Freein von Liebert, is a lady of touching plainness, but fortunately in 1774 when she sat for her portrait she put on the entire contents of her jewel case, a rare record of a lady's full panoply from that informal age.

Where, as in some cases, the new illustrations reproduce objects discussed in the text, a plate reference has been inserted in the appropriate place.

I should like to express my gratitude to the following persons and institutions for permission to reproduce works of art in their care: Kunstsammlungen, Augsburg; Historisches Museum, Bâle; British Museum; Hungarian Museum of Fine Arts, Budapest; Hungarian National Museum, Budapest; Fitzwilliam Museum, Cambridge;

PREFACE

Germanisches Nationalmuseum, Nuremberg; Mrs. Phyllis Phillips; Baron von Thyssen-Bornemisza; Musée des Beaux-Arts, Valenciennes; Victoria and Albert Museum. Finally, I should like to thank Mr. R. W. Lightbown of the Victoria and Albert Museum for the assistance he has kindly given me in preparing this new edition.

1970   J. E.

Contents

Illustrations

————————•◦✿◦•————————

Where the photograph of an object from a Museum is reproduced without further acknowledgment it is by courtesy of the Museum authorities. Those from the Victoria and Albert Museum are Crown Copyright.

ILLUSTRATIONS

(*b*) Silver buckle found on the island of Visby. *c.* 1220. ? Rhenish. National Historical Museum, Stockholm.

5. Detail of statue of a Queen, from Corbeil, showing ring-brooch and crown. Musée du Louvre. Phot. Commission des Monuments historiques.

6. (*a–c*) Pendant. An Islamic crystal fish set in a Western mount of silver, nielloed and gilt. Fish *c.* 1200 (?), mounts *c.* 1300. With screw stopper. (*Slightly enlarged.*) Victoria and Albert Museum. Crown copyright reserved.

(*d*) Brooch. Silver-gilt, ornamented with lions and eagles on foliage. Hungarian (?) thirteenth century. Victoria and Albert Museum.

7. (*a*) Buckle. Gold, nielloed with a battle scene. Hungarian, second half of the thirteenth century. (*Slightly enlarged.*) Found with four gold buttons at Kiskun-majsa-Kúgyóspuszta. Hungarian National Museum, Budapest (No. 61.64).

(*b*) Fragment of a crown. Four gold plaques decorated with gold filigree and set with pearls, turquoises, garnets and sapphires. (*Slightly reduced.*) Hungarian, second half of the thirteenth century. Hungarian National Museum, Budapest (No.55.427.l.c.).

(*c*) Fragment of a brooch matching the crown. Gold set with turquoises, garnets and sapphires. (*Slightly reduced.*) Hungarian, second half of the thirteenth century. Hungarian National Museum, Budapest (No. 55.427.2.c.).

8. Ring brooches, British Museum. Thirteenth and fourteenth centuries.

(*a*) Engraved gold, set with rubies and emeralds. Early thirteenth century. Franks Bequest.

(*b*) Gold, set with rubies and emeralds: from Enniscorthy Abbey. Inscribed: +AMES : AMIE : AVES M PAR CES PRESENT.

(*c–d*) Silver : both back and front are shown. Both are inscribed with versions of the amuletic inscription IHESUS NAZARENUS REX JUDAEORUM.

9. (*a*) Crown holding relics sent from Constantinople in 1205. Cathedral Treasury, Namur. Phot. A.C.L., Brussels. (*Slightly reduced.*)

(*b*) Crown given by Saint Louis to the Dominicans of Liége. Before 1270. Musée du Louvre. (*Slightly reduced.*)

10. (*a*) Crown worn by Richard Earl of Cornwall for his coronation as King of the Romans at Aachen in 1257. Treasury of Aachen Cathedral. (*Reduced.*)

(*b*) Jewel of St. Hilary. Sardonyx cameo of Augustus in a setting of silver gilt set with rubies, sapphires and pearls, once dedicated as an ornament on the silver bust-reliquary of St. Hilary in the Treasury of Saint Denis. Early thirteenth century. Bibliothèque Nationale, Paris.

11. (*a*) The Schaffhausen Onyx. An antique Roman cameo of Peace, set in a frame of gold with little figures of lions among jewels in high raised collets. The back is engraved with the figure of a man in civil dress, holding a hawk, and an illegible inscription.

(*b*) Side view. Second half of the thirteenth century. Musée de Tous-les-Saints, Schaffhausen. Phot. courtesy of Monsieur W. U. Gûyàn.

12. (*a*) Reliquary Cross of jewelled gold. Late thirteenth century. Palazzo Pitti, Florence. Phot. Alinari.

(*b*) Gold double cross, from a figure of Christ in Røskilde Domkirke. Late thirteenth century. National Museum, Copenhagen.

(*c–d*) Reliquary pendant of the Holy Thorn, enamelled gold set with two large bean-shaped amethysts. Late thirteenth century. Given to the British Museum by Mr. George Salting.

13. (*a–b*) Gold ring-brooch. 'The Kames Brooch.' *c.* 1300. Formerly in the possession of Sir Malcolm Macgregor of Macgregor. National Museum of Antiquities, Edinburgh.

(*c*) Gold ring brooch set with rubies and sapphires, the back nielloed. *c.* 1300. Victoria and Albert Museum.

14. (*a*) Gold ring brooch found near Doune Castle, wreathed and inscribed in black letter + ave de+ moy mercie+ pite moun coer en+ vous repoce. *c.* 1400. National Museum of Antiquities, Edinburgh.

(*b*) Silver brooch inscribed IHESVS NASARENE, fourteenth or fifteenth century. Franks Bequest, British Museum.

(*c*) Gold brooch with projecting setting for jewel. *c.* 1400. British Museum.

(*d*) Gold brooch with lobed ring. Fourteenth century. Victoria and Albert Museum.

(*e*) Gold brooch with cabalistic inscription. Fourteenth century. British Museum.

15. (*a*) Gold ring-brooch set with rubies and sapphires. Fourteenth century. Victoria and Albert Museum.

(*b*) Gold brooch set with pearls, cabochon sapphires and emeralds. Early fourteenth century. British Museum. (From the Londesborough Collection.)

(*c*) Silver ring-brooch from Norham, with gilt rosettes and collars. Fourteenth century. National Museum of Antiquities, Edinburgh.

16. The Glenlyon brooch. Silver gilt set with amethysts, the back inscribed CASPAR . MELCHIOR . BALTASAR . CONSUMATUM. Scottish. ?*c.* 1500. British Museum. (*Reduced.*)

17. (*a*) The Loch Buy brooch. Silver, set with rock crystals and pearls. Scottish. Sixteenth century. British Museum.

(*b*) Gold brooch set with a cameo and rubies. Late fourteenth century. Victoria and Albert Museum.

18. (*a*) Gold heart brooch inscribed VOUS ESTES MA IOY MOUNDEINE. Late fourteenth century. British Museum.

(*b*) Gold brooch set with four sapphires and three small pearls. Late fourteenth century. British Museum.

(*c*) Gold heart brooch, once enamelled with peacocks' feathers. Inscribed NOSTRE ET TOUT DITZ A VOSTRE PLESIR. Fourteenth century. Victoria and Albert Museum.

(*d*) Gold heart brooch ornamented with flowers and foliage. Fourteenth century. British Museum.

19. (*a*) The Founder's Jewel, left by William of Wykeham to New College, Oxford, in 1404. Late fourteenth century. New College, Oxford. Phot. Ashmolean Museum.

(*b*) Gold brooch in the form of a pelican, set with a ruby, standing on a scroll set with a small pointed diamond. Burgundian? Fifteenth century. British Museum.

(*c–d*) Gold reliquary pendant engraved with figures of saints and the motto A MON DERREYNE. *c.* 1400. British Museum.

20. Wheel-shaped fourteenth-century gold brooch set with jewels and ornamented with grotesque figures, in the fifteenth century applied to a larger plate of gold also jewelled and ornamented with eagles and lions of gold. Found in the Motala river near Kumstad. National Historical Museum, Stockholm. (*Reduced.*)

21. The Fleur-de-Lys clasp of the French Regalia: enamelled gold set with sapphires and amethysts. Fifteenth century. Musée du Louvre. Phot. Giraudon. (*Reduced.*)

22. (*a–e*) Brooches of the early fifteenth century dedicated in the Cathedral of Essen. Phot. Rijksmuseum, Amsterdam.

(*a*) A wreath of flowers; the projecting leaves once went all round the brooch. One of seven.

(*b*) With a star; some pearls missing.

(*c*) With a hart; the foliage once went all round the rim.

(*d*) With an eagle.

(*e*) With a hart; a cluster of pearls missing.

(*f*) From the bed of the Meuse, set with a sapphire, diamond and three rubies. Franks Bequest, British Museum.

23. Brooches dedicated in the Cathedral of Essen. Early fifteenth century.

(*a, c*) Ladies in a garden.

(*b*) Pelican in her piety.

(*d*) Huntsman.

Phot. Rijksmuseum, Amsterdam.

24. Reliquary brooch, silver gilt with gems and opaque enamels. German, *c.* 1375. Musée de Cluny. Phot. Giraudon. (*Reduced.*)

25. The Bridal Crown worn by Princess Blanche, daughter of Henry IV of England, at her marriage to the Elector Ludwig III in 1402. Wittelsbach Treasure, Residenz Museum, Munich. Phot. Residenz Museum. (*Reduced.*)

ILLUSTRATIONS

26. (*a*) Dress ornaments. Silver-gilt. From the 'Budapest Find'. Hungarian, fifteenth century. Hungarian National Museum, Budapest (No. 1878/9/3-4-5, 9).
    (*b–d*) Pendant triptych. Gold, the doors set with crystal panels, enclosing figures of the Virgin and Child and two angels in *émail en ronde bosse*. French, *c.* 1400. Collection of Mrs. P. Phillips.

27. Miniatures of (*a*) the White Rose Jewel (1916.478), and (*b*) the Three Brothers Jewel (1916.475) captured at Grandson in 1476 from Charles the Bold. Reproduced by courtesy of the Historisches Museum, Basle.

28. Detail of the *Virgin* by Gerard David. National Gallery.

29. Jewel border from a Flemish Book of Hours. *c.* 1500. Bibliothèque Nationale, MS. Latin 1166.

30. Detail of the portrait of Margaret of Denmark, Queen of Scotland, by Van der Goes, 1476. H.M. the Queen, Holyrood Palace. Phot. Annan, Glasgow.

31. Anne de Beaujeu. Detail from the triptych of the Maître de Moulins. *c.* 1498. Moulins Cathedral. Phot. Giraudon.

32. Detail from the portrait of Margaret of Austria, Duchess of Savoy, 1483. Musée de Versailles. Phot. Giraudon.

33. Portrait of a woman. French *c.* 1500. Musée du Louvre. Phot. Giraudon.

34. Miniature painted about 1500 of the gold aigrette set with pearls and rubies looted from the tent of the Duke of Burgundy at Grandson in 1476. Historisches Museum, Basle.

35. Buckle and mordaunt, inscribed VIRTUS VIN. Italian, fifteenth century. Victoria and Albert Museum.

36. (*a*) Buckle and belt-end of nielloed silver, the end inscribed AMORE. Italian, fifteenth century. Private collection.
    (*b*) Reliquary pendant, silver nielloed and gilt: on the obverse IHS. Italian, fifteenth century. Private collection.

37. Reliquary pendants of the fifteenth century.
    (*a*) Pendant triptych, enamelled gold with a cameo of the Nativity. Burgundian, middle of the fifteenth century. Cleveland Museum of Art, Cleveland, Ohio. Purchase from the J. H. Wade Foundation.
    (*b*) Silver gilt diptych with the Virgin and Child and the Crucifixion in relief on an enamelled ground. German, late fifteenth century. Victoria and Albert Museum.

38. (*a*) Pendant triptych reliquary; French, late fifteenth century. A. de Rothschild gift. Musée du Louvre.
    (*b*) Rosary of agate beads opening to show enamelled reliefs of the Life of Christ. Probably Italian, early sixteenth century. A. de Rothschild gift. Musée du Louvre. Phot. Giraudon. (*Slightly reduced.*)

39. Pendant mirror of Margaret Duchess of Burgundy. Silver gilt and gold, enamelled with Christ's entry into Jerusalem. *c.* 1470. Formerly in the J. C. Robinson Collection. Private Collection.

40. Cross found at Middlefart, Denmark, the back engraved with figures of the Blessed Virgin, St. Paul, St. Simon and St. Christopher. Early sixteenth century. National Museum, Copenhagen.

41. (*a*) Hat badge. Gold, with head of St. John the Baptist (enamelled white) on a charger (enamelled red). Inscribed: INTER NATOS MVLIERVM NON SVREXSIT. (*Enlarged.*) French, early sixteenth century. Victoria and Albert Museum.

    (*b-c*) Front and back of a reliquary pendant of enamelled gold. North Italian, *c.* 1500. Metropolitan Museum, New York.

42. The Reliquary Pendant of St. Thomas More; enamelled gold. Sixteenth century. Stonyhurst College. Phot. courtesy of the Revd. the Rector, Stonyhurst College.

43. Pilgrims' Signs, painted on a page of a Flemish Book of Hours, *c.* 1500. Sir John Soane's Museum, MS. 4, fol. 112v. Phot. Fine Art Engravers Ltd.

44. (*a*) Cameo of Lorenzo de' Medici. *c.* 1490. Bibliothèque Nationale.

    (*b*) Cameo of Ludovico Sforza. *c.* 1500. Bibliothèque Nationale.

    (*c*) Cameo of Jean, Duc de Berry. Early fifteenth century. British Museum.

    (*d*) Drawing of a pendant with a table diamond held by a nymph and satyr, offered for sale to Henry VIII by John Carolo of Antwerp in 1546. Record Office, S.P. 1, 213, f. 168.

45. Portrait of Battista Sforza by Piero della Francesca. *c.* 1480. Uffizi, Florence. Phot. Archives Photographiques.

46. (*a*) Hat medallion of enamelled gold, with the Conversion of St. Paul. Once belonging to Don John of Austria. Probably Italian. Middle of the sixteenth century. Waddesdon Bequest, British Museum.

    (*b*) Hat medallion of enamelled gold with the Judgment of Paris, in a rim of garnets. Probably Italian, middle of the sixteenth century. Waddesdon Bequest, British Museum.

    (*c*) Hat medallion of enamelled gold with a battle scene. Probably Italian, and before 1560. Cabinet des Médailles, Bibliothèque Nationale.

    (*d*) Hat medallion of enamelled gold with Apollo driving the horses of the Sun. Italian, *c.* 1540. Musée Condé, Chantilly. Phot. Bernard, Chantilly.

47. (*a–b*) Hat ornament of enamelled gold. It shows St. John and St. Mary Magdalene; the doors behind them open to reveal the veil of St. Veronica and Annunciation figures. The rim is inscribed CON FEDE UNA SOLA AMO. Italian, *c.* 1500. Metropolitan Museum, New York.

    (*c*) Hat ornament of enamelled gold, with the Entombment and angels holding the

Robe of Christ and the Crown of Thorns. Italian *c.* 1500. Metropolitan Museum, New York.

48. (*a*) Brooch from a Florentine picture of the Virgin and Child. *c.* 1490. National Gallery.

(*b*) Pendant from Lorenzo Lotto's *Lucrezia*. *c.* 1520. National Gallery.

49. (*a*) Model of the back of a seal made for Cardinal Giovanni de Medici by Lautizio di Perugia. Florentine *c.* 1500. Victoria and Albert Museum. (*Reduced.*)

(*b*) Gold repoussé medallion for a cap brooch. Italian, sixteenth century. Fitz-william Museum, Cambridge. (*Twice actual size.*)

50. Designs for pendants by Hans Holbein. *c.* 1530. British Museum.

51. Designs for chains by Hans Holbein. *c.* 1530. British Museum.

52. (*a*) Hat medallion of enamelled gold with the figure of St. John the Baptist in the wilderness, in a border of pearls and diamonds in enamelled settings. Italian, early sixteenth century. Metropolitan Museum, New York.

(*b*) Hat medallion of enamelled gold, with the figure of St. John the Divine. Italian, early sixteenth century. Kunsthistorisches Museum, Vienna. Phot. Fine Art Engravers Ltd.

53. Portrait of Caterina Cornaro (1454–1510), Queen of Cyprus, by Gentile Bellini, *c.* 1500. Budapest Museum of Fine Arts.

54. Detail of portrait of Bianca Maria Sforza, wife of the Emperor Maximilian I. School of Bernardin Strigel, *c.* 1510. Kunsthistorisches Museum, Vienna. Phot. Archives Photographiques.

55. Detail of the portrait of Isabella of Austria by Jan Gossaert. Formerly in the collection of Count Zozilas Tarnowski at Dyrkow. *c.* 1520. Copyright Medici Society.

56. Detail of the portrait of Eleanor of Austria, Queen of France. Spanish School, *c.* 1525. Musée Condé, Chantilly. Phot. Giraudon.

57. Portrait of Henry VIII by Hans Holbein, *c.* 1536. Lugano, Villa Favorita, collection of Baron von Thyssen-Bornemisza. Reproduced by courtesy of Baron von Thyssen-Bornemisza.

58. Detail of the portrait of Anne of Cleves by Holbein. *c.* 1540. Louvre. Phot. Braun, Mulhouse.

59. Engraved designs for pendants by Virgil Solis of Nuremberg. *c.* 1540. Victoria and Albert Museum.

60–1. Designs for pendants by Etienne Delaune. *c.* 1560. Ashmolean Museum, Oxford.

62. (*a*) Cap jewel of enamelled gold set with rubies, emeralds and diamonds, with St. George and the Dragon. Probably German. Middle of the sixteenth century. Waddesdon Bequest, British Museum.

(*b*) Cap jewel of enamelled gold, with David bearing the head of Goliath. Middle of the sixteenth century. National Museum, Copenhagen.

63. (*a*) Hat medallion of enamelled gold with Leda and the Swan, the head and body of Leda of chalcedony. The back bears the arms and devices of Francis I. Probably French, *c.* 1540. Kunsthistorisches Museum, Vienna.

(*b–c*) Back and front of a pendant with the figure of Prudence, the head and arms of chalcedony. The back is enamelled with Diana after an engraved design by Etienne Delaune. Probably French, middle of the sixteenth century. Metropolitan Museum, New York.

64. (*a*) Cameo of St. George and the Dragon with details in enamelled gold, in a mount of enamelled gold set with rubies and diamonds. Middle of the sixteenth century. Kunsthistorisches Museum, Vienna.

(*b*) Cameo of Hercules in a mount of enamelled gold set with rubies. Middle of the sixteenth century. Bibliothèque Nationale.

(*c*) *Enseigne* of enamelled gold with the story of Judith and Holofernes. English *c.* 1550. Wallace Collection, London.

65. (*a*) Medallion from a hat ornament of enamelled gold, with the Adoration of the Magi. German, *c.* 1540. Cabinet des Médailles, Bibliothèque Nationale.

(*b*) Portrait pendant of the Emperor Charles V, gold and enamel on a bloodstone background in a rim of lapis lazuli. *c.* 1540. Metropolitan Museum, New York.

66. Chain and pendant found in the tomb of Caterina Jagellonica, Queen of Sweden, d. 1583. The pendant of enamelled gold with a crowned C in rubies. Treasury of Upsala Cathedral. Phot. courtesy of the Dean of Upsala. (*Reduced.*)

67. Pendant of enamelled gold with AA in table diamonds and a crown with rubies, made for Anna of Saxony, *c.* 1560. Formerly in the Green Vaults, Dresden. Phot. Landesbildstelle Sachsen.

68. Detail from the portrait of his wife by Cranach. *c.* 1530. Roscoe Collection, Walker Art Gallery, Liverpool.

69. Portrait of Henry VIII by Holbein, 1540. National Gallery, Rome. Phot. Royal Academy.

70. Pendant book cover of gold enamelled in black and white with the worship of the Brazen Serpent and the Judgment of Solomon. English, middle of the sixteenth century. British Museum.

71. Pendant book cover of gold enamelled in many colours with the Creation of Eve and a scene of nymphs surprised while bathing. Middle of the sixteenth century. Victoria and Albert Museum.

72. IHS pendants.

ILLUSTRATIONS

(*a*) Diamonds in a setting of enamelled gold. End of the sixteenth century. Cabinet des Médailles, Bibliothèque Nationale.

(*b*) Diamonds in a setting of enamelled gold. *c.* 1600. Victoria and Albert Museum.

(*c*) Diamonds in gold setting. *c.* 1600. Private collection.

73. Drawings of a carcanet, *cotière* and pendants by Hans Mielich of Munich. *c.* 1570. Hefner-Altneck Collection, Munich. After Hefner-Altneck.

74. Portrait of Elisabeth of Austria, wife of Charles IX of France. French School, *c.* 1570. Musée du Louvre. Phot. Archives Photographiques.

75. Detail from the portrait of the Infanta Isabella Clara Eugenia, *c.* 1570, by Alonzo Sanchez Coello. Prado, Madrid. Phot. Anderson, Rome.

76. Portrait of Mary Tudor by Hans Eworth. Fitzwilliam Museum, Cambridge.

77. Portrait of Queen Elizabeth. *c.* 1575. National Portrait Gallery.

78. Head-dress. Gold, set with pearls. Nuremberg, *c.* 1600. (*Reduced.*) Germanisches National-Museum, Nuremberg.

79. Back and front of a Sea-Dragon pendant of enamelled gold, set with baroque pearls and emeralds. Probably German, *c.* 1575. Waddesdon Bequest, British Museum. (*Slightly reduced.*)

80. Back and front of a Sea-Horse pendant of enamelled gold set with emeralds. Probably German, *c.* 1575. Waddesdon Bequest, British Museum.

81. (*a*) Merman pendant formed of a baroque pearl set in enamelled and jewelled gold, brought by Lord Canning from India. Perhaps Italian, *c.* 1580. Victoria and Albert Museum.

(*b*) Lizard pendant of enamelled gold set with a baroque pearl. Spanish, *c.* 1580. Salting Bequest, Victoria and Albert Museum.

82. (*a*) Mermaid pendant of enamelled gold set with emeralds. Probably German, *c.* 1580. Waddesdon Bequest, British Museum.

(*b*) Mermaid pendant of enamelled gold set with rubies. German, *c.* 1580. Private collection.

(*c*) Pendant of a nereid and child, enamelled gold set with baroque pearls, emeralds and rubies. Probably German, *c.* 1580. Waddesdon Bequest, British Museum. (*All slightly reduced.*)

83. Back and front of a dragon pendant in enamelled gold and pearls. Spanish, *c.* 1570. Musée du Louvre.

84. Spanish bird pendants, *c.* 1580.

(*a*) Crowned eagle in enamelled gold, the body formed of a baroque pearl. Wallace Collection, London.

(*b*) Pelican, set with a carbuncle. From the Treasury of the Virgen del Pilar, Saragossa. Victoria and Albert Museum.

ILLUSTRATIONS

(c) Parrot, set with a jacinth, from the Treasury of the Virgen del Pilar, Saragossa. Victoria and Albert Museum.

85. Front and back of a pendant with the figure of Charity in enamelled gold, set with diamonds, rubies and emeralds. German, c. 1590. Waddesdon Bequest, British Museum.

86. Front and back of a pendant with the Adoration of the Magi in enamelled gold set with diamonds and rubies. German, c. 1610. Waddesdon Bequest, British Museum.

87. (a) Pendant of enamelled gold with the figure of Justice, set with table-cut diamonds. German, late sixteenth century. Metropolitan Museum, New York.

(b) Pendant of enamelled gold with the Incredulity of St. Thomas. German, late sixteenth century. Wallace Collection, London.

88. (a) Pendant of enamelled gold with the Annunciation; once in Horace Walpole's Collection at Strawberry Hill. Perhaps Italian. Late sixteenth century. Waddesdon Bequest, British Museum.

(b) Pendant of enamelled gold with Hercules and the daughters of Atlas. Late sixteenth century. Victoria and Albert Museum.

89. Chain and pendant of gold enamelled with scenes of the Passion. German, c. 1580, perhaps made for the Emperor Rudolf II. Rothschild Bequest, Musée du Louvre.

90. (a) Cameo of Lucretia, mounted in enamelled gold. German, c. 1600.

(b) Cameo of a negress, mounted in enamelled gold. German, c. 1600.

(c) Cameo of Omphale in a rim of rubies. German, c. 1600. Vienna, Kunsthistorisches Museum. Phot. Fine Art Engravers.

(d) Hat ornament of a cameo of a negro king in a rim of rubies. c. 1580. Cabinet des Médailles, Bibliothèque Nationale.

91. Sixteenth-century ship pendants.

(a) Crystal hull and enamelled gold rigging. Metropolitan Museum, New York.

(b) Enamelled gold and pearls, probably Venetian. (*Reduced.*) Victoria and Albert Museum.

(c) Crystal hull in enamelled gold mount. Victoria and Albert Museum.

92. Portrait cameos of Mary Queen of Scots:

(a) Pendant of enamelled gold set with a cameo of Mary Queen of Scots. c. 1565. The Duke of Portland.

(b) Cap-brooch with cameo of Mary Queen of Scots in a rim of enamelled gold set with rubies. c. 1560. Cabinet des Médailles, Bibliothèque Nationale, Paris. (The pendant pearl is a later addition.)

(c) Heart-shaped pendant of enamelled gold set with a cameo of Mary Queen of Scots. c. 1565. National Museum of Antiquities, Edinburgh. (*Slightly reduced.*)

93. The Heneage Jewel, given by Queen Elizabeth to Sir Thomas Heneage, in recognition of his services as Treasurer at War against the Spaniards. The miniature dated

1580, the jewel probably 1588: both probably by Nicholas Hilliard. Victoria and Albert Museum.

94. Silver belt inscribed MAREN KNVDSDATTER. 1608. National Museum, Copenhagen.

95. (*a*) Ovoid pendant of gold enamelled in blue with touches of other colours and set with rubies and pearls. German, *c.* 1600. Metropolitan Museum, New York.

(*b*) Pendant of enamelled gold set with rubies and pearls, with a figure of David harping. Spanish? *c.* 1610. Victoria and Albert Museum.

96. (*a*) Aigrette of enamelled gold set with rubies and diamonds. German, *c.* 1615. Waddesdon Bequest, British Museum.

(*b*) Jewel of enamelled gold set with rubies, said to have been lost by Charles I on the field of Naseby. German, *c.* 1615. Sir John Soane's Museum, London.

97. (*a*) Pendant of Princess Maria Eleanora of Sweden. German, *c.* 1620. Myntkabinett, Stockholm.

(*b*) Links from a necklace of enamelled gold set with pearls and diamonds. German, *c.* 1620. Formerly Pierpont Morgan Collection. Phot. Victoria and Albert Museum.

98. (*a*) Aigrette of enamelled gold set with emeralds. Italian? *c.* 1600. Victoria and Albert Museum.

(*b*) Pendant with Daniel in the lions' den, the back enamelled in the style of Mignot, *c.* 1600. Musée du Louvre.

99. Designs for aigrettes set with rubies and emeralds, by Arnold Lulls, jeweller to Anne of Denmark. *c.* 1610. Victoria and Albert Museum.

100. Portrait of a Princess, by Alonzo Sanchez Coello. Alexander Shaw, Esq., Buenos Aires. Phot. Giraudon.

101. Portrait of Dorothée de Croy, Duchesse de Croy et d'Arschot (1575–1662), painted in 1615, by Frans II Pourbus. Musée des Beaux-Arts, Valenciennes.

102. Portrait of Maria Capponi (1578–1656), wife of Guido Pecori. Florentine, unknown painter, *c.* 1600.

103. Two miniature cases, *c.* 1610. Fitzwilliam Museum, Cambridge.

(*a–b*) Enamelled in tawny red and set with diamonds, containing a miniature of Anne of Denmark ascribed to Hilliard.

(*c*) Enamelled and set with rubies and diamonds, containing a miniature of an unknown man by John Hoskins; the fretted lid ornamented with a knot and inscribed FAST THOVGH VNTIED.

104. Back and lid of a miniature case containing a portrait of Queen Elizabeth; the lid set with diamonds and the back enamelled in colours after a design by Daniel Mignot. English, *c.* 1610. Victoria and Albert Museum.

ILLUSTRATIONS

105. (*a*) Gold miniature case with champlevé enamel in the style of Mignot. *c.* 1610. Victoria and Albert Museum.

(*b*) Gold miniature case with champlevé enamel. *c.* 1610. Waddesdon Bequest, British Museum. (*Both slightly reduced.*)

106. (*a*) Gold miniature case with champlevé enamel in white and black. *c.* 1620. Private collection.

(*b*) Design for miniature case by Jean Toutin of Châteaudun, 1619.

107. *Email en résille sur verre. c.* 1620.

(*a*) Back of the case containing an engraved silver portrait of Princess Mary of Austria, daughter of Philip II of Spain. Formerly Pierpont Morgan Collection.

(*b*) Oblong pendant with Apollo and Daphne. Waddesdon Bequest, British Museum.

108. (*a*) Watch case by Klotz of Augsburg, end of the sixteenth century. Fitzwilliam Museum, Cambridge.

(*b*) Watch case of enamelled gold in the style of Daniel Mignot. *c.* 1620. Victoria and Albert Museum.

(*c*) Watch case of enamelled gold. French, *c.* 1640. The watch by Nicholas Bernard, Paris. Formerly in the Pierpont Morgan Collection.

109. Watch of enamelled gold set with sapphires. French, *c.* 1620. British Museum.

110. Spanish Bird Pendants. *c.* 1620. Fitzwilliam Museum, Cambridge.

111. Spanish Devotional Jewels. *c.* 1625.

(*a*) Victoria and Albert Museum.

(*b*) Wallace Collection.

112. Design for a diamond pendant, with three hanging pearls, by Arnold Lulls. *c.* 1610. Victoria and Albert Museum.

113. Gold pendants set with amethysts. *c.* 1630.

(*a*) Private collection.

(*b*) Victoria and Albert Museum.

114. Gold pendant set with diamonds with touches of black and white enamel. *c.* 1625. Private collection.

115. Portrait of Claudia de' Medici by Sustermans. *c.* 1625. Uffizi, Florence. Phot. Anderson.

116. Spanish crosses. *c.* 1620.

(*a*) Private collection.

(*b–c*) Victoria and Albert Museum.

117. (*a*) The Lyte Jewel of enamelled gold set with diamonds, containing a miniature of James I given by him to Thomas Lyte of Lyte's Cary, Somerset. *c.* 1620. British Museum.

(*b*) Plaque of *email en résille sur verre*. French, *c.* 1620. British Museum.

118. Jewels in enamelled pea-pod style.

(*a*) Back of the case of a miniature by Peter Oliver, 1625, enamelled after a design by Pierre Firens. Victoria and Albert Museum.

(*b*) Cameo of Louis XIII as a child in an enamelled frame. *c.* 1610. Bibliothèque Nationale.

(*c–d*) Cameo of Lucius Verus in a frame in the style of Pierre Marchand, enamelled in white and green and set with small diamonds. *c.* 1620. British Museum.

119. Watches in enamelled pea-pod style. *c.* 1620.

(*a–b*) By Claude Pascal, The Hague. Victoria and Albert Museum.

(*c*) By Vautyer, Blois. Victoria and Albert Museum.

120. (*a–b*) Watch by Daniel Bouquet set with rose diamonds and enamelled with coloured flowers in low relief on a black ground. *c.* 1665. British Museum.

(*c*) Watch case of fretted and chased gold enamelled in pale colours. French. *c.* 1650. Victoria and Albert Museum.

121. (*a–b*) Watch by Jacques Huon of Paris decorated in painted enamel with flowers in pinkish grisaille on a black ground. *c.* 1660. Victoria and Albert Museum.

(*c*) Cameo in a frame of enamelled flowers. French, *c.* 1670. Bibliothèque Nationale.

(*d*) Watch decorated with flowers in champlevé enamel. *c.* 1670. Victoria and Albert Museum.

122. Detail from the portrait of Lady Rich by Anthony Van Dyck, *c.* 1635, in the collection of Lady Lucas. Phot. National Gallery.

123. Portrait of the Duchesse de Longueville. *c.* 1640. Musée de Versailles. Phot. Archives Photographiques.

124. (*a–b*) Coffin pendant of enamelled gold inscribed 'Through the Resurrection of Christe we be all sanctified'. English, *c.* 1600. Found at Torre Abbey, Devon. Victoria and Albert Museum.

(*c*) Back of a badge of the Order of Malta, enamelled with the Holy Family. French, *c.* 1670. Victoria and Albert Museum.

125. (*a*) Brooch with enamelled figures representing Jacob and Rachel at the Well on a ground of black. English, *c.* 1650.

(*b*) Pendant enamelled with portraits of Charles I and Charles II. English, middle of the seventeenth century.

(*c*) Watch case of gold filigree. English, *c.* 1640.

(*d*) Slide for ribbon, enamelled with a death's head and cross-bones. English, *c.* 1640.

(*e*) Memorial buckle with hair under crystal, dated 1728. English.

(*f*) Coffin pendant of enamelled gold. English, *c.* 1640. Private collection.

126. (*a*) Miniature case enamelled with flowers. English or Dutch, *c.* 1660.

(*b*) Back of miniature case set with emeralds. (*See* Plate 127 (*a*).)

(*c*) Back of an enamelled miniature of a lady, with R.W.P. engraved on a matted ground within a wreath of flowers in the style of Gilles Légaré. French, *c.* 1670.

(*d*) Back of memorial buckle. (*See* Plate 125 (*e*).) Private collection.

127. (*a*) Miniature case set with emeralds between leaves of white enamel with touches of black. Probably French, *c.* 1670. Private collection.

(*b*) Necklace set with rose-cut crystals, the back enamelled in pale blue with touches of black. Probably Dutch. Middle of the seventeenth century.

128. Pendant and earrings set with topazes and diamonds. Spanish, middle of the seventeenth century. Private collection.

129. Portrait of Henrietta of England, Duchess of Orléans. French, *c.* 1665. Musée de Versailles. Phot. Giraudon.

130. (*a*) Engraved designs for enamel by Gilles Légaré, 1663.

(*b*) Watch case in pale blue enamel with touches of black and white. *c.* 1670. Victoria and Albert Museum.

131. (*a*) Jewel of gold set with diamonds and ornamented with white enamel, dedicated by the Marquis de Navarens at the Shrine of the Virgen del Pilar at Saragossa in 1679. Victoria and Albert Museum.

(*b*) Necklace of gold enamelled in black and white, the pendant set with diamonds and a cabochon sapphire. French, *c.* 1670. Victoria and Albert Museum.

132. (*a*) Enamelled back of a miniature case formerly containing a miniature of Louis XIV. French, *c.* 1680.

(*b*) Enamelled back of a miniature case. French, *c.* 1680.
Private collection.

133. Enamels of the late seventeenth century:

(*a–b*) Watch in black and white enamel. French, *c.* 1680. Nelthropp Collection, Guildhall Museum.

(*c*) Back of a miniature case in chased gold. English, *c.* 1710. Victoria and Albert Museum.

(*d*) Miniature case enamelled in the style of Louis Roupert on a matted gold ground. *c.* 1680. Victoria and Albert Museum.

(*e*) Another, on a ground of black enamel. *c.* 1680. Private collection.

134. Breast ornament or *crochet* set with emeralds with flowers of enamel. From the Treasury of the Virgen del Pilar. Spanish, early eighteenth century. Victoria and Albert Museum. (*Slightly reduced.*)

135. (*a*) Pendant set with coloured topazes and emeralds. Spanish, *c.* 1680.

(*b*) Arrow brooch set with diamonds and emeralds. French, *c.* 1670.

(*c*) Slide for a ribbon set with table-cut diamonds. French, *c.* 1670.

(*d*) Pendant set with rubies, emeralds and diamonds. Spanish, *c.* 1680. Private collection.

136. *Parure* of crystals from the waxen funeral effigy of Frances Stuart, Duchess of Richmond. English, *c.* 1702. Westminster Abbey. (*Slightly reduced.*) Phot. Victoria and Albert Museum.

137. (*a–b*) Back and front of pendant set with crystals, the back enamelled and set with an enamelled portrait of William of Orange. English or Dutch, *c.* 1690. H.M. the Queen. (*Slightly reduced.*)

138. Pendant of diamonds in scroll settings of gold. From the Treasury of the Virgen del Pilar. Spanish, early eighteenth century. Victoria and Albert Museum.

139. Stomacher of rose-cut crystals. Probably English, *c.* 1710. Private collection. (*Slightly reduced.*)

140. (*a*) Bow brooch set with white topazes. Spanish, early eighteenth century. Victoria and Albert Museum.

(*b*) Bow and bird pendant set with crystals. Spanish, early eighteenth century. Victoria and Albert Museum.

141. (*a*) Brooch in asymmetrical rocaille design set with rubies and diamonds. Italian or German, *c.* 1740. Private collection.

(*b*) Brooch set with chrysolites. Portuguese, *c.* 1760. Victoria and Albert Museum.

142. Hat clasp set with brilliants and a green diamond, made for Augustus III of Saxony in 1740. Phot. Landesbildstelle Sachsen.

143. Order of the Golden Fleece in diamonds and rubies made for Augustus III of Saxony, *c.* 1740. Phot. Landesbildstelle Sachsen.

144. Detail from the portrait of Maria Amalia Christina, Queen of Spain, by Anton Raphael Mengs. *c.* 1760. Musée du Louvre. Phot. Arch. Phot.

145. Detail from the portrait of Queen Charlotte from the studio of Allan Ramsay. *c.* 1762. National Portrait Gallery.

146. Flower spray brooches.

(*a*) Set with chrysolites. Spanish or Portuguese, *c.* 1770.

(*b*) Made by Duval at St. Petersburg for the Empress Catherine the Great. *c.* 1760. Private collection.

147. Bouquet of enamelled gold set with diamonds. Dedicated to the Virgen del Pilar of Saragossa by Doña Juana Ravasa. Spanish, *c.* 1770. Victoria and Albert Museum.

148. *Demi-Parure* of brooch and earrings set with chrysolites. Spanish, *c.* 1760. Victoria and Albert Museum.

149. *Parure* of diamonds and topazes. Spanish, middle of the eighteenth century. Private collection.

150. Breast ornament set with foiled amethysts and topazes. Spanish, *c.* 1770. Private collection.

151. Necklace with alternative pendants in diamonds and topazes. French, *c.* 1760. Private collection.

152, 153. *Parure* of blue and white sapphires. French, *c.* 1760. Private collection.

154. Part of a suite of three diamond bows. English, *c.* 1770. Victoria and Albert Museum. Phot. Fine Art Engravers Ltd.

155. (*a*) Necklace of crystals. English, *c.* 1790.
(*b–c*) Pair of bracelet clasps with the initials of Marie Antoinette and her device of doves in diamonds on a ground of blue paste. French, *c.* 1770. Victoria and Albert Museum.

156. Watch and chatelaine made by Thuilst for Queen Anne, of engraved gold set with mother of pearl and garnets with rims of black and red enamel. *c.* 1705. Fitzwilliam Museum, Cambridge.

157. Gold watch and chatelaine by James Rowe of London. 1758. Fitzwilliam Museum, Cambridge.

158. Gold chatelaine and *étui*, the hook plate chased with a seated Britannia and the *étui* with Mars and Venus. English, *c.* 1740. Private collection.

159. (*a*) Chatelaine of base metal, with *chinoiseries* in gilt on a silvered ground. English, *c.* 1760. London Museum. (*Slightly reduced.*)
(*b*) Chatelaine of base metal with rayed designs in gilt on a silvered ground. English, *c.* 1760. London Museum. (*Slightly reduced.*)

160. *Étui* and chatelaine of agate mounted in gold. English, *c.* 1770. Victoria and Albert Museum.

161. Gold watch and chatelaine in enamelled gold, the watch with the French hallmark for 1772–3. Fitzwilliam Museum, Cambridge. (*Slightly reduced.*)

162. (*a*) Buckle of gold set with rose-cut crystals. English, *c.* 1740.
(*b*) Gold cross set with crystals. Perhaps Flemish, *c.* 1740.
Victoria and Albert Museum.

163. (*a*) Waist buckle, set with marcasites. French, *c.* 1760.
(*b*) Shoe buckle, set with sapphires and diamonds. French, *c.* 1750.
(*c*) Shoe buckle, set with blue and white pastes. Spanish, *c.* 1770.
Private collection.

164. (*a*) Detail from a bracelet formed of plaques of Bilston enamel. English, *c.* 1775. Victoria and Albert Museum.
(*b–c*) Buckles of cut steel. English, *c.* 1775. Private collection.

177. Brooch of diamonds and rubies, designed as a bouquet of wild roses and a butterfly. English, c. 1830. Mr. Nyburg, Antique Art Galleries.

178. Convolvulus brooch set with small turquoises. French, c. 1840. Victoria and Albert Museum. Phot. Fine Art Engravers.

179. Diamond spray of lilac. French, 1867. Formerly in the collection of the Empress Eugénie. After Vever.

180. Diamond and pearl brooch made by Lemonnier for the marriage of the Empress Eugénie. 1853. After Vever; the actual jewel 24 cm. long.

181. Brooch set with diamonds from the Crown Jewels for the Empress Eugénie. 1853. Musée du Louvre.

182. 'Gothic' brooches. French, c. 1840. Musée des Arts Décoratifs, Paris.

183. *Parure* in coloured gold. French, c. 1830. Musée des Arts Décoratifs, Paris. Phot. Giraudon. (*Slightly reduced.*)

184. Mid nineteenth-century bracelets:
    (*a*) Flexible gold snake, the head set with rubies and diamonds. French, c. 1820.
    (*b*) Gold snake, the head set with diamonds. French, c. 1830.
    (*c*) Gold, set with emeralds and pearls, with lines of enamel in tawny red. English, c. 1860.
    (*d*) Gold, with delicate applied filigree. English, c. 1870.
    Private collections.

185. *Demi-parure* of gold filigree set with pearls and rubies, linked by strings of small pearls. English, c. 1840. Private collection.

186. *Demi-parure* of enamelled gold set with chrysoprases. French, c. 1830. Victoria and Albert Museum.

187. (*a*) Vinaigrette pendant in chased gold; the coronet top opens on a vinaigrette, the foot drops to show a setting for hair under crystal. English, c. 1840. London Museum.
    (*b*) Necklace of linked circular plaques of gold enamelled and set with crystals and amethysts. Perhaps Swiss, c. 1835.
    Private collection.

188. Necklace and pendant cross. Gold, enamelled black and green, set with garnets and pearls. Designed by A. W. Pugin and made for his third wife, Jane Knill. English, 1848. Victoria and Albert Museum.

189. (*a*) Neckband. Gold, enamelled green and white, set with a ruby, diamonds, turquoises and pearls. Designed by A. W. Pugin for his third wife, Jane Knill, and made by John Hardman and Co. Exhibited at the Great Exhibition of 1851. English, 1848–50. Victoria and Albert Museum.
    (*b*) Brooch. Gold, enamelled green, set with turquoises, garnets and pearls.

ILLUSTRATIONS

Designed by A. W. Pugin and made for his third wife, Jane Knill. English, 1848. Victoria and Albert Museum.

190. *Parure*. Silver-gilt, enamelled white with strokes of black, and set with pearls, garnets and green garnets. Made by Schichtegroll, Vienna, and shown at the Paris Exhibition in 1855. Victoria and Albert Museum.

191. Necklace of seven strands of small pearls mounted with gold enamelled in black and white, with a pendant to match, set with an aquamarine and small rubies. By Giuliano, *c*. 1870. Private collection.

192. (*a*) Bracelet. Gold, with filigree decoration in the Etruscan style. Probably made by Pasquale Novissimo for Carlo Giuliano, *c*. 1880. Victoria and Albert Museum.

(*b*) Bracelet. Gold, set with red agate scarabs. Made by Castellani of Rome. Second half of the nineteenth century. Victoria and Albert Museum.

(*c*) Bracelet. Gold, with applied decoration representing Ashur-bani-pal, King of Assyria, sacrificing on his return from a lion hunt, after Assyrian sculptures in the British Museum. By John Brogden, London. English, *c*. 1851. Shown at the Great Exhibition, 1851. Victoria and Albert Museum.

FIGURES IN THE TEXT

ILLUSTRATIONS

CHAPTER ONE

The Early Middle Ages

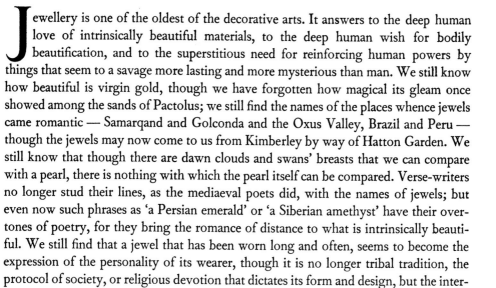

Jewellery is one of the oldest of the decorative arts. It answers to the deep human love of intrinsically beautiful materials, to the deep human wish for bodily beautification, and to the superstitious need for reinforcing human powers by things that seem to a savage more lasting and more mysterious than man. We still know how beautiful is virgin gold, though we have forgotten how magical its gleam once showed among the sands of Pactolus; we still find the names of the places whence jewels came romantic — Samarqand and Golconda and the Oxus Valley, Brazil and Peru — though the jewels may now come to us from Kimberley by way of Hatton Garden. We still know that though there are dawn clouds and swans' breasts that we can compare with a pearl, there is nothing with which the pearl itself can be compared. Verse-writers no longer stud their lines, as the mediaeval poets did, with the names of jewels; but even now such phrases as 'a Persian emerald' or 'a Siberian amethyst' have their overtones of poetry, for they bring the romance of distance to what is intrinsically beautiful. We still find that a jewel that has been worn long and often, seems to become the expression of the personality of its wearer, though it is no longer tribal tradition, the protocol of society, or religious devotion that dictates its form and design, but the interplay of fashion, chance and taste. Jewels, indeed, though they may seem alien to an age of austere functionalism, still play a living part in our civilisation. To understand that part we must understand their history.

To follow that history in full would need many volumes; to analyse the development of the technique of jewels, the rise and fall of the beliefs in their magic, many more. The present book surveys a field limited in time from the end of the eleventh century to the middle of the nineteenth, and limited in space to the more civilised parts of Europe. It begins when the cycle of European economic life once more made it possible for artistic creation to break through the shackles of tribal tradition; it ends in 1870. The latter date is made precise by three events: in 1868 South African diamonds, that by their quantity were to commercialise fine jewels, were first offered on the Paris market; in 1869 the first mechanically made collet setting was produced, to introduce an element of mass production into gem-set jewels; and in 1870 the fall of the Second Empire brought to an end the centuries of court patronage that had made Paris the chief focus of the decorative arts, through a long era of European history.

It is as a decorative art that jewellery is here considered, and as an art confined to ornaments actually worn upon the person. Magical jewels are not considered;[1] goldwork as concerned with other things than personal ornaments is entirely omitted. Neither the jewelled shrines of the middle ages nor the jewelled snuffboxes of the eighteenth century receive any consideration. Furthermore, ecclesiastical jewels (except those that are secular in origin), the insignia of the Orders of Knighthood, and finger rings, have been omitted: each deserves consideration in a separate book.

Even within the limits thus laid down, a further simplification is needed. Jewels can be divided into two great categories, the creative and the traditional. The distinction goes far back in history: there is an obvious and fundamental contrast between the jewellery of Minoan Crete, freely composed on a basis of naturalistic imitation of leaves and flowers, shells and insects, and that of the tribes of the great Migrations, complex and enigmatic in design, changing only from tribe to tribe, so that its distribution in graves can be used as evidence of tribal movements. The contrast seems to be based upon a contrast of social organisation: such a settled and autonomous state as an island monarchy is under no necessity to express the corporate identity of its people, which can find full expression in its characteristic civilisation; but a tribe, forced by economic or military conditions to wander over the face of the earth, finds a need to make even its jewels a mark of its common life. Traditional form and ornament, based on the creative work of happier days, have a sanctity of association and come to have a secondary sanctity as marking the common origin and interest of the tribe. Nomadic conditions, too, do not encourage creative invention; and tribal, as opposed to national, art is almost always traditional.

The jewellery of the post-Roman period held two main stylistic elements: one northern and specifically barbarian, most familiarly represented by the clumsy horse-headed and saucer brooches of gilt bronze: and one, mainly southern, ultimately derived from the traditions of higher civilisations, and represented by the techniques of filigree gold, cloisonné garnet work and the use of cabochon gems — the first a part of the great Mediterranean heritage, and the second a perpetuation of the no less Mediterranean tradition of cloisonné enamel in other materials. Progress in jewel design was achieved by the gradual victory of the more civilised of these two elements over the more primitive.

In some measure this more civilised element found its natural field in the simpler forms of jewels that belonged to the same Mediterranean tradition. Such ornaments as the disc brooches from Kingston and Faversham are themselves the perpetuation of a

[1] I have already written on the subject in *Magical Jewels of the Middle Ages and the Renaissance*, Oxford, 1922.

late Empire form,[1] and it is not unnatural that they should be ornamented in techniques and styles that have no less civilised an ancestry. These techniques, moreover, had not only an Imperial tradition behind them, but also used materials that were inherently precious. There seems, in the countries where both styles are found, to have been a certain class-distinction in their use: the Mediterranean techniques (if the adjective may be used in a very general sense) of filigree and cloisonné were characteristic of the governing class, the barbarian technique of gilt bronze of the governed. Yet exceptionally (for example in the sixth- or seventh-century brooch inscribed with the name of Uffila found at Wittislingen on the Danube)[2] the traditional northern horse-headed and radiated types were adorned with the more sophisticated and costly ornamentation. A similar rationalisation of design inspires the jewels of the Merovingian age.[3]

Such work seems to be associated with the stage when a tribe settles down and starts on the road that will one day lead to nationhood. At that point creative work is once more attempted: not for everyone, but for the kings who have taken the place of the tribal leaders. The splendid jewels found in the cenotaph at Sutton Hoo admirably illustrate the moment of transition: they are obviously linked in form and technique with tribal jewels, yet they are both more magnificent and more free in design. No one hesitates for a moment in recognising them as the funerary commemoration of a king.

This stylistic stage was usually first reached at the moment when the tribe was brought into touch with the great and stable civilisation of the Christian Church. Such votive jewels as the crown dedicated by Agilulf at Monza early in the seventh century, a richly jewelled arcaded circlet with figures of Christ, two angels, and the apostles in the arcades,[4] brought the iconography of the Christian church into the decorative tradition of the jeweller; and the change was confirmed in the work of the sainted goldsmiths of the same century, Eloi, Alban of Fleury and Théau, who made the reigns of Dagobert and Clotaire III the great age of jewelled shrines. In the eighth century St. Bilfrid of Lindisfarne did like work in England; in the ninth Isenric of St. Gall established a tradition of fine goldwork in his monastery which was carried on into the tenth century by the more famous Tutilo and Notker.[5] In the tenth century, indeed, the names of

---

[1] See T. D. Kendrick, *Anglo-Saxon Art to A.D. 900*, 1938, p. 64; he considers that they should nearly all be ascribed to the sixth century (p. 71).

[2] National Museum, Munich; Clifford Smith, p. 62 and Plate XII, 7.

[3] These can best be studied in the Musée des Antiquités Nationales de la France at Saint-Germain-en-Laye.

[4] See Texier, s.v. Agilulphe. The crown was looted by the armies of Napoleon and stolen from the Bibliothèque Nationale in 1804. A second crown formed from a relic of a nail from the Cross dedicated by Queen Theodolinda at the same time was reset in the fourteenth century and is said to have been looted by the Russians with the rest of Mussolini's treasure in the late war.

[5] Texier, however, exaggerated the importance of the monastic goldsmiths; see Swartwout, *The Monastic Craftsman*, 1932, p. 25, and Appendix 3.

monkish goldsmiths are recorded all over Europe: in our own country Mannius of Evesham, Anketil of St. Albans and Leo of Ely are still remembered.[1] The great Paliotto of Sant'Ambrogio of Milan, in major part dating from about 835, and the Crosses of Oviedo, dedicated in 808 and 874, may stand as examples of the votive offerings on which they were chiefly engaged.

Long before this such ecclesiastical work had influenced more personal jewellery and had helped to establish a style that was long to remain in favour. Such crosses as that found on the body of St. Cuthbert in Durham Cathedral,[2] and that found at Ixworth, though they date from the fifth and seventh centuries, may yet be taken as the precursors of mediaeval jewellery. A yet freer stage is represented in such later Saxon ornaments as the Alfred Jewel and the rings of Ethelwulf, King of Wessex[3] and of Alfred's sister Ethelswith, Queen of Mercia.[4] A European parallel is afforded by the legendary amulet of Charlemagne[5] containing relics of the Virgin's hair and the True Cross, said to have been buried with him at Aix-la-Chapelle in 814, and re-discovered when the tomb was opened by Otto III in 1000 and preserved in the treasury of the Cathedral until it was given by the Canons to the Empress Josephine in 1804 to wear at her coronation.[6] Each side is set with a great cabochon sapphire in a foliated collet that rises from a rim of gold, enriched with embossed work and rather coarse filigree and settings of garnets, carbuncles, emeralds and pearls. The wide edge is similarly adorned. The rich setting represents a more developed stage of the decoration of the Merovingian circular and lobed brooches found in France;[7] it finds a parallel on a few contemporary episcopal rings with enormous circular bezels,[8] and on the central medallion of the Cross of the Angels at Oviedo.[9]

After the end of the seventh century, indeed, the cloisonné technique died out and cabochon gems, filigree and enamel held the field; the change may owe something to the development of the arts of sculpture and illuminated manuscripts and to the

---

[1] Mr. C. C. Oman tells me that St. Dunstan was not claimed as a goldsmith before the Conquest.

[2] Found in 1827; now in Durham Cathedral Library. On these see T. D. Kendrick in *Antiquaries' Journal*, XVII, 1937, p. 283.

[3] Found at Laverstock, Wilts., in 1780. British Museum.

[4] Found near Aberford, Yorks. British Museum.

[5] See Sir Martin Conway in *Antiquaries' Journal*, II, 1922, p. 350; and *Jahrbuch des Vereins von Alterthumsfreunden im Rheinlande*, Bonn, 1866, pp. 265–72.

[6] It later passed by inheritance from his mother to the Emperor Napoleon III: his widow gave it shortly before her death to the Archbishop of Rheims, as the only reparation it lay in her power to make for the 1914 bombardment of his cathedral. See Blaise de Montesquiou-Fezensac in *Art de France*, II, Paris, 1962, p. 66.

[7] An important series is in the Musée des Antiquités Nationales de la France at Saint-Germain-en-Laye.

[8] One from Saint Denis now forms part of the knop of the *main de justice* of the French regalia in the Louvre. Another, found in a tomb at Déols, is in the Museum of Châteauroux.

[9] See H. Schlunk in *Art Bulletin*, XXXII, 1950, p. 93.

consequent appreciation of relief on the one hand and of varied colour on the other. A similar stage of development is reached a little later in the countries lying further to the north. Germany[1] and Scandinavia in the tenth and eleventh centuries produced traditional jewels of great beauty, half tribal and half creative; a splendid brooch, for instance[2] (Plate 1a) keeps the traditional round form, bossed like a shield, but elaborates it into a composition of real beauty. The lobes and bosses, though they keep something of the traditional arrangement of the earlier brooches with knobs of bone and garnet, are all treated in pure goldwork. Another group of round brooches[3] of which the Towneley Brooch, (Plate 1b) is an example, show the traditional type transmuted into a more civilised form by their translation into the technique of enamel.

Once Christianity was accepted by Western Europe, a new stability and a new integration brought the contradictions of the transitional style to an end. The deliberate return to the classical past that inspired Carolingian and, still more, Ottonian art was perhaps most easily achieved in goldwork, that among the decorative arts had always retained the largest part of the technical heritage of the classical age.

The links between Ottonian Germany and Byzantium brought fresh elements into that heritage. An eleventh-century necklace of cameos, hanging from linked chains[4] to form a decoration over the whole breast, is German in technique and provenance, but recalls the jewels which the Empress Theodora wears in the Ravenna mosaics. The treasure of the Empress Gisela found at Mainz,[5] dating from the middle of the century, included a rather similar necklace, lunette earrings of gem-set filigree, clearly oriental in type, and the splendid Eagle brooch (Plate 2a) in which the bird-brooches of an earlier age inspired a new and imperial ornament. The brooch was elliptical, four inches high and rather less across; the eagle in the centre, decorated in cloisonné enamel, broke through the encircling ring, which was adorned with eight flowers similarly enamelled in translucent green, turquoise blue, white and yellow. Two brooches found at Mainz in 1896 and now in the Hessisches Landesmuseum at Darmstadt, may also be linked with the Empress: a pair of brooches (Plate 2b) of gold filigree set with pearls, amethysts and sapphires, that still keep something of barbaric tradition in their form, though a finer technique and more splendid jewels have given it new beauty. A third brooch that may come from the same hoard is in the Alterthums Museum of Mainz. The lovely

---

[1] e.g., the find from Hiddensoë near Rügen, now in the Provincial Museum of Stralsund.

[2] In the Victoria and Albert Museum.

[3] The finest are in the Berlin Museum and the British Museum: see Meyer, p. 19 and Plate 6, and Dalton in *Proc. Soc. Ants.*, XX, 1903–5, p. 64.

[4] Formerly in the collection of Freiherr Max von Heyl at Darmstadt; Bassermann Jordan, Fig. 86.

[5] Falke, Fig. IV. They were in the Berlin Schloss Museum and are believed to have been destroyed in 1945.

combination of gold, purple and blue that appears in all of them owes something to the colouring of contemporary illuminated manuscripts.

Such jewels have an imperial and hieratic beauty that makes them as stately and as noble as any ornaments designed for church use. They sometimes, indeed, ended in the service of the Church. A splendid golden pax in the Collegiate Church of San Lorenzo at Chiavenna, made from the upper leaf of a twelfth-century gospel cover,[1] is set with eight pairs of brooch-like circular medallions and a central cross, that are in obvious relation with the secular jewels of the time, and may even have been originally made for personal use and afterwards dedicated. The crown on the gold statue of the Virgin at Essen, with its adornment of threaded pearls, cameos and cabochon jewels in elaborate settings of a filigree sort, is secular in spirit. The Roman agate cameo in the treasury of Aosta Cathedral, in a setting of filigree and pearls, is delicate enough for personal use: its date is certainly not later than about 1200 (Plate 3). The elegant scrolling whorls of goldwork are as accomplished as the sculpture on a Romanesque Cathedral.

In France and England less progress seems to have been made in the eleventh and twelfth centuries in the fabrication of personal ornaments; feudal wars devastated the one and the Norman invasions impoverished the other. In both countries, too, the available craftsmanship and the available wealth in gold and gems seem to have been primarily dedicated to the service of the Church. The Church, indeed, had its own tradition of style and iconography in goldwork, which had little influence on jewellery; the *Schedula diversarum Artium* of Theophilus, though it gives instructions for making vessels for secular as well as for ecclesiastical use, makes no mention of personal jewels. Yet the ecclesiastical tradition soon enriched the secular. The goldsmiths' shops of the great Abbeys occasionally provided training for secular goldsmiths; and, where these shops were only able to work at a repairing level, work was given out to lay goldsmiths. About 1124 the shrine of St. Alban was entrusted to a monastic goldsmith and a lay assistant, Salamon, who seems later to have become the royal goldsmith: he and his descendants until the early fourteenth century were the Abbey goldsmiths of Ely.[2]

By 1180 the secular goldsmiths of London were numerous enough to have banded themselves together into a company; the guild was heavily amerced as adulterine in that year.[3] Jean de Garlande in his description of the great bridge of Paris, written about 1200,[4] describes the goldsmiths at work in their shops there, sitting at their little counters in front of their furnaces, making cups of gold and silver, brooches, jewels, bracelets and clasps, and setting jewels in rings.

Curiously enough, however, the goldsmiths and jewellers were never differentiated

---

[1] Dr. Yvonne Hackenbroch considers it to be north Italian work made under German influence. *Italienische Email des Frühen Mittelalters*, p. 39.
[2] Oman, *Goldsmiths*, p. 219.   [3] Herbert, II, p. 121.   [4] Gay, s.v. Orfèvres.

into separate guilds, either in Paris or London, probably because they used almost identical techniques. In both cities the goldsmiths absorbed the jewellers into their mystery; the *Livre des métiers* drawn up by Etienne Boileau between 1258 and 1269 to regulate the Paris guilds has plenty to say about the goldsmiths and their work,[1] but nothing about jewels or jewellers. It was only in the French provinces that jewellers occasionally had their own guild, usually allied with that of the mercers,[2] which suggests that they dealt in what we should now call 'costume jewellery' made of base metal.

In the late twelfth and early thirteenth century there was no great influx of jewels from their fountain-head in the East into Western Europe. The Seljuk invasions and a series of Crusades were disturbing Asia, and the Spanish Crusades breaking the trade of Arab Spain. The minds of the Emperors Frederick Barbarossa and Henry the Lion were set rather on conquest than on the arts; they must have acquired great treasures in the course of their conquests, but no record of the jewels among them remains. A great number of relics were coming to Europe from the East, and the finest jewels available were used for their shrines rather than for personal adornment. The monk Hugo of Oignies stands as the great master of this age. It was a time when in Western Europe the cameos and intaglios inherited from the Romans played an unusually large part in jewellery; and such engraved gems rarely demand or receive more than a simple rim of gold when they are set for personal use.

Yet this very rarity gave gems a greater prestige than ever before. An incredible number of *Lapidaries*[3] were written in Latin and French, in verse and prose, to describe their appearance and their alleged magical virtues; and few poems were complete without a description of fabulous riches that included all the twelve stones of the Apocalypse.

Jewels are essentially a part of dress; the history of the two is inextricably interwoven. The Carolingians had inherited something of Byzantine tradition in the flowing robes of the Imperial caste, and, with these, jewels little less magnificent than those of the Eastern Empire could be worn; but the long period of political insecurity that followed the break-up of the Empire brought most of such magnificence to an end. Such clothes as are worn by the warriors of the Bayeux tapestry are incompatible with any great display of jewels.

A few years before 1100 the tunic of the men began to lengthen, and the trend continued in the time of political *détente* that followed. Yet the long, high-necked, sleeved

---

[1] Cap. XI. The *Livre de la Taille* of 1292 shows more than 120 lay goldsmiths at work in Paris. Three are named as English; seven or more are from Limoges. See Texier, s.v. Histoire.

[2] e.g., at Alençon, Évreux, Lille, Saumur and Tours. Lacroix-Seré, p. 166.

[3] These works derive ultimately from Greek sources. See de Mély, *Lapidaires Grecs*; Joan Evans, *Magical Jewels*, p. 15, *et seqq.* The Christian tradition of the virtues of gems was carried on in every country of Europe; see Evans, op. cit. p. 31 *sqq.*; L. Pannier, *Les Lapidaires français*, Paris, 1882; P. Studer and J. Evans, *Anglo-Norman Lapidaries*, Paris, 1924; J. Evans and M. Serjeantson, *English Mediaeval Lapidaries*, Early English Text Society, vol. 190, 1933.

under-dress, and shorter-sleeved over-tunic that were worn by both sexes, though they might themselves be richly adorned with embroidery, left little scope for jewels. The belt that was worn by men and married women and the ring brooch that fastened the tunic at the neck, were the only jewels that naturally formed a part of it, though a coronet or other head ornament might also be worn. Belts, however, seem rarely to have been richly decorated at this time, though their buckles were, a little later, often chased with figures in a fashion that makes them exquisite miniatures of contemporary sculpture. A clasp of gilt bronze[1] (Plate 4a) with figures of a king and queen each with an attendant, is purely sculptural in style, and may even be by the great artist Nicholas of Verdun. A thirteenth-century silver clasp from Sweden[2] may also serve as an example, with its clasp chased with leafage and the plate that joins it to the belt adorned with the figure of a lady welcoming a knight and his attendant (Plate 4b). Belts with hanging jewelled ends came into fashion; Mahaut, Countess of Burgundy, wears one on her seal of 1239.[3] Similarly the *surceinte* that was in fashion at the end of the century[4] was often jewelled. The fact that such ornaments were peculiarly subject to the changes of fashion and were made of precious metal that could easily be melted down and recast, serves to explain the rarity of their survival.

The brooches that clasped the underdress at the neck, both for men and women, varied greatly in size and shape. The statue of the Queen of Sheba from Corbeil,[5] dating from the middle of the twelfth century, wears an enormous cluster brooch (Plate 5); a similar statue of about 1170 from Saint-Loup-de-Naud has a solid lozenge-shaped brooch. Adelaïs de Champagne, who died in 1187, wears a ring-brooch with a jewelled ring on her effigy at Joigny. It closely resembles one in the Franks Bequest[6] (Plate 8a) with an engraved ring set with eight cabochon jewels alternately emeralds and rubies; a ninth is set in the head of the pin. There is no catch for the pin; it was held in place against the ring by the natural pull of the stuff through which it passed.

The most usual adornment for thirteenth- and fourteenth-century ring-brooches was inscriptions, usually of a kind which shows that they were love gifts.[7] Such are: IO SVI FLVR DE FIN AMVR;[8] † IEO: SVI: FER MAIL : PUR : GAR : DER : SEIN † KE : NVS : VILEIN NI METTE MEIN;[9] BEL AMIE NE. ME : VBLIE : MIE — on a gold brooch set with emeralds;[10] † IE SVI CI EN LIV DAMI ; or PENSEET DE LI PAR KI SUE CY.[11] The AMOR VINCIT OMNIA that Chaucer later set on the brooch of Madame Eglantine his Prioress

[1] In the Metropolitan Museum, New York. [2] National Historical Museum, Stockholm.
[3] Demay, p. 97. [4] Gay, s.v. Surceinte.
[5] Now in the Louvre. [6] British Museum.
[7] See Joan Evans, *English Posies and Posy Rings*, 1931, p. 1, *et seqq.*; *Arch. Journ.*, III, 1846, p. 77; XVI, 1859, p. 181; LXXIII, 1916, p. 299.
[8] 'I am a flower of perfect love.' British Museum. [9] British Museum, from Writtle, Essex.
[10] In the City and County Museum, Lincoln. [11] Formerly collection of Dr. Philip Nelson.

is found on several examples;[1] and a brooch shaped, like hers, as an A, bears the inscription IO . FAS . AMER . E . DOZ . AMER as well as the cabalistic AGLA[2].

Sometimes the inscriptions wish the wearer well, like the ✝ BENEET SEIT QVI ME PORTE on a brooch at Aylesbury,[3] or complete an amatory inscription with an amuletic formula, as on the brooch inscribed AMI AMET DE LI PENCET . IHESVS NAZARENVS REX IVDAEORVM.[4]

Such devotional inscriptions as appear on these brooches seem for the most part to be prophylactic and magical in intention:[5] the names of the Three Kings,[6] which protected against the falling sickness; the *titulus* of the Cross of Christ, that preserved from sudden death; and the Angelic Salutation. More cabalistic inscriptions of the names of God were also used, as on the 'fermaile d'or del viele manere, et escriptz les nons de Dieu en chescun part d'ycelle fermaile', which John of Gaunt inherited from his mother.[7]

The thirteenth-century fashion in dress for both men and women was not favourable to the wearing of many jewels. It was a time of heavy draperies of sculptural simplicity, made from the woollen cloth that had become one of the chief industries of Flanders and Champagne. Luxury lay less in jewels or embroideries than in the linings of rich furs and in the fine quality of the cloth. It was an age when both men and women passed much of their time in going from fief to fief and from castle to castle, and most clothes approximated to travelling attire in warmth and simplicity. Their collars and mufflers made necklaces needless and the bodices fastened close with buttons. It is only in the romances that unusual jewels appear, like the earrings that fill two lines[8] in the *Roman de la Rose*:

Et met à ses deux oreilletes
Deus verges d'or pendans greletes.

Already, too, fine jewels were recognised as constituting in some sort a badge of rank. The *Ordonnances* of 1283 forbid *bourgeois* and their ladies from wearing precious stones, belts of gold or set with pearls, or coronals of gold or silver.[9] Even men and women of noble birth wore their finest jewels only on state occasions, and on their heads. The grandest coronets seem to have been worn by women. Eleanor of Provence owned a

[1] e.g. one in the Museum of Shakespeare's Birthplace, two in the British Museum, and one from Poitou in the Nantes Museum, which has on the reverse AMIE . AMI . AMITIE.

[2] Roach Smith, *Collectanea Antiqua*, IV, p. 109, now in the collection of Mr. John Hunt.

[3] Museum of Bucks Archaeological Society. Cf. a gold brooch with ✝ BIEN . AIT . QVI . ME . PORTE in the Museum of Nantes.

[4] Private collection.   [5] See Joan Evans, *Magical Jewels*, p. 121.

[6] e.g. 1380 inventory of Charles V: 'Ung fermail d'or esmaillé d'azur au nom des 3 roys d'une part et de AVE MARIA d'autre.' Gay, s.v. Fermail.

[7] Armitage Smith, *John of Gaunt*, Appendix, p. 427. *Testamenta Vetusta*, p. 141, wrongly translates 'fermail' as chain.

[8] 21965–6   [9] Texier, s.v. Cercles.

great number of garlands and chaplets for the hair, of the richest kind: she had nine when she married Henry III in 1236 and bought eleven more later.[1] Sixty-five years later the inventory of the Countess of Artois[2] includes four crowns of jewelled gold, one very rich, fourteen 'chaplets', or coronets, and ten 'tressons' or jewelled bandeaux. A simple crown of hinged plaques of silver gilt, set with pastes, with six rather rudimentary fleurs-de-lis rising from the circlet, has survived[3] to show the type. The larger crowns were formed of eight, twelve or more jewelled plaques hinged together.[4]

An eight-sided crown, now at Namur (Plate 9a) which is set with two relics of the Crown of Thorns, is said to have been sent from Constantinople by the Emperor Henry to his brother Philip, Marquis of Namur, in 1205; it is probable that only the relics were so sent, for the eight-sided crown does not look Byzantine. The enrichment of the filigree ground by the application of little stamped flowers of gold, and the mixture of plain rimmed settings with those formed by foliated claws, are characteristic of Mosan and French work of the first half of the thirteenth century. It may be compared with the early thirteenth century crown made for the reliquary of St. Oswald at Hildesheim:[5] a crown made for its purpose but evidently representing the kind of coronal ordinarily worn by great men. It is decorated with square plaques of enamel set in gold, surrounded by filigree scrolls relieved with cabochon gems in raised settings.

Another votive crown that is evidently based on a secular model is that (Plate 9b) given by Saint Louis, together with a cross and a reliquary, to the Dominicans of Liège.[6] It is formed of eight silver-gilt plaques with fleur-de-lis terminals linked by as many winged angels. The plaques are decorated with oak leaves, and are set with cabochon jewels and classical intaglios. The whole is a little heavy and austere, for all its magnificence; it is the product of an age when the gold work of shrines and reliquaries was more advanced than that of personal ornaments.

The cameos and intaglios of ancient Rome had been commonly used through the early Middle Ages as ornaments for shrines and reliquaries; the crown worn by Richard Earl of Cornwall when crowned King of the Romans at Aachen in 1257 (Plate 10a), preserved in the Cathedral Treasury, shows them applied, together with cabochon gems, to the ornament of a ritual coronal. All, cameos and intaglios alike, are set in rims strengthened by four claws. The design of the crown suggests that it was originally completed by four crockets and four fleurs-de-lis, and that the imperial arch was added for the occasion of the Coronation.

Cameos, indeed, were held to be among the richest of jewels in the thirteenth century.

[1] Barrera, p. 40–41. [2] Richard, p. 233.
[3] In the Musée du Cinquantenaire, Brussels; Clifford Smith, Plate XVII, 9.
[4] Marguerite of Hainault in 1298 had one of 14 pieces (Richard p. 382), and Blanche de Perthes in 1301 one of 16 (Gay, I, p. 325, s.v. Chapeaux couronnes).
[5] In the Cathedral Treasure; Braun I, Fig. 41. [6] Now in the Louvre.

PLATE II

(*a–b*) Brooch. Gold, set with cameos. English (?), *c.* 1300.
Found at Oxwich Castle, Glamorganshire
(*c*) The Swan Badge. French (?), mid fifteenth century.
Found at Dunstable

PLATE III

Rosary. Enamelled gold, consisting of fifty enamelled *Ave* beads, six
lozenge-shaped *Paternoster* beads and a large rounded knop. Each bead
is hollow and is decorated on front and back with a subject identified
by an inscription. English, fifteenth century

Their classical subjects were often interpreted in the light of Christian iconography, and the lapidaries attributed magical virtues to them. They were in consequence in some demand for personal ornaments to be constantly worn.[1] A thirteenth-century brooch from Canterbury is set like a contemporary seal[2] with an antique gem engraved with a faun drawing a thorn from the foot of another, in a plain rim inscribed AMOR VINCIT FORTITVDINEM.

Several more splendid brooches of the time survive that display ancient cameos in late thirteenth-century settings. One (Plate 10b) is set with a magnificent sardonyx of the Emperor Augustus; it is framed in an irregular oval of rubies and emeralds, each held by four claws, with trefoils of pearls between. It once formed part of the silver reliquary bust of St. Hilary in the treasury of the Abbey of Saint Denis.[3] The fact that its setting is of silver gilt and not of gold suggests that it was made for this purpose and not for personal use; yet the whole ornament is eminently wearable and may at least be taken to represent a secular type.

A second ornament, now arranged to be sewn on to a garment, is the great onyx now belonging to the municipality of Schaffhausen.[4] It is set with an antique cameo of Peace, which is framed in a jewelled setting that exemplifies how elaborate the technique of the jeweller had become in the second half of the thirteenth century (Plate 11). The stones are raised in high collets with rubbed-over rims strengthened by four projecting claws rising from the collet and forming ribs down its sides. The four pearls that occur at regular intervals are in similar raised settings with four tiny projecting leaves alternating with leaf-claws. Among the forest of jewels lurk tiny figures of lions, exquisitely made. The whole is an unparalleled example of the jeweller's work of its time. A rather later brooch in the Victoria and Albert Museum (Plate 17b) has an onyx cameo in the centre in a leafy setting, with an outer rim of more elaborate leafage set with rubies. It recalls the three ouches of similar design recorded in the 1313 inventory of the jewels of Piers Gaveston.[5]

Some of the most beautiful personal jewels of the thirteenth century are reliquaries meant to be worn round the neck. A cross in the Palazzo Pitti at Florence[6] has a cruciform crystal for its central adornment; this is set in heavy gold with a corded rim and

---

[1] The belt of lion's skin adorned with cameos that formed part of the treasure of Piers Gaveston in 1313 (Gay, s.v. ceinture) was doubtless magical in intention. Cf. Albertus Magnus, de Virtutibus animalium, I, 3, p. 162 'Si ex pelle leonis fiant corrigiae, percinctus ex illis non timebit hostes'.

[2] Proc. Soc. Ants., VII, 1878, p. 368. It cannot have been converted from a seal for the inscription is not reversed.

[3] See Babelon, Catalogue des Camées de la Bibliothèque Nationale, p. 107.

[4] See J. J. Oeri, Der Onyx von Schaffhausen.

[5] Rymer, Foedera, II, pt. 1, p. 203. Cf. the 1363 inventory of the Duke of Normandy: 'Un fermail où il a un camahieu d'une dame qui se baigne.' Texier, s.v. Camahieu.

[6] Set in the fifteenth century in a frame of jewelled silver gilt.

terminal settings of cabochon gems in raised collets of varied kinds. The importance of crosses of Byzantine form in Crusading times brought a two-armed form into fashion[1] both for processional and reliquary crosses for church use and for pendant crosses for personal wear. A beautiful example (Plate 12b) in jewelled gold was dedicated by its owner or his heirs and hung round the neck of an image of Christ in Røskilde Cathedral.[2] The most precious relic to travel west after the crusades was the Crown of Thorns which Saint Louis bought from Baldwin, Latin Emperor of Constantinople. He detached a few single thorns from it to give to members of his family, and one of these was a little later mounted by the King of Aragon between two large cabochon amethysts set in gold, enamelled in translucent colours with scenes from the Passion.[3] It is a tiny thing, yet has all the glow of colour and of religious feeling that we find in the Sainte Chapelle (Plate 12c–d).

Rosaries, too, came gradually into more common use,[4] and were more often made of precious materials.[5] Raoul de Clermont, for example, in 1302 had a rosary with aves of jet with the larger beads, or paternosters, of crystal and another of Scotch pearls and garnets.[6] They grew yet more varied with the course of the century. In 1372 Queen Jeanne d'Évreux had a rosary of a hundred pearls with ten 'seignaux' of gold;[8] and in 1381 Adam Ledyard, a London jeweller, had in his stock paternoster beads of white and yellow ambers, coral, jet and silver gilt, and aves of jet and blue glass as well as cheap sets of maple-wood (mazer) and white bone for children.[7]

At the same time other devotional jewels were coming into fashion. The Pope in the first year of his Pontificate, and every seven years after, blesses at Easter little wax roundels stamped with the Paschal Lamb and the image of a saint.[8] In the fourteenth century a fashion arose of setting these roundels as pendants; that they were usually framed only in silver gilt suggests that they were not often worn, perhaps only during pregnancy.[9] Mahaut d'Artois had two thus set in 1312;[10] others, also set in silver though

[1] See Joan Evans, *Art in Mediaeval France,* 1948, p. 58.

[2] It is now in the National Museum, Copenhagen.

[3] Formerly in the Pichon Collection; given to the British Museum by Mr. George Salting in 1902.

[4] The earliest recorded is that dedicated by Godiva c. 1040: William of Malmesbury *de Pont.* lib IV, c. 4, quoted Texier, s.v. Chapelets.

[5] Strictly speaking a rosary should consist of three chaplets, each of 15 *dizaines* of Ave Marias and 15 Paternosters (see Texier, s.v. Chapelet) but in the Middle Ages the number of beads varied.

[6] Gay, s.v. Patenôtres.

[7] Riley, *Memorials of London,* p. 455. The street names of Paternoster Row and Ave Maria Lane remain (though the streets lie in ruins) to show where the Rosary makers had their shops, not far from the jewellers' street of Cheapside.

[8] Texier, s.v. Agnus Dei states that the practice goes back at least to the sixth century.

[9] cf. the French royal accounts for 1393. 'Pour 5 petits tableaux d'argent dorez appelez Agnus-Dei, que les femmes portent quant elles sont grosses, et l'en met en chascun un pain beneist à chanter'. Gay, s.v. Agnus Dei.

[10] Richard, p. 242.

jewelled, are recorded in the wills of the Queen of France in 1372 and of Charles VI in 1399.[1] One survives in the Victoria and Albert Museum: a roundel issued by Urban VI between 1378 and 1389, in a fifteenth-century German case.

The amount of jewellery worn increased slowly with the progress of the thirteenth century. In 1272 Henry III deposited as security with his sister in Paris many rings, sixty-nine belts adorned with gold or jewels, and forty-five *fermails* or ring-brooches, including one 'cum duobus amantibus'[2] — a kind of brooch with the ring formed as two human figures, that is represented in surviving base metal brooches of slightly later date.[3] Marguérite of Hainault on her marriage to the Count of Artois in 1298[4] received as wedding gifts, besides two crowns and a number of jewelled coronets, a fleur-de-lis brooch set with jewels, enamelled on the back, and a belt of seventy-six jewelled pieces.

A list of jewels once belonging to Blanche of Castile (1188–1252), Queen Regent of France,[5] includes a gold crown set with rubies, emeralds, and large pearls; another set only with oriental pearls; a third with rubies and emeralds; and a great crown used for her coronation set with large balas rubies, surrounded by emeralds, pearls, oriental sapphires and rubies. Her brooches showed considerable variety: she had three *fermails* or ring-brooches set with gems; two square brooches, one with a large balas and one with a large sapphire in the middle, each surrounded by alternating gems and pearls; and 'duo firmacula aurea qui dicuntur tasseux', set with rubies and emeralds: presumably a pair of brooches linked by a chain, such as is used to fasten mantles on the Gothic sculpture of the time. She had two larger brooches or 'ouches'; one shaped as an eagle, set with rubies and emeralds,[6] and one with figures of a King and Queen wearing mantles of fleurs-de-lis.[7]

The tastes of men might be simpler. In 1299–1300[8] the only notable jewels of King Edward I were two golden ouches set with cameos, a *fermail* with a ruby and small garnets that he usually wore, another with rubies and emeralds that his Queen had given him, some belts of silk harnessed with gold, and a gold pendant set with a large sapphire

---

[1] Laborde, *Glossaire*, p. 122.   [2] Rymer, *Foedera*, 1st ed., 1878.
[3] e.g. in the Museum of Archaeology, Cambridge.   [4] Richard, p. 382.
[5] *Liber Quotidianus*, p. 353.

[6] cf. one found at Mainz, in 1908, in the collection of Baron von Heyl zu Herrnsheim at Worms, $2\frac{1}{8}$ inches high (Clifford Smith, p. 136) and one recorded in the inventory of Humphrey de Bohun, Earl of Hereford, 1322; *Arch. Journ.*, III, 1846, p. 348.

[7] 'Una nouchia auri cum imaginibus Regis et Regine de armis Francie cum petraria diversa.' Cf. the brooch which Mahaut d'Artois gave to her son-in-law the King of France in 1319: 'un joyau d'argent esmaillié a un Roy d'une part et une Royne d'autre, et un rubis au milieu, et un aneau d'or,' and that 'à la semblance des deux rois de France et de Behaigne' owned by the Duke of Burgundy in 1397. Laborde, *Glossaire*, p. 313.

[8] *Liber Quotidianus*, pp. 345, 348, 351.

'ad pendendum circa collum' — that is to say, to be worn next the skin, so that its supposed magical powers might benefit the wearer.[1] When his tomb was opened in 1774[2] his body was dressed in a mantle fastened by a ring-brooch set with stones in raised collets, with the head of its pin shaped like an acorn. The stole round his neck was sewn with small pearls in an interlaced pattern round quatrefoils of finely chased gilt metal, with each petal, and the centres, set with a paste in a raised collet. His gloves were each sewn with a jewelled quatrefoil.[3] The whole parure exemplifies the essential simplicity of the jewels of the time, only modified by an approximation to the greater splendour of ecclesiastical use. It was the age of the dominance of Gothic architecture; and such architecture, piling space on space and basing all its ornament on real or apparent structural forms, offered comparatively little inspiration to the designer of jewels. Even the arts of pure decoration were dominated by the schemes of illuminated manuscripts and stained glass, both planned as a series of medallions of minute figure subjects: schemes which could be followed by the enameller only on a rather larger scale than that of personal ornaments.

[1] cf. '. . . un saffir que li cuens pandoit a son col' in the 1266 inventory of the Count of Nevers (Gay, s.v. Pent-a-col) and the eight pendants with sapphires owned by Queen Clémence in 1328. Laborde, *Glossaire*, p. 436.

[2] Gough, *Sepulchral Monuments*, I, pt. 1, p. 4.

[3] cf. the enamelled roundels in *émail de plique* from the tomb of Jean de Tanlay, Bishop of Le Mans, died 1294, at the Abbey of Preuilly, Seine et Marne, now in the Louvre.

CHAPTER TWO

The Gothic Period

The early fourteenth century was a time of delicate lyricism in all the decorative arts. The love of romance that found expression in amatory inscriptions, the feeling for natural beauty that was expressed in every art from monumental sculpture to illumination and embroidery, the taste for a rather mannered elegance, were all reflected in the design of jewels. Precious stones gradually became more abundant as the trading cities of Italy strengthened their contacts with the Eastern marts; pointed and table cut diamonds came to add sparkle to the lustre of cabochon gems; enamel grew more brilliant as the art of translucent enamel in many colours was developed and more applicable to figure work as *émail en blanc* was used;[1] and the technique of gold work was enriched by such new processes as *pointillé* engraving on gold.

The increased supply and demand for precious stones soon led to their use being regulated by law. By 1331 an edict had been passed in Paris against the use of paste gems[2] and in 1355 jewellers were forbidden to use river pearls and oriental pearls together and to put tinted foil under an amethyst or carbuncle to improve its colour.[3] On the other hand, the development of the goldsmith's craft was officially recognised; the goldsmiths of London were given their Charter by Letters Patent in 1327[4] and those of Paris, whose association had long prospered as a religious community, bought a house to serve as their hall in 1405.[5]

In the 1300s luxury began to creep into the French court, that had long been dominated by the austere tradition established by Saint Louis. Clothes were made from cloth of delicate and exotic dyes; brocades were used for yet more splendid dress; and everything, from architecture to mantles, was made on a richer plan with more complicated decoration. So profound a change was naturally reflected in the sumptuary art of jewellery. The wearing of jewels had become, indeed, a definite mark of rank, and as such was restricted by law. In 1363 Edward III of England's Statute *de victu et vestitu*

---

[1] It is mentioned in the 1399 inventory of Charles VI.

[2] Gay, s.v. Doublet. False pearls (except those made of silver beads) had been forbidden by Étienne Boileau in the *Livre des Mestiers* (between 1258 and 1269).

[3] Laborde, *Glossaire*, pp. 129, 437.   [4] Herbert, II, p. 121.

[5] Gay, s.v. Orfèvres.

decreed that handicraftsmen and yeomen were not to wear 'ceynture, cotel, fermaille, anel, garter, nouches, rubaignes, cheines, bendes, sealx u autres chose dor ne dargent', nor their wives and children either; knights were not to wear rings or brooches made of gold or jewelled with precious stones; and only esquires with land or rent of 200 marks a year and merchants and their families with goods and chattels of £500 value were to be permitted to wear apparel reasonably garnished with silver, and their wives apparel for the head garnished with stones. In Castile the sumptuary decrees were yet more strict. In 1380 Juan I forbade all his subjects except Infantas to wear dresses of cloth of gold or silk, or jewels and ornaments of gold or silver, pearls or precious stones. The ordinance was repeated in 1404.[1] There is little evidence to show how strictly such laws were enforced, but their very existence has its significance.

Royal and noble personages wore more and richer jewels than ever. In 1349 Queen Jeanne d'Évreux gave her best jewels to the Convent of the Grands Carmes of the Place Maubert at Paris, to be kept in the church until her death and then sold to pay for the buildings. The list of them[2] well illustrates the parure of a great lady: her crown with five small on five large fleurons, all richly jewelled; her fleur-de-lis brooch that she wore at her wedding and her coronation, set with sixteen rubies, fourteen emeralds and twenty-five pearls; her coronation girdle similarly set, and her 'tressons' for every-day use in her hair. Nor were these all her jewels; the inventory made in 1372 after her death[3] includes a crown with ten fleurons set with emeralds; two smaller crowns; four-teen coronals, three very rich — one jewelled chiefly with emeralds, one chiefly with balas rubies, and the third with sapphires; two jewelled 'ataches' or clasps, a pair of lozenge-shaped fermails, three large brooches — one round, one with a cameo in the middle, and one square — and a number of lesser brooches, circlets and belts.

Fleur-de-lis brooches such as Jeanne d'Évreux wore at her wedding and coronation were almost heraldic in intention, and seem to have been worn only by the royal family. Margaret of Hainault bought a fine one in 1323[4] and Charles V owned six splendid ones at his death in 1380.[5] The one that survives as part of the Regalia of France (Plate 21) is a little later, but well exemplifies the type. An idea of a great lady's crown may be gained from the jewelled crown of the late fourteenth century that adorns the Reliquary of St. Ursula in the Church of Castiglion Fiorentino,[6] with stones in high collets.

The marriage of Duke Philip of Burgundy to the widow of Philippe de Rouvre

---

[1] Davillier, 119.   [2] Montaiglon, *Archives de l'Art français*, I, 1861, p. 448.
[3] Leber, *Coll. des meilleures dissertations*, XIX, 1838, p. 120.   [4] Gay, s.v. Fermail.
[5] Labarte, p. 35. By 1488 the King of Scotland had one. Thomson, p. 5.
[6] See A. della Vita in *Dedalo*, I, 1920–1, p. 423. The Reliquary belongs to the Conservatorio di Santa Chiara. The Crown was probably made to be dedicated; it is set with sham pearls and pastes. The base is enamelled in a window-tracery design.

marked another stage in the growth of magnificence. She adored jewels, and those she bought and those her husband gave her set new standards of luxury for Europe. Even its vocabulary changed: the word *jouel* or *joyau* which had hitherto been used for the elaborate centrepieces of royal and lordly dinner tables, was henceforward used for jewels as we know them.[1] The inventory made in 1380[2] after the death of Charles V lists eight splendid crowns of his own, eight of his queen's, and twenty-six others, besides lesser coronals, all richly jewelled; a number of belts, no less rich, and a variety of brooches with eagles, griffins, stags and other decorative subjects. Louis d'Anjou in 1380 had a great crown, two lesser crowns, two small ones, seven 'grands cercles', two little circlets and endless 'fronteaux' and other head ornaments.[3]

French influence and Edward II's own taste for luxury brought similar standards of magnificence into fashion in England. In 1324 the King had ten crowns, five described according to their 'mestres peres' or predominating stones, two circlets and three chaplets.[4] The inventory of Edward III's mistress Alice Perrers records nearly twenty-two thousand pearls.[5] When Richard II married Isabella of France in 1396, the wedding presents[6] show an even higher standard of luxury. The bridegroom gave her a 'cercle de demi-ront' or frontlet set with large balases, sapphires and pearls; the Duke of Gloucester a crown of eight fleurons, and a jewelled eagle, 'd'or blanc'; the Duke of Aumale 'un cercle de pierrerie fait à manière de jardins'; other courtiers rich brooches: she already had a very rich fleur-de-lis *fermail* set with jewels and pearls. At Dover and at Canterbury she received yet other crowns on her arrival; at Eltham Richard gave her a collar of diamonds, rubies and large pearls, a belt of golden feathers to be worn baldrick-wise, a set of six eaglet buttons of jewelled gold, and a chaplet formed of clusters of large pearls set like roses and sewn on red velvet, with hanging buds, white, green and gold, and a circlet set with pearls, diamonds and rubies. The Earl Marshal gave her a mirror in a jewelled frame and a pearl studded belt, the City of London a jewelled circlet, the Duke of Brittany a cluster brooch with a great ruby in the middle surrounded by pearls and the Duke of York another with a diamond similarly set.

The description of the *chapel et coiffe* illustrates the fact that a stronger element of fashion was coming into the design of women's jewellery, especially in head ornaments. Already in 1360 we read in the inventory of Jeanne de Boulogne of 'un chappel à la nouvelle guise',[7] richly jewelled. The inventory of the jewels of Louis d'Anjou and his duchess, drawn up in 1379–80, describes various fanciful and fashionable head orna-ments, such as the Duchess' 'atour d'Espaigne': a garland of stones and pearls set on

[1] The change took place about 1390. Gay, s.v. Jouel.   [2] Labarte, p. 12.
[3] Moranvillé, p. 557 *et seq.*   [4] Palgrave, III, p. 138.
[5] Devon, *Issues of the Exchequer*, II, 209.
[6] Douët d'Arcq, *Choix de pièces inédites rélatives au règne de Charles VI*, 1864, p. 273.
[7] Gay, I, p. 325, s.v. Chapeaux couronnes.

flat hinged gold, its centre decorated with a rose of seven large pearls, and hanging pieces on either side.[1] She likewise owned a rich jewelled horned head-dress, of the kind that came into fashion about 1360 'garnished with very fine stones, rubies, sapphires, pearls, diamonds set in gold'.[2] Even ordinary felt hats were sewn with stones and enamels.[3]

Belts in their turn came under the influence of fashion with men's adoption of the short fitted pourpoint about 1340. They were studded with plaques of gold or enamel on a ground of silk or gold tissue; they were hinged together like a coronal, or hung with bells. Of belts so hung in the inventory of Philippe le Bon, two are said to be intended to be worn over plate armour, and the other when dancing.[4] Wide and heavy belts remained in fashion, worn further and further down, until about 1367, when they were ousted by a narrow belt worn at the true waistline, with its ornament often concentrated in the clasp and mordant.[5]

It is probably partly because of the increasing influence of pure fashion that few of the modish jewels of the fourteenth century have survived. A lady's belt buckle now in the Museum of Hungarian History at Budapest is formed of two rosettes linked by three clusters, all set with pearls.[6] Its beauty makes one regret the disappearance of the rest yet more.

The innumerable head ornaments of the fourteenth century are hardly represented in our own time except by one or two votive examples which are severer and more archaic in style than those recorded in the inventories. The Crown of St. Henry at Munich[7] perpetuates the tradition of the crown dedicated by St. Louis at Liége (Plate 9b) in its heavy fleurs-de-lis, set with cameos and gems in settings of Gothic leafage, divided by airy pinnacles of angels. The votive crown given to the head reliquary of St. Cornelius at Aachen by Johannes von Levendaal, Abbot of the Cornelimünster from 1355 to 1381, is rather lighter and equally beautiful.[8]

In general, however, fourteenth-century design tended away from traditional forms towards greater freedom. The fourteenth century witnessed a steady development of the ring-brooch towards a less utilitarian design. The simplest forms continued in use chiefly in base metal. The *Dit du Mercier* shows that the use of ring-brooches was passing to people who could not afford them of precious metal. The mercer declares:

---

[1] Moranvillé, p. 568.   [2] ibid., p. 567.
[3] See the hat of Mathilde d'Albret described in 1366. Laplagne-Barris in *Revue de Gascogne*, XV, 1874, pp. 501, 503.
[4] Gay, s.v. Ceinture.
[5] e.g. in 1408 the mordant of the King s belt was enamelled 'de deux paons qui font la roue'.
[6] Pásztory-Alcsuti, Fig. 4.   [7] Royal Treasury; once in the Bamberg Domschatz.
[8] O. von Falke and H. Frauberger, Fig. 122 and p. 138.

THE GOTHIC PERIOD

J'ai fermaillez d'archal dorez,
Et de laiton sorargentez,
Et tant les aim cax de laiton;
Sovent por argent le met on.

Many museums contain examples in gilt latten with inscriptions of the kind that had been fashionable on gold brooches some fifty years before.[1] In remote countries such as Scotland the simple ring-brooch remained in fashion until far into the age of the Renaissance; even in Gloucestershire it is said to have been worn as part of the traditional country-woman's dress as late as the eighteenth century.[2]

The ring-brooch was modified when made in more precious metal for more sophisticated wearers. Such a brooch as one from the Pichon collection in the Victoria and Albert Museum (Plate 13c) shews rubies and sapphires set in high collets and arranged as the blossoms of a wreath of delicate gold leaves.[3] The back is adorned with leafage in niello. A different version of the same theme, with a flatter ring, is represented by a brooch from Denmark.[4] On a third brooch[5] of the same kind the rubies and emeralds with which it is set are larger and more irregular in form, and break the regularity of the ring. The yet more elaborate golden foliage is here a link to bind them together; two lions in high relief emerge from the foliage. Sculptural influence is no less evident in the Kames Brooch (Plate 13a–b) now in the National Museum of Antiquities at Edinburgh which has a ring formed of six dragons each biting the hindquarters of the beast before him. Their eyes are formed of dots of clear yellow enamel, which has an extraordinary effect on the pure gold. The back is inscribed with an amuletic inscription in Lombardic letters.[6] A flat-ringed brooch in the Carrand Collection[7] has a rather similar amuletic inscription on the front[8] enamelled between bands of colour broken by four Vernicles in gold.

In other brooches the outline of the ring is modified; one found in the Water of Ardoch near Doune Castle[9] (Plate 14a) has the circle twisted like a heraldic wreath, and adorned alternately with a cord and an inscription in black letter:

[1] A good collection is in the Musée des Antiquités de la Seine Inférieure at Rouen; see Coutil.

[2] Similarly annular and heart-shaped brooches were popular in the Vendée in the eighteenth century and are still worn. See M. Pézard in *Art Décoratif*, I, 1908, p. 36.

[3] cf. a fragment from a similar brooch in the British Museum.

[4] From Grønsbeksgaarden, Bringstrom. National Museum, Copenhagen.

[5] Carrand Collection, Bargello Museum, Florence. Clifford Smith, Plate XX,6.

[6] IESVS : NAZARENVS : CRVCIFIXVS : REX : IVDEORUM : IASPER : MELPCHIOR — A. The pin is inscribed ATROPA.

[7] Bargello Museum, Florence; Clifford Smith, Plate XX, 2.

[8] IESVS AVTEM TRANSIENS PER MED (Luke IV, 30). This text was thought to be a protection against thieves.

[9] Now in the National Museum of Antiquities, Edinburgh. See *Proc. Soc. Ants. Scotland*, VIII, 1871, p. 330.

THE GOTHIC PERIOD

†ave de † moy mercie † pite
moun coer en † vous repoce.

This fourteenth-century corded-ring type of brooch is oddly modified in one instance
to form a reliquary for a thorn from the Crown of Thorns: the pin protects the relic;
other relics are set under stones on a plate that fills in the space between ring and pin;
and the rim is inscribed with details of what these relics are. The back is enamelled with
the scene of Christ's flagellation and with figures of a knight and a lady kneeling in
adoration.[1]

The very form of the ring was sometimes changed: a ring-brooch in the British
Museum (Plate 14b) has an octagonal ring, while one in the Victoria and Albert
Museum has the ring formed of six lobes[2] (Plate 14d). A silver gilt brooch in the Nantes
Museum is formed of two interlacing triangles with projecting heads and hands,
giving a star-shaped effect. Another in the British Museum, probably dating from
early in the fifteenth century, has four lobes curved inwards, each decorated with
a cabochon sapphire in a rectangular setting. The head of the pin is studded with three
pearls.

To break up the ring of the brooch into lobes and to add projections was an obvious
way of enriching the design of the annular type. A brooch in the British Museum (Plate
15b) has the ring expanded into eight lobes, four filled with hollow bosses of gold
chased with cockatrices, and four with cabochon jewels in raised settings, the rims
marked by four decorative ribs that simulate claws. Beyond the lobes project eight more
jewels: four pearls pinned down on to flower-shaped calyxes[3] and four stones in plain
rimmed settings. A few rings, however, were made with settings projecting from the
ring to hold a stone (Plate 14c); a variant has clasped or praying hands instead, a type
mentioned in the will of Philippa Countess of March who died in 1378.[4] Another version

---

[1] Silver gilt, 6 cm. across; now in the Cluny Museum, Paris. It is said to have come from the Abbey
of Poissy. The inscriptions read: DE CARCERE QUO INTRATUS-DE VACE QUO LAVAT MANUS. DE
KATHERINAE TUMBA. DE PILLARI QUO ALLIGATUS. DE DOMO QUA NATUS. DE PRECEPS QUO
INCLUSUS.

[2] For a later example with six lobes see the Kindrochet Castle brooch: *Proc. Soc. Ants. of Scotland*,
LX, 1925–6, p. 118 and LXI, 1926–7, p. 177.

[3] cf. Roman de la Rose, line 21358:
Une corone d'or grelete
Ou moult ot precieuses pieres
Et biaus chastons a quatre querres
Et a quatre demi compas.

[4] 'Un fermayl bleu avec deux maings tenang un diamant'. *Proc. Soc. Ants.*, VII, 1878. Cf. Inventory
of Charles V, 1380; a little brooch 'a deux mains qui s'entretiennent'. Laborde, *Glossaire*, p. 312. One
found at Ixworth has a head and open arms closing at the hands: C. Roach Smith, *Coll. Antiqua*, III,
p. 253.

of this form keeps the annular shape but has it broken by a pair of clasped hands; a gold example said to have been found near Lanercost[1] is inscribed in black letter:

Pe then my trought I plight
And to Pe Mary his moder bright

The type with clasped hands is most commonly represented in silver examples of late date from the Northern countries.[2] Another Northern type[3] has its ring studded with daisy-like flowers of metal that project beyond the frame; one from Norham has the flowers and the collars between gilded in contrast to the silver ring (Plate 15c).

The long series of Scottish brooches, continuing into the eighteenth century, perpetuates the ring-brooch tradition with little change. Exceptionally the Glenlyon brooch[4] (Plate 16), formerly belonging to the Campbells of Glenlyon, has a central bar on which the two pins rest. The back is engraved in black-letter with the names of the Magi and CONSVMATVM — the last saying of Christ. The more usual type, well represented by the Loch Buy brooch[4] (Plate 17a) is set with crystals and river pearls in high collets; in this instance a central crystal fills in the hole of the ring. A similar survival of the annular form, and a similar tendency ultimately to fill the whole, may be followed in the Scandinavian countries.[5]

In the more highly civilised countries the same process of development away from the annular form proceeded along various lines. Heart-shaped brooches of annular type came into fashion early in the fourteenth century.[6] They were obviously intended as gifts between lovers and often bear amatory inscriptions. One is inscribed in black-letter *Is thy heart as my heart;*[7] others bear the motto *Sans departer.*[8] Among the jewels Joan of Navarre, wife of Henry IV, forfeited in 1423,[9] were two, one inscribed *A ma vie de coer entier*, the other *A vous me lie*. A surviving gold heart-shaped brooch in the British Museum (Plate 18a) has the heart-ring twined with a ribbon; on one side it shows leaves, on the other the inscription VOUS ESTES MA IOY MOUNDEINE — You are my earthly joy. A gold heart-brooch in the Victoria and Albert Museum, chiselled and once enamelled with peacocks' feathers, has the inscription on the back: NOSTRE ET

[1] cf. two other gold brooches now in the Museum of the Society of Antiquaries of Newcastle-upon-Tyne.
[2] Examples in National Museum of Antiquities, Edinburgh; Nordiska Museum, Stockholm; and National Museum, Copenhagen.
[3] See *Archaeologia Aeliana*, 4th series, IV, 1927, p. 104.
[4] In the British Museum. See also the Brooch of Lorne, Paton, *Scottish National Memorials*, p. 34.
[5] Examples may be seen in the National Museum, Copenhagen, and in the Historical Museum of Stockholm. See too Rosenberg, *Niello*, p. 58, for German examples.
[6] In 1385 Hugh, Earl of Stafford left one to his daughter Joan. *Test. Vet.*, I, 119.
[7] *Arch. Journ.*, XI, 1854, p. 71.   [8] e.g. Nelson Collection, from Warwickshire.
[9] *Archaeologia*, LXI, 1909, p. 170.

TOUT DITZ A VOSTRE PLESIR (Plate 18c). One in the British Museum (Plate 18d) has a less regularly shaped heart outline and is adorned with flowers and leafage in relief. Such inscriptions were even set on jewels containing relics: a reliquary pendant (Plate 19c–d) of about 1400 in the British Museum is inscribed *a mon derreyne*.

The general development of the ring-brooch in the fourteenth century may perhaps be best expressed in terms of its approximation to the ouch, or brooch formed of a roughly disc-shaped ornament affixed by a pin fastening with a catch, as a modern brooch is. Once the ring-brooch was no longer thought of as depending on the pull of the stuff against the ring for holding its pin in place, the distinction hardly existed. It is only round about the year 1300 that the phrase 'fermail à couvercle' is used.[1] The stage is clearly marked by the use of ribs to cross the central space, so as to give a wheel form.[2] A fine wheel-brooch,[3] with its rim adorned with little dragons and sirens, with a further group of grotesque figures clustered round the central stone, has been set at a later date on a plate of gold to form a yet larger brooch of an entirely solid kind (Plate 20). Two others of silver gilt set with pastes are mounted on a mitre belonging to Lady Herries.[4] Another rather later brooch, of which the straight spokes are to some extent disguised by the jewels in fretted settings that are applied to them, is preserved in the treasury of the Cathedral of Split (Fig. 1). The same kind of decoration may be found on lobed brooches of gilt silver and bronze,[5] and on a lozenge-shaped brooch with cross-bars in the Carrand Collection.[6]

The inventory of Queen Clémence of Hungary drawn up in 1328 includes a brooch shaped as an M, set with a ruby and other small stones, and another formed as a B with a figure of St. John.[7] This type of jewel is still exquisitely represented for us by the Founder's Jewel which William of Wykeham left to New College, Oxford, in 1404, formed as a crowned Lombardic M with the Virgin and Angel of the Annunciation framed in the double arch of the letter (Plate 19a). The letter itself is jewelled with cabochon emeralds and rubies, with three pearls at the top of its arch; its central stem bears the lily of the Annunciation rising from a vase formed from a shaped stone. The lilies are enamelled in white, the angel's wings in translucent green. It may be that this brooch was designed as a cope clasp or morse;[8] it is equally likely, in view of Queen Clémence's B with St. John, that it was once a secular jewel. The bands of hinged

---

[1] e.g. Inventory of the Comtesse d'Artois, 1301; Richard, p. 233.

[2] See Joan Evans, 'Wheel shaped brooches', in *Art Bulletin*, XV, 1933, p. 197.

[3] Found in the Motala river near Kumstad, Sweden. National Museum, Stockholm.

[4] See *Proc. Soc. Ants.*, XXIV, 1912, p. 127.

[5] In the National Museum, Copenhagen, and in the University Museum of Archaeology at Cambridge, found at Topler's Hill, Edworth, Beds.

[6] Bargello Museum, Florence.   [7] Douët d'Arcq, *Nouveau recueil*, p. 42, No. 26, p. 43, No. 33.

[8] cf. the cope clasp of a golden M set with cameos and jewels which figures in the 1379 inventory of Charles V. Gay, s.v. M.

FIG. 1. Wheel-brooch, early fifteenth century, Cathedral of Split

plaques of basse-taille enamel and blue paste and crystals that now adorn Wykeham's mitre started life as a lady's girdle.[1]

The other brooches included in the inventory of Queen Clémence are clusters — a favourite fourteenth-century type of brooch, represented by a surviving example in the National Museum of Copenhagen[2] set with sapphires and pearls — and brooches formed of pairs of birds, one of two parrots and one of two magpies. Cluster brooches continued in fashion all through the century, and are represented in great magnificence in the inventories of Queen Jeanne de Boulogne, 1360,[3] Jean le Bon, 1364,[4] and Louis d'Anjou, 1380.[5] On his wedding in 1369 the Duke of Burgundy bought in Paris and gave his mother a splendid brooch of the kind, set with four great pearls, four great diamonds, and a ruby in the middle.[6]

Already these cluster brooches were being developed to give greater prominence

---

[1] The fact has been pointed out by Mr. Charles Oman.
[2] Two smaller ones found in the Meuse are in the Franks Bequest, British Museum.
[3] Douët d'Arcq in *Bibliothèque de l'Ecole des Chartes*, XL, 1879, p. 545.
[4] Bapst, *Testament de Jean le Bon.*   [5] Moranvillé, p. 572, *et seqq.*   [6] Prost, I, p. 176.

to the central stone or motif. In 1377 the Earl of Huntingdon lost a brooch of gold set with a large sapphire and pearls, with an image of St. George under the sapphire;[1] in 1360 Louis d'Anjou had one set with five large balas rubies, two large sapphires and eight pearls, with the centre of chased and enamelled gold representing four lions climbing ladders set against a tree on a mound,[2] and another with pearls in groups of three arranged in a cluster with the figure of a stag pursued by a hound in the centre. Gradually the cluster form was forgotten and brooches were designed as plaques of enamelled gold in more or less important rims of jewels, like those with a selvage man, and a lady holding a parrot, belonging to Jeanne de Boulogne in 1360,[3] and those with a griffin of gold set with a sapphire and rubies, a lion, and St. George, belonging to the Duchess of Brittany in 1370.[4] At the marriage of his daughter in 1387 the Duke of Burgundy gave the bridegroom a jewelled brooch with a falcon; the Duchess one with the figure of a lady; the Countess of Montbéliard had one with a rose, Jeanne d'Oiselet one with a unicorn, and the Duke himself wore one with a sun.[5] Six years later the bride owned brooches with goldfinches, sheep, dogs, and squirrels, all of richly jewelled gold.[6] The fashion was not confined to France and England. In 1389 Valentine de Milan on her marriage to the Duke of Orléans brought with her from Italy[7] brooches with a doe and fawn, a roe deer, a dove in a sun, a pelican, a lady harping[8] and another holding a large ruby.[9] The general tendency was for these ouches to grow larger and larger; one of the numerous ones belonging to Charles V was later given to the Pope for use as a cope-morse.[10] Such brooches continued in fashion for some fifty years. The surviving examples appear to be of the first half of the fifteenth century, yet they so clearly represent a fourteenth-century type and style that their natural place is with the jewels of that time. That the fifteenth-century ones are indeed of the first half of the century, and not, as is sometimes supposed, later is, I think, proved by the presence of such brooches in the pictures of Stephan Lochner, who died in 1457.[11] The largest

[1] *Archaeologia*, 1909, LXI, p. 164.   [2] Laborde, *Glossaire*, p. 113.
[3] Gay, s.v. Fermail; Bapst, *op. cit.*   [4] Rymer, *Foedera*, III, pt. 2, p. 1056.
[5] Prost, II, p. 311.   [6] Gay, s.v. Fermail.
[7] Nearly a hundred years later the Este Treasure included an immense number of jewels 'fatto ala todescha' with figures of an archer, a griffin, a mermaid, etc. that seem to have been of this type. Campori, p. 3.
[8] A brooch with the same subject is recorded in the Duke of Burgundy's inventory of 1389. Gay, s.v. Fermail.
[9] Graves, p. 62. Ten years later she had further acquired brooches with a phoenix, an angel with grey feathers, a white violet set with pearls and sapphires, and the royal badge of a flying stag; ibid, p. 94. For a later list see that of the jewels found in the Treasury on the accession of Henry IV of England. Palgrave, III, p. 313.
[10] Laborde, *Glossaire*, p. 312. They included brooches with eagles, griffins, stags and storks.
[11] His 'Dombild' Virgin in Cologne Cathedral wears a brooch with a maiden and a unicorn; see Clifford Smith, p. 145. The type continued in use in silver gilt almost into the sixteenth century: e.g. one in the Clemens Collection, Kunstgewerbe Museum, Cologne. Moses, Fig. 509.

collection of surviving brooches of this kind is that of those dedicated in the Cathedral of Essen.[1] Each is built up on a more or less circular tube of gold decorated with leaves of enamelled gold or with pearls on wires. Seven of them (of which one is reproduced in Plate 22) are alike, and may possibly have once been linked to form a necklace.[2] The others represent the current designs recorded in inventories: stags, stars, eagles, pelicans, huntsmen, and ladies sitting in gardens with the rays of the sun behind them.[3] A circular brooch now in Florence[4] is enamelled with a dromedary. A brooch from the Meuse, in the Franks Collection in the British Museum (Plate 22f) shows a woman holding a sapphire; it offers a parallel with the ouche 'd'un aungell blanc tenant en sa mayn un saphir feble garnisez de vi. perles enterfoiles' recorded in an inventory of the jewels delivered on his accession to Henry IV.[5]

The culmination of the series is the splendid brooch, dating from the middle of the fifteenth century, in the Imperial Treasury at Vienna[6] (Colour Plate I),[*] in which the traditional design of a pair of lovers is set in a delicate golden wreath forming a kind of park-paling round them. Their faces and hands are enamelled white; the man's hair is partly of gold wire; their dress a rather pale cold blue. The ground is filled in with minute flowers and foliage in high relief. Between their heads is a triangular diamond and beneath it a cabochon ruby. The two pearls that counter-balance these are pinned through; the three at the base of the jewel are set à potences with little projections on either side. A rather later version[7] of the same theme, that has lost the surround, is in a private collection: the cast figures, the less delicate hair and features, show by contrast how admirable is the quality of the Vienna brooch. The Duke of Burgundy could command the highest technical skill, and got it.

Such brooches were not usually inscribed, unless in explanation of their subject. An elaborate and richly jewelled brooch belonging to Louis d'Anjou, however, ornamented with figures of angels singing Alleluia was inscribed in the old-fashioned way:

> *Cuer de vray ami*
> *Doit avoir mercy*

[1] See Verhaegen in *Revue de l'Art Chrétien*, 3rd ser., V, 1887, p. 276; Clifford Smith, p. 143; Humann I, p. 376.

[2] They may be compared with one now set as a pendant on the collar of the bust reliquary of Ste. Valérie at Chambon-Sainte-Valérie, Creuse.

[3] A further collection, now mounted as a necklace, was in 1947 the property of the Brummer Gallery, New York. See *Bulletin of the Cleveland Museum of Art*, Cleveland, Ohio, XXXIV, Nov. 1947.

[4] Carrand Collection, Bargello. Clifford Smith, p. 146, Plate XVII, 12.

[5] Palgrave, *Kal. & Inv. of Exchequer*, III, p. 345.

[6] See Falke in Staatliche Museum Berlin, *Verzeichnis der Neuerwerbungen seit 1933*, Nos. 164 and 167.

[7] Dr. Erich von Strohmer informs me that another version is in the Boston Museum of Fine Arts; I have not seen it.

*In black and white in the Dover edition. 63

and another, no less rich, with St. Michael overcoming the devil, bore the inscription *C'est pour le mieulx, bien me doit plaire.*[1]

For state occasions royal and noble persons were apt to wear brooches shaped as eagles, a traditional form which, it may be remembered, is found as early as the eleventh century[2] and was represented among the jewels of Eleanor of Castille. Thomas Beauchamp Earl of Warwick mentions two such brooches in a will made not long before his death in 1369;[3] the 1363 inventory of the Duke of Normandy mentions 'le grant aigle d'or de MonSeigneur', set with two great rubies and six lesser ones, two great sapphires and several diamonds and large pearls; the Duchess of Brittany had two in 1376;[4] the Earl of Huntingdon one of plain gold and two of pearls, one large with a chaplet of pearls round it,[5] and Richard II in 1379 four.[6] The type is now best represented by two brooches, one in the Cluny Museum[7] (Plate 24) and one given by Charles d'Anjou, King of Hungary, to the treasury of the Cathedral of Aachen.

These vaguely heraldic brooches were succeeded by others that were specifically designed as badges. In 1376 the Duchess of Brittany had one shaped as an ermine set with pearls,[8] in 1360 Louis d'Anjou had another with a little boar on a terrace, on a white rose, inside a garter inscribed with the motto of the Order of the Garter.[9] In 1379 Richard II pawned five brooches (*nouches*) with his badge of the white hart studded with rubies on the shoulders, like those the angels wear on the Wilton Diptych; four others with griffins, five with white dogs with rubies on the shoulders, and one with four boars azure.[10]

These badge-brooches soon came to have a political significance, particularly in England, where they were used in less precious materials as the marks of the vast retinues of great lords and by implication as the badges of political factions. Leaden badges in the British Museum, mostly of the fifteenth century and probably once gilt, include the royal rose and fetter-lock, the crowned ostrich feather of Norfolk, the Warwick bear and ragged staff, the white hart of Richard II lodged within palings, a talbot, fleur-de-lis, and a shield with the collar of SS. One with a cock has a scroll inscribed 'Follow me Kocrel' and one with a cat and mouse the legend: 'Vi sis mus.'[11] Similar badges in the Musée de Cluny represent those of du Guesclin and Charles V, the St. Andrew Cross of the Burgundians and the dolphins of the Armagnacs.

In both England and France these badges were also developed into those collars of livery which served to distinguish royal persons and those they delighted to honour,

[1] Moranvillé, p. 574. It was one of the Duke's mottoes.
[2] See above, p. 43.
[3] *Test. Vet.*, 79.
[4] Rymer, *Foedera*, III, pt. 2, p. 1056.
[5] *Archaeologia*, LXI, 1909, p. 164.
[6] Riley, *Memorials*, p. 429.
[7] The outer is rim set with relics.
[8] Rymer, *Foedera*, III, pt. 2, p. 1056.
[9] Gay, s.v. Fermail.
[10] Riley, *Memorials*, p. 429.
[11] For a fuller list see Clifford Smith, p. 110.

and were later merged into the collars of the Orders of Knighthood and office.[1] The history (even now imperfectly known) of the English collar of SS exemplifies the course of development of one such collar. It was used by John of Gaunt[2] and his dependants,[3] and then passed to his son and heir, Henry of Lancaster, later Henry IV of England. John Gower the poet on his effigy in Southwark Cathedral wears a collar of SS of his livery with the swan pendant used by Henry in virtue of his first wife Mary Bohun.[4]

Yet it was also used by John of Gaunt's nephew Richard II, who had a collar of SS worked with SOUVENEZ VOUS DE MOI, which he used as his motto at the Smithfield Joust.[5] Henry seems to have added this motto to the ancestral SS, at least by implication, in 1396–7. He then[6] had a collar of SS adorned with hanging flowers of 'souveigne vous de moy' — presumably forget-me-nots; these became associated with the SS and are alluded to in descriptions of similar collars as 'flores domini'. In 1407, when he was King, he paid a huge sum to a London goldsmith, Christopher Tyldesley, for another collar of gold adorned with the motto SOVEIGNEZ, enamelled letters of S and X and a quantity of rich jewels; it had a triangular clasp hanging from it, set with a great ruby and four large pearls.[7] At an uncertain date the same goldsmith made him another collar of twenty-four SS pounced with the word SOVERAIN with a clasp set with a balas ruby and six pearls.[8] Can he have changed the motto *soveignez* for *soverain* on his accession? It would seem not, for as Earl of Derby he used SOUVERAYNE on his seal (1385) and the motto reappears on the tester of his tomb in Canterbury, together with that of the Queen A TEMPERANCE.[9]

By this time, at all events, the collar of SS was established as that of the royal livery. Its pendant often represented family or political badges, such as the white lion of March, the black bull of Clare, the swan of de Bohun, or the Beaufort portcullis.[10]

With the accession of Edward IV it was rivalled by his collar of alternate suns and roses,[11] such as appears on the portraits of Sir John Dunne and his wife in the triptych by Hans Memlinc.[12] They wear it, as is usual, with the white lion of March as pendant; in the time of Richard III his silver boar replaced the lion. The inventory of the jewels of Sir John Howard, made in 1466,[13] described a collar made of thirty-four suns and roses of gold fixed on a band of black silk, with a pendant of gold set with a sapphire.

[1] On these see W. St. John Hope, *Heraldry for Craftsmen and Designers*, p. 292; A. P. Purey Cust, *The Collar of S.S.*

[2] *Arch. Journ.*, XXXIX, p. 376.

[3] e.g. on the effigy of Sir John Swinford, d. 1371, in Spratton Church, Northants.

[4] Hope, op. cit., p. 298.   [5] ibid.   [6] ibid.

[7] The 'nouche' of the original is presumably the elaborate clasp, usually with pendant, of which Hope illustrates examples. ibid. p. 299.

[8] ibid. p. 300.   [9] See Hope, op. cit., p. 300.   [10] See Joan Evans, *English Jewellery*, p. 53.

[11] See Hope, op. cit., p. 304. It is combined with the Fitz Alan oak leaves on the effigy of Joan Countess of Arundel at Arundel, c. 1487.

[12] In the collection of the Duke of Devonshire.   [13] Royal Commission Hist. MSS. 7th Report, p. 537.

With the accession of Henry VII the collar of SS was revived, with a portcullis or Tudor Rose pendant.[1] By this time it had ceased to be a personal ornament and had become a badge of office in the King's Household. It is still worn by certain of Her Majesty's judges and, exceptionally, by the Lord Mayor of London.

The Collar of SS has had an unusually long history. It is often forgotten how many other collars of livery were in existence in England in the late fourteenth and early fifteenth century. The effigy of Sir Thomas Markenfield, who died about 1390,[2] shows him wearing a collar of park palings widening out to enclose a couchant hart: an adaptation of the badge of Richard II to form a collar. Anne of Bohemia, Richard's consort, seems to have used a collar of her ostrich feathers. A brooch with such a collar found in the Treasury on Henry IV's accession is described as being of the 'livere de la Roigne que Deux assoille'. When her widower married Isabella of France in 1396 his new bride received among her presents a collar which included her predecessor's badge among its adornments: it was formed of broom-pods with roundels between, each charged with a rosemary pearl-set and an ostrich with a ruby on its shoulder.[3] Henry VI again, in 1446 owned 'a Pusan of gold called ye riche coler, conteynyng XVI culpons or peces, upon ye whiche beth viij antelopes, garnysshed wt. xx grete perles . . . and viij crownes of gold eche of hem enameled wt. a reson of UN SAUNZ PLUIS'.[4]

The royal collars of France were no less rich and varied. In 1389 the Duke of Burgundy had a collar of five white fleurs-de-lis and another of nineteen doves enamelled white.[5] Four years later he was using his badge of the bell for the collars of livery worn by his household.[6] In 1405 his political badge of the carpenter's plane to some extent superseded this;[7] and then in 1412 the Duke paid for a collar of hop leaves and flowers all of gold set with stones and pearls.[8] Yet when the great Burgundian order of the Golden Fleece was founded its collar was formed of yet another Burgundian badge, the *briquets de Bourgogne*.

The King of France's collar of the broom-pods, which may be that worn by Richard II on the Wilton Diptych,[9] was invented (or possibly revived) in 1378; in its turn it never became standardised. Sometimes it is described as made of two round cords or tubes, powdered with broom-pods and flowers in branches with clusters of pearls between and letters forming the King's motto JAMÈS hanging;[10] sometimes as having *pièces d'euvre* with the motto JAMÈS in openwork joined by heavy links and with hanging bells and a broom-pod pendant at either end.[11] The inventory of the jewels of the Duchess of

[1] Hope, op. cit., p. 306.   [2] At Ripon; Hope, p. 309.
[3] Douët d'Arcq, *Choix de pièces inédites relatives au règne de Charles VI*, II, 1864, p. 275.
[4] *Archaeologia*, XXI, 1827, p. 35.   [5] Laborde, *Glossaire*, p. 220.
[6] Gay, s.v. Collier.   [7] Laborde, *Ducs*, I, 21.
[8] ibid., I, 58.   [9] See Joan Evans in *Arch. Journ.*, CV, 1948, p. 1.
[10] M. Clarke, *Fourteenth Century Studies*, p. 281; Evans, loc. cit., p. 4.   [11] In 1398. Gay, s.v. Collier.

Orléans in 1456 gives evidence of the existence of at least three other collars of livery: one with crosses of St. Andrew and her motto, another with her device of *chantepleures* and her motto; and a third 'a façon de l'Ordre de Clèves' with clouds charged with her badges and hanging pansies enamelled in violet and white.[1] The whole suggests, as was no doubt the case, that a royal donor making a present of his collar of livery to a relative who himself (or herself) had badges and mottoes, might modify his own customary design to include some of them.

A similar and even greater freedom in the use of badges and heraldic devices is evident in other jewels which had not the significance of collars of livery, such as the belt belonging to the Duchess of Brittany in 1376,[2] formed of eight bars of gold ornamented with white eagles, linked by plaques charged with greyhounds bearing shields. In 1390, again, the King of France had a belt of black silk studded with forty-four golden broom-pods, each hung with three little bells, fastened by a buckle and mordant to match. Seven years later the Queen had a belt all of gold without any stuff, adorned with thirty-two broom blossoms each set with a ruby or a sapphire, joined by as many clusters of eight pearls set on a white flower and a green broom-pod. In the next year[3] the King had a belt harnessed with five plaques enamelled with his four livery colours of black, white, green and red, each enamelled with his motto JAMÈS; the buckle engraved with branches with flowers and pods of broom, and the mordant with a tiger.[4]

Yet more often the only heraldic element incorporated in a jewel was a motto, such as the BONNE FOY on a brooch of Charles V's[5] in 1380 or the LOYAULTE PASSE TOUT on a belt of the Duchess of Touraine's nine years later.[6]

Saint Louis had considered that the men of his court who wore robes embroidered with their arms were unduly luxurious. A hundred and fifty years later dresses were no longer embroidered with mere silk, but were sewn with jewels. The *surcot* that had become the official uniform of a great lady on state occasions usually had its plastron front adorned with a series of brooches or *ataches*, sometimes hinged together to form a chain. The dress itself was sometimes sewn with jewels; in 1362 a thief stole from Yolande de Bar a scarlet *cotte* with the sleeves edged with garnets and pearls set in gold in groups of four, and the neck-piece of a cloak buttoned with wreaths of violets made of large pearls, and a cloak with its button-holes worked with vines, the leaves of gold and the grapes of large pearls. Two years later Jean le Bon had a long *houppelande* or house-coat of blue brocade, 'orfraisiée d'orfevrerie', round the sleeves and collar and on the breast.[7] New wealth had brought in new standards of luxury.

---

[1] Laborde, *Ducs*, III, p. 377.   [2] Rymer, *Foedera*, III, pt. 2, p. 1056.   [3] Gay, s.v. Ceinture.
[4] A different belt with similar elements of decoration is recorded for 1403.
[5] Laborde, *Glossaire*, p. 312.
[6] Gay, s.v. Affiche. Both mottoes occur among those of Louis d'Anjou. Moranvillé, p. XXIX.
[7] Bapst, *Testament de Jean le Bon*, p. 49.

CHAPTER THREE

The Later Middle Ages

The later Middle Ages are in some sense a time of transition in the history of jewels. Not only were gems themselves available in greater quantities, but greater skill was being developed in their cutting. The natural octahedron of the diamond had long been cut in two to give the pointed diamond, and in the fourteenth century this had begun to be flattened to give the table form; more elaborate cutting was now attempted. In 1412 the Duke of Burgundy owned[1] a large diamond 'de quatre losenges en la face dudit dyamant et de quatres demies losenges par les costez dudit dyamant'; another 'plat de six costés', as well as table-cut stones like mirrors. Two years later the inventory of the Duc de Berri[3] records a 'gros dyament poinctu taillié à plusieurs lozanges'. Guillebert de Metz, in his description of Paris in 1407, mentions 'La Courarie' where the diamond cutters live, and names Herman as one of the most skilful of them.[3] In 1420 the Duke of Burgundy[4] owned 'deux petis dyamens plaz aus ij costez fais a iiij quarrez'; 'un bon dyamant taillié à quatre quarrés en façon de losange'; and 'un dyamant taillé à plusieurs faces'. By this time the diamond cutters of the Low Countries were recognised as highly skilled men. In a case heard at Bruges in 1465[5] about an amethyst sold as a balas ruby, four men — Jean Belamy, Chrétien van de Scilde, Gilbert van Hitsberghe and Leonard de Brouckère — appeared as expert witnesses and are specifically called 'diamantslypers'.[6]

The development of jewel-cutting naturally tended to shift the emphasis in the design of jewels from gold and its techniques of filigree and enamel to gems and their glow and glitter. Yet the older tradition was very strong and deep-rooted, and the change was a very slow one, needing more than one century for its completion. In the late fifteenth century a fashion arose of portraying jewels in the margins of illuminated manuscripts.

---

[1] Texier, s.v. Diamant.

[2] Pannier in *Rev. Arch.*, 1873, XXVII, p. 39; it had been given by the Chapter of Chartres Cathedral to the Duc de Berri.

[3] Gay, s.v. Diamant. By 1497 there were diamond cutters at Lyons.

[4] Laborde, *Glossaire*, 251.   [5] Laborde, *Glossaire*, 251.

[6] Robert de Berquen, in his *Merveilles des Indes*, 1661, p. 12, says that it was his ancestor Louis de Berquen who in 1476 found how to cut diamonds with their own powder. This is obviously untrue, but he may perhaps have improved the process.

THE LATER MIDDLE AGES

The Grimani Breviary is perhaps the most famous example.[1] What is particularly notable is that the jewels portrayed are for the most part lozenge-cut and cabochon gems in simple gold rims surrounded by pearls.[2] Another Book of Hours[3] (Plate 29) has its Annunciation picture bordered with ten pendants — one a cross, three lozenge-shaped, and the rest variations on the cluster — all elegant, all richly jewelled and crocketted with pearls and all, though extremely skilful, designed by a man more interested in jewels than in the art of the goldsmith. It cannot be said that the art of gem-cutting was the predominant factor in fifteenth-century jewel-design; the important thing is that for the first time it took its place as one of the factors in the art.[4]

In the fourteenth century jewels had been linked with architecture only in their use of naturalistic and heraldic decoration; towards its end the forms and proportions of Flamboyant and Perpendicular architecture begin to leave their impress even on things so small as jewels. A loftier proportion, more liny mouldings, even the reproduction of architectural niche-work and tracery on a minute scale, make a clear distinction between the two epochs, even though certain survivals from the earlier period in less aristocratic jewels make it difficult to establish a perfectly clear chronological division.

The crown which Blanche of England, daughter of Henry IV, wore on her marriage to the Elector Ludwig II in 1402 (Plate 25) is a splendid instance of the new style. It is formed of twelve brooch-like medallions of delicate tracery, each centred with a jewel and studded with three other jewels and three clusters of pearls to form a double triangle. From these greater and lesser pinnacles rise alternately, that seem to have lost their traditional fleur-de-lis form in a loftier and more architectural development of their design. It affords an interesting parallel with the crown given by the Duke of Burgundy to his daughter on her marriage to the Duke of Savoy in 1403, with a circlet garnished with eight 'fermailles', surmounted by four great and four lesser floriated pinnacles, all jewelled with indescribable richness.[5] At the wedding of Antoine de Bourgogne in 1402 a golden crown ornamented with sixteen brooch-like medallions of this kind was undone and the pieces given to sixteen of the ladies and gentlemen present.[6]

The general tendency in the fifteenth century was to lower the pinnacles of crowns

[1] See also Otto Paecht, *The Master of Mary of Burgundy*, 1948, frontispiece and Fig. 23b.

[2] e.g. Grimani Breviary, fol. 18 v. A few pages have pictures of enamelled flowers with jewelled centres (e.g. fol. 172, fol. 175, fol. 181). Slightly more elaborate settings are shown on fol. 53 v and 56 v.

[3] Bibliothèque Nationale MS Latin 1166.

[4] It is perhaps worth noting that jewels were beginning to be counterfeited on a greater scale. The *Segreti per colori* of 1440 (ed. Merrifield, II, 509) gives recipes for making false pearls, using small shells and fish scales to give them lustre.

[5] A detailed description will be found in Plancher, *Histoire de la Bourgogne*, III, Dijon, 1748, p. CCXVI. It may be compared with such splendid painted crowns as that of the *Madonna of the Chancellor Rolin* in the Louvre; those of the angels on the wings of the Van Eyck altarpiece at Ghent; and those of the altarpiece (perhaps by Burgkmair) of the Virgin and female saints at Frankfurt.

[6] Gay, s.v. Chapeaux couronnes.

and to assimilate them into the circlet of the crown. Such a crown as that worn by Margaret of York at her wedding to the Duke of Burgundy in 1468[1] keeps the tradition of floriated pinnacles; but this was a ceremonial ornament made especially for the marriage. Jeanne de Laval, in Nicolas Froment's *Burning Bush*, painted between 1475 and 1476,[2] wears a rather massive crown with low fleurons closely set to form a cresting to the circlet. Even the crowns worn by the Virgin in pictures show a similar tendency. The Virgin Jean Foucquet painted for Étienne Chevalier about 1457[3] has high fleurons mounted on twisted stems, each a trefoil set with jewels in chased collets, with lesser trefoils of pearls between; the crown given by Enguerrand Charonton to his Virgin of 1453,[4] though less elegant, has lofty pinnacles formed as fleurs-de-lis. But Gerard David's *Virgin* in the National Gallery (Plate 28), painted towards the end of the century, shows her wearing a crown with low pinnacles made of twisted branches that form an integral part of the design of the circlet.

By the last quarter of the century great ladies had come to treat their crowns as a part of their general head-dress. From about 1380 women's hair-dressing had grown more and more complicated; the hair was puffed and padded out over the ears and kept in shape by a golden net. The inventory of Margaret Duchess of Burgundy in 1405[5] includes richly jewelled *coiffes* for covering the padded hair as well as crowns and *fleurs de couronnes* for the wide circlets that surmounted it. Chaucer in his *Legende of Good Women*[6] describes such an attire:

> ... *She was clad in roiall habite grene;*
> *A fret of golde she had next her here,*
> *With florouns small; and, I shall not lie,*
> *For all the world, right as a daisie*
> *Icrowned is with white levis lite,*
> *So were the florounis of her crowne white,*
> *For of a perle fine orientall*
> *He white coroune was imakid all.*
> *For which the white coroune above the grene*
> *Ymade her like a daisie for to sene,*
> *Considered eke her fret of golde above.*

The portrait of Margaret of Denmark, Queen of Scotland, by Van der Goes[7] (Plate

---

[1] She dedicated it to the Treasury of Aachen Cathedral in 1475.
[2] In the Cathedral of Aix-en-Provence.   [3] In the Antwerp Museum.
[4] In the Musée de l'Hospice, Villeneuve-lès-Avignon.
[5] Dehaisnes, p. 855.   [6] I, 214.
[7] In the collection of Her Majesty the Queen at Holyrood House; at present lent to the National Gallery of Scotland.

30) shows her hair held in by side pieces of golden network, hung with pearls, with a solid rim that helps to support the toque-like coronal, similarly pearl-hung, that sweeps down in a great curve on to her lofty forehead. The portrait of Anne de Beaujeu on the Moulins triptych (Plate 31) shows a much simpler outline, but the heavily jewelled rim of the *coiffe* forms a part of the crown and seems to be hinged on to it.

The low-necked dresses that came into fashion in the middle of the century made a necklace or a chain and pendant a decorative necessity. Margaret, wife of John Paston, wrote to him in 1455[1] to ask him for 'sommethyng for my nekke', since when Queen Margaret of Anjou had come to Norwich she had had to borrow a cousin's 'devys', 'for I durst not for shame go with my be[a]ds among so many fresch jauntylwomen'. Nine months later she renewed her request, and asked for a girdle as well. We do not know what, if anything, John Paston gave her; when she died in 1484 she did not own necklace or pendant, though she had six broad girdles harnessed with gold and silver, as well as 'demysaints' and other girdles with long hanging ends.[2]

Yet for long the great ladies of France and England had been wearing necklaces, collars and pendants of considerable richness. As early as 1319 the French crown jewels included 'une belle gorgerette d'or semée de diamans et de pelles blanches sus veluyau vert'.[3] In 1455 the Countess of Arundel bequeathed to her daughter a golden collar with a jewelled pendant,[4] and in 1469 the Duchess of Brittany died owning a golden collar enamelled in black, white and purple, with Fs and Ms, friar's knots and white and purple pansies.[5] The portrait by Van der Goes of Margaret of Denmark, Queen of Scotland (Plate 30), shows her wearing a necklace of two rows of pearls divided by clusters of stones, with a jewelled pendant of triangular form with a large pendant pearl. The triptych by the same painter[6] given to the Spedale di Santa Maria Nuova at Florence by Tommaso Portinari, the Medici agent in Bruges, depicts his wife wearing a necklace of interlaced gold branches and enamelled roses of three colours: red centred with a sapphire, white centred with a ruby, and blue centred with a pearl.[7] The same picture shows his daughter wearing a necklace practically identical with that worn by Queen Margaret.

Yet more fanciful necklaces are described in royal inventories. The Duke of

[1] Quoted Hartshorne in *Arch. Journ.*, LXVI, 1908, p. 88.
[2] Gairdner, *Paston Letters*, III, p. 461. A necklace with five massive pendants is shown on the brass of Isabella Cheyne, d. 1485, in Blickling Church, Norfolk.
[3] Marolles et Soultrait, *Inventaire des titres de Nevers*, 1873, col. 619.
[4] Clifford Smith, p. 113.
[5] La Borderie, p. 46. It sounds like a mourning jewel, but she was not a widow when she died.
[6] Now in the Uffizi; a similar necklace appears on her portrait in the Altman Collection, Metropolitan Museum, New York.
[7] cf. the collar of white roses and columbines owned by the Comtesse de Montpensier in 1474. Boislisle, p. 9.

Burgundy in 1467[1] owned 'ung collier d'or, esmaillié de vert, de blanc et de rouge, à petites paillectes d'or branlans, et est pour servir à femmes en manière d'un poitrail'. In 1499, again, Margaret of Austria owned a heavy collar of gold formed of twenty-seven pieces and twenty-seven points, with a network over all enamelled in black, white and light red; and another of forty-three roses with diamond centres joined by little snakes all enamelled, given her by Ferdinand the Catholic. A collar of another kind, formed of hinged plaques, is depicted as worn by one of the Magi in Quentin Matsys' *Adoration* at New York.[2]

Purely ornamental pendants, too, grew more and more important. A fashion for heart-pendants followed on that for heart-brooches; at her death in 1469 the Duchess of Brittany owned a golden heart set with a lozenge-shaped diamond and a ruby, a diamond and three pearls, and a large diamond shaped as a heart, on which was a St. Margaret.[3] In 1488 the Duke had a whole section of his inventory devoted to such pendants;[4] one was inscribed IL NEST TRESOR QVE DE LIESSE. We have seen how Margaret Paston in 1455 had to borrow a 'devys' or pendant to make herself fit for company. In 1467 we find Sir John Howard giving his wife two such 'devices' of jewelled gold, as well as a chain of gold with a 'lokke' and a pair of beads and a collar of thirty-four roses.[5] The loot from Charles the Bold's tent, when it was taken by the Swiss at Grandson in 1476, included a white rose pendant centred with an immense balas ruby, that was probably a present to him from Edward IV of England[6] on his marriage in 1469. A portrait of Margaret of Austria, Duchess of Savoy, painted as a child by the Maître de Moulins in 1483 (Plate 32), shows her wearing a flat cluster pendant of nine stones, with three pendant pearls, while the Maître de Moulins' picture of Suzanne de Bourbon, painted about 1490,[7] shows her wearing a very large pendant set with two fine stones in enamelled scrolls, that form a fleur-de-lis with a pendant pearl. The portrait of a woman in the Louvre of about ten years later (Plate 33) shows her wearing a very large pendant with an enamelled figure of St. John, seated, between six large jewels.[8] Various other portraits by the Maître de Moulins show rather heavy pendants with superb gems in simple settings. The most famous of such jewels was that set with the three rubies known as the Three Brothers, which Charles the Bold inherited from his father in 1467 and lost at the battle of Grandson[9] in 1476; it was later acquired

---

[1] Texier, s.v. Collier.

[2] cf. the collar with a great enamelled central clasp on a reliquary of 1473 in the Cornelimünster at Aachen. O. von Falke and H. Frauberger, p. 138 and Fig. 122.

[3] La Borderie, p. 47.   [4] La Nicollière, p. 433.   [5] Hartshorne in *Arch. Journ.* LXVI, 1908, p. 88.

[6] See Burckhardt in *Anzeiger für Schweizerische Alterthumskunde*, XXXIII, 1931, p. 257 and Deuchler.

[7] Private collection.

[8] She also wears a collar of hinged plaques and has a devotional medal tucked into the front of her bodice. Her cap is edged with pearls and gems.

[9] See Commines, *Mémoires*, Bk. V, cap. 1.

by Henry VIII. A drawing of it made after its capture (Plate 27b) shows it as a rather inelegant jewel, with the great gems that adorn it baldly set.[1]

Many of these pendants, indeed, were so far famous and unique as to have names. Ludovico il Moro, Duke of Milan, had a jewel with a great diamond and three pendant pearls called 'Il Lupo', valued at 12,000 ducats; a balas called 'Il Spico' worth 25,000 ducats, and others with pet names such as 'el buratto', 'la semprevia', 'de la Moraglia'.[2]

Such pendants were not infrequently worn in the hat; other jewels were exceptionally designed for the same purpose. A curious stiff aigrette was among the jewels looted from the tent of the Duke of Burgundy after the battle of Grandson in 1476; a drawing of it made about 1500 shows it set with rubies, diamonds and pearls (Plate 34).

Just as the low-cut bodices encouraged the use of necklaces and pendants, so the wide loose sleeves of the fifteenth century encouraged the use of bracelets. As early as 1415 the trousseau of Mary of Burgundy included a bracelet set with six small sapphires and six pearls in a gold setting enamelled with flowers, with the inner side powdered with spots of white, green and red enamel.[3] The inventory of Philippe le Bon in 1420 includes three bracelets,[4] one enamelled with bands of the colours of his livery and set with twelve good pearls, fastening with a hanging lock of beryl set with two diamonds; another made like a towel, enamelled white, set with diamonds and rubies, with a hanging ring; and a third made as a circlet with an enamelled inscription round it. By 1428 the fashion had reached England; in that year Henry VI owned a bracelet formed of the figures of two women enamelled white, each holding a flower made of four diamonds, with a jewelled cluster above their heads.[5]

Other jewels of luxury included such extravagant trifles as the Duke of Burgundy's marten skin with ruby eyes, a diamond at the muzzle and teeth and nails of gold,[6] and all kinds of fanciful trifles to hold musk and ambergris and other scented things. Birds modelled out of scented clay were imported from Cyprus; the Duke of Burgundy had six silver cages in which to put them.[7] Balls of musk were harnessed with gold; one in 1380 was enclosed in golden hoops set with pearls and jewels with a sapphire at the bottom, and was hung from a cord with two knots of pearl.[8] In 1379 Charles V had a ball of ambergris covered with gold wrought in fleur-de-lis and niche work.[9]

Such fancies, however, were of less importance in the history of jewellery than the

---

[1] In the Historisches Museum of Bâle. See Burckhardt, loc. cit.
[2] Malaguzzi-Valeri, I, p. 387.   [3] Gay, s.v. Bracelet.
[4] Gay, s.v. Bracelet.   [5] Palgrave, *Kal. and Inv.*, II, p. 128.
[6] Texier, s.v. Collier de fourrure; in 1467. The fashion reappears in the second half of the sixteenth century.
[7] Laborde, *Ducs*, II, 132; in 1467, but inherited from his father.
[8] Gay, s.v. Pomme de Musc; inventory of the Château de Cornillon.
[9] Gay, s.v. Ambre. In 1467 the Duc de Berri had two others. The Guild of Corpus Christi of York owned a 'pila aurea vocata musce ball' given by Ellen Gare, who was widowed in 1439. Skaife, p. 290.

more commonly worn jewels of the time; and these were either practical, such as belt buckles, or devotional, such as reliquary pendants.

Fashions in belts varied most frequently of all. In 1422 the courtly fashion was for long girdles of hinged plaques, usually jewelled.[1] In 1509, at the marriage of Henry VIII to Catherine of Aragon, the fashion was to wear the belt 'traverse' from shoulder to waist.[2]

Humbler folk contented themselves with harnessing a belt of leather or stuff with precious metal. A fifteenth-century Italian belt of gold tissue in the Victoria and Albert Museum has a buckle and studs of gilt metal, the plate decorated in niello and inscribed VIRTVS VIN (cit) (Plate 35); another is inscribed AMORE (Plate 36a). Similarly John Baret of Bury had a girdle with buckle and pendant of silver, inscribed GRACE ME GOVERNE: his 'reson' or motto.[3] The majority of the surviving buckles are decorated with late Gothic tracery. The type survived well into the sixteenth century as one of the 'épreuves de maîtrise' for admission to girdlers' guilds; many of the very elaborate ones were probably made as master-pieces, in the strict literal sense of the word.

The chief use of architectural style in fifteenth-century jewellery was in the devotional pendants, that by their very nature approximated to the architecturally designed gold work that was being produced in great quantities for ecclesiastical reliquaries and shrines. Such reliquaries as represent the scenes of Nativity and Crucifixion that figured in the church retables of wood and alabaster and stone are necessarily in close touch with greater ecclesiastical art, though they were made for personal wear. Yet many reliquary pendants of the kind so far exploited the possibilities of the goldsmith's technique as to surpass (at least in virtuosity) the achievements of the sculptor. The inventory of the jewels of Louis d'Anjou made in 1380[4] has a section devoted to 'petis reliquiaires d'or à porter sur soy', one of which, although it is described as 'tres petit', was wrought in the most delicate and complicated manner. It was flat and more or less oval in shape. It had a branch round it in open work, from which fruited eleven fine pearls, each weighing about two carats and a half. It opened in front with two little doors, with rubies above and below, enamelled in colours with the Annunciation outside, and inside with St. Peter and St. Paul. Their opening revealed a little image of Our Lady in a golden mantle, holding the Child, dressed in white. The back of the jewel was enamelled with the image of the Christ of Pity surrounded by angels; below it was a space for relics. Reliquaries of this type, if rather less elaborate, continued in fashion all through the fifteenth century. The inventory of Philippe le Bon, Duke of Burgundy, made about 1458,[5] includes a number of 'tableaux' hung by chains, and enamelled with such

---

[1] Gay, s.v. Mordant.　　　　　　　　　　　　　　[2] Hall's *Chronicle*, I, 5.
[3] Will of 1463; Tymms, *Bury Wills and Inventories*, p. 16.
[4] Moranvillé, p. 587.　　　　　　　　　　　　　　[5] Pinchart, *Archives*, I, 19.

subjects as the Resurrection, St. Mary Magdalen, the Entombment, the Annunciation, the Virgin, St. John the Evangelist, and St. George and the Dragon. The inventory of the jewels of the Duke of Brittany in 1488[1] includes a little 'bullete' of gold with St. Margaret on one side and a marguerite on the other with a relic of the saint between, which he used to wear on a ribbon round his neck. In 1497, again, the Countess of Angoulême[2] owned a round jewel with a crucifix on one side and Our Lady on the other, containing relics.

Nearly all these types are represented in surviving jewels. None exactly represent the very rich kind of reliquary owned by Louis of Anjou; the nearest approximation to it is a triptych of the middle of the fifteenth century,[3] probably of Burgundian work (Plate 37a). The central core of the reliquary is an early cameo of the Nativity. It is set in a heavy gold rim inscribed: DOMINVS DIXIT AD ME FILIVS MEVS ES TV EGO HODIE GENVI TE. The cameo is covered by two shutters of gold[4] enamelled inside with minute scenes from the life of the Virgin and on the outside with two prophets from her ancestry bearing scrolls with their prophecies of her glory. On the back is enamelled a scene of St. Anne teaching the Blessed Virgin to read. The triptych — an almost square oblong with a rounded top — hangs from three plain gold chains.

A simpler and rather earlier Rhenish triptych pendant in the Louvre[5] (Plate 38a) has little reliefs under canopies of eight scenes of the childhood of Christ in silver gilt, behind shutters enamelled with figures of St. Barbara and St. Adrian on gilt backgrounds adorned with *pointillé* scroll work. Another in the same collection, a good deal later in date, is a book-shaped diptych with St. John the Evangelist and St. Joseph with the Child Christ enamelled on the covers, and a scene from the life of St. Ildefonso and a relic within.

The general tendency towards the end of the fifteenth century and at the beginning of the sixteenth was towards a circular form for devotional and reliquary pendants. The fashion was curiously linked with that for wearing a circular mirror for vanity's sake. As early as 1380 the jewels of a daughter of Charles V who had died[6] included a reliquary pendant enclosing the Navitity and a mirror, all in a jewelled frame. Ten years later the King of France gave his Queen as a New Year's gift a hinged tablet of gold enamelled within with the Entombment on one side and the Virgin and Child on the other, and without having an image of the Virgin on one side and a mirror on the other.[7] The

---

[1] La Nicollière, p. 415.   [2] Sènemaud, p. 63.

[3] Lent by Messrs. Rosenberg and Stiebel of New York to the Exhibition of goldwork held at Cleveland, Ohio, in 1947. See *Bulletin of the Cleveland Museum of Art*, November 1947. It is now in the Museum, purchased from the J. H. Wade Fund.

[4] Two shutters of the same kind, enamelled with figures of saints in relation with those of the Moulins triptych, are in the Wallace Collection.

[5] A. de Rothschild gift.   [6] Labarte, p. 49.   [7] Gay, s.v. Jouel.

pendant mirror of Margaret Duchess of Burgundy survives[1] (Plate 39) to show the
strange assortment; one side has a plaque enamelled with the Entry into Jerusalem in a
frame of elegant foliage, the other a steel mirror framed in the legend JE LAI EMPRINS :
BIEN EN AVIENGNE, set at the back of the foliage. A considerable number of circular
reliquary pendants were produced in Germany in silver and silver gilt, set with crystals
with relics behind,[2] reliefs in metal,[3] or medallions of mother of pearl.[4] In such circular
pendants might also be set an *Agnus Dei*, for the popularity of these continued un-
broken throughout the late Middle Ages and the Renaissance. Other objects much
favoured in the fifteenth century for pendants were, like relics, prophylactic. Gentile
Bellini's portrait of Caterina Cornaro (Plate 53) shows so great a lady as an ex-Queen
of Cyprus wearing a *touche* or *espreuve* of unicorn's horn, which was believed to be
especially efficacious against poison.

Circular devotional pendants continued universally popular in Western Europe
into the third decade of the sixteenth century. A fine reliquary pendant from the Pierpont Morgan Collection (Plate 41b), now in the Metropolitan Museum in New York,
with an enamelled group of the Annunciation in high relief within a border of formal
foliage, is probably North Italian. The back is elegantly designed in interlaced circles.[5]
It may be compared with the famous reliquary pendant worn by St. Thomas More and
now preserved as a relic at Stonyhurst College (Plate 42), to which it was bequeathed
by his descendant, a Jesuit Father, in 1773. It is enamelled on one side with the figure
of St. George and on the other with the emblems of the Passion and the figure of Christ
by the open sepulchre. Round the rim, which is enamelled with pansies and has a
delicate corded edge, is the inscription: O PASSI GRAVIORA DABIT HIS QVOQVE
FINEM.[6]

Such reliquaries were far from being the only devotional jewels in use in the late
Middle Ages. Such an inventory as that made on the death of Dame Agnes Hungerford
in 1523[7] includes few jewels that are not devotional: 'a flowre of golde, full of sparkes of

[1] Sir J. C. Robinson Collection, Private Collection.

[2] e.g. one in the National Museum, Munich. Clifford Smith, Plate XVIII, 1, p. 121.

[3] A good example in silver, with the symbols of the evangelists on the rim, the Holy Family on one
side and the Crucifixion on the other, has long been in the Danish Royal Collection. It is now in the
National Museum of Copenhagen.

[4] e.g. one in the A. de Rothschild gift, Louvre; another from the Treasury of Euger nr. Herford,
Westphalia, Clifford Smith, Plate XVIII, 2; and one carved with the Nativity and set in silver gilt
belonged to the Corpus Christi Guild of York in 1465. Skaife, p. 287. Some good examples are in the
Clemens Collection, Kunstgewerbe Museum, Cologne. Exceptionally other materials were used; e.g.
the 'petit rondelet d'écaille de licorne, taillée à l'ymage Nostre Dame qui tient son enfant', that the
Duke of Burgundy owned in 1467. Laborde, *Glossaire*, 362.

[5] cf. the engraved designs by Jacob Honervogt, Bibliothèque Nationale, Estampes, Le 41.

[6] It does not look of English manufacture and should be compared with a hat medallion of the same
subject in the Kunsthistorisches Museum, Vienna.

[7] *Archaeologia*, XXXVIII, 1860, p. 370.

dyamondes set abowte with perles, and the Holy Gost in the mydste of yt'; a table with St. Christopher; two brooches with St. Catherine, and 'a tabulle, hangyng of hit the Passion of Crist'.

Rosaries, too, took on a new importance. In 1467 Charles the Bold inherited some thirty-five rosaries of coral, crystal, gold, jet, amber and chalcedony.[1] In 1498 chalcedony was the fashionable stone;[2] a little later jacinth, lapis and crystal. A list of the property of the Guild of Corpus Christi at York in October 1465[3] describes many of carved coral. Some rosaries were extremely long: in 1488 the King of Scotland inherited from his father 'the grete bedis' containing 122 beads and a knop, all of gold.[4] It seemed that all such jewels (in England at all events) had been melted down, when a few years ago a splendid example was discovered in a chest that belonged to the old Yorkshire Catholic family of Langdale of Houghton Hall.[5] It consists of fifty small *Ave* beads, six *Paters* or gauds and a larger knop, all of gold engraved and nielloed with the figures of saints to make a kind of calendar of devotion (Colour Plate III).[*]

In the fifteenth century the larger paternoster beads that divided rosaries into decades grew more varied; a French knight taken prisoner at Agincourt had a gold rosary with 'signes' shaped as hearts, and another with daisies and sabots.[6] The fifteenth-century effigy of a lady in Bangor Cathedral holds a rosary with five brooch-like pendants of irregular size and shape attached to it, and the illuminations of the Grimani Breviary portray one with acorn-shaped gaudees and St. James's shell paternosters.[7]

In England a fashion arose in the middle of the century for ladies to wear their rosaries necklace-wise; the inventory of the jewels of Sir John Howard, made in 1466, includes a pair of beads for a gentlewoman's neck, gauded with eight 'gawden' of gold and eight pearls.[8] By 1514 'paternostre' was beginning to be used to indicate any large gold bead, even in an ordinary necklace.[9]

The most interesting rosaries of the late fifteenth and early sixteenth centuries are perhaps those formed of beads each of which opens like a reliquary pendant to show two scenes carved or enamelled within. One of the earliest recorded is that in the inventory of the Duke of Savoy drawn up in 1498.[10] with beads of chalcedony opening to show figures in silver-gilt protected behind crystal plaques. A splendid surviving example, probably Italian, in the Louvre (Plate 38b), has agate beads that open to show enamelled reliefs of the life of Christ. Another, evidently by the same hand, was formerly in the

[1] Laborde, *Ducs*, II, 130.   [2] Gay, s.v. Patenôtres.
[3] Skaife, p. 290.   [4] Thomson, p. 5.
[5] See E. Maclagan and C. C. Oman in *Archaeologia*, LXXXV, 1935, p.1. It was acquired in 1934 by the Victoria and Albert Museum. Mr. Oman in *Country Life*, CIII, 1948, p. 1076 shows reason to believe that it belonged to Lord William Howard, third son of the fourth Duke of Norfolk.
[6] Bourbon in *Bull. Arch.*, 1884, p. 325.   [7] fol. 188 v.
[8] Royal Commission on Historical MSS, seventh report, p. 537.
[9] Merlet, p. 371.   [10] Gay, s.v. Patenôtres.   [*]In black and white in the Dover edition.

Pierpont Morgan Collection;[1] its onyx beads opened to show enamelled groups illustrating the life of the Virgin. The short decade rosary of Henry VIII, now in the collection of the Duke of Devonshire, shews a similar virtuosity in carved boxwood; it is probably of Flemish manufacture. The ten *Ave* beads are each carved with a scroll with an article of the Creed and five medallions. On one medallion appears the Apostle associated with that article, and on another his Old Testament prototype. The large *Paternoster* bead is carved with the King's name and the royal arms; it opens to show minute carvings of the Mass of St. Gregory and of the Virgin and Child enthroned in a glory. The Cross has a crucifix on one side and the four Evangelists and the Four Doctors of the Church on the other. The decade hangs from a finger ring with the Garter motto and the inscription POENI DEI ADJVTORIVM MEVM.

Crosses not only formed part of rosaries but were also commonly worn as pendants. The exquisitely delicate *pointillé* work which adorns the cross of about 1400 found at Clare Castle cannot be judged from a reproduction.[2] The more showy types, fashionable later in the century, are elaborated both in the lobing of the cross and in its purely decorative treatment (Plate 40). The cross made for St. Ulrich of Augsburg in 1494 has a central rose, surrounded by four rubies and a diamond in each arm on a rose setting with groups of pearls.[3] The whole is framed in lopped branches of gold. A similar frame of twined lopped branches of matted gold is used for another cross set with five cabochon rubies and a table diamond in heavy quadrilobed settings relieved by a little foliage in dark translucent green with four white flowers in the angles. The back is ornamented with green enamelled leaves behind the rubies and a red flower behind the diamond. Even the ring is delicately chased as a knopped branch. The same knopped branches are shown in the delightful pendant which Lucas Cranach gives to St. Catherine in his famous altarpiece in her honour of 1506.

No less characteristic devotional jewels were the *enseignes*, pilgrims' signs[4] that were worn in the hat: the religious parallel to the brooches of livery that marked the wearer's secular allegiance. These were normally made and sold at the actual place of pilgrimage; moulds for casting them are now in the Guildhall Museum and the British Museum, and a forge for working the metal for them has been found at Walsingham Priory, one of the great pilgrimage churches of England. A French royal ordinance of 1394 grants a

[1] Williamson, Catalogue No. 13.

[2] It is at present lent from the English Royal Collection to the British Museum. See *Arch. Journ.*, XXV, 1868, p. 60, and Victoria and Albert Museum, *English Mediaeval Art Exhibition*, 1930, No. 883. It is illustrated in the *Illustrated London News* of May 16th, 1936. For a rather later cross found in the New Forest see *Proc. Soc. Ants.*, XXIV, 33.

[3] Rücklin, II, plate 47.

[4] On the whole question, see John Evans, in *Proceedings of the Society of Antiquaries*, second series, XXII, 1908, p. 102 and T. Borenius, *Mediaeval Pilgrims' Badges*, Sette of Odd Volumes, XC, 1930; and Catalogue of Exhibition at Ironmongers' Hall, II, 1861, p. 309, *et seqq*.

charter to those who sell *enseignes* to pilgrims at Mont St. Michel[1] and a letter of re-mission of 1392 records that on Easter Monday 'afiches et autres joueles de plont' were sold in the market of Saint Quentin.[2] The greater number of them — and almost all that survive — are of lead or pewter, perhaps once gilt; but the records show that great personages had them of precious metal. When the Duke and Duchess of Burgundy visited the shrine of Our Lady of Boulogne in 1420[3] they bought four gilt *enseignes* and sixteen silver ones for themselves and their retinue; when the Comte de Charolais visited the shrine in 1456 he bought five, all of gold.[4]

Langland[5] describes a pilgrim with

> *An hundred of ampulles*
> *On his hat seten,*
> *Signes of Synay,*
> *And shelles of Galice,*
> *And many a crouche on his cloke,*
> *And keyes of Rome,*
> *And the vernicle be fore,*
> *For men showlde knowe*
> *And se bi his signes*
> *Whom he sought hadde.*

A pilgrim in a piece of sculpture of about 1420 in the Museum of Évreux wears a round knitted hat with a turned up brim stuck with badges of the Veronica and the Keys of Rome. In 1490 King Charles VIII paid a goldsmith of Embrun for no less than forty-two images of Our Lady of Embrun which were sewn to a scarf of cloth of gold lined with scarlet.[6]

The ampullas of St. Thomas of Canterbury and Our Lady of Walsingham, the shells of Compostella,[7] the horn of St. Hubert, the comb of St. Blaise, the wheel of St. Catherine, the foot of St. Victor and the effigies of Saints such as the Virgin, St. Julian, St. Martin and St. Thomas Becket, are to be found in many Museums.[8] An interesting collection of them is painted in the margin of a Flemish Book of Hours in Sir John Soane's Museum (Plate 43). This well illustrates the difference between the continental and English examples; the former are fairly plain solid medallions of regular shape, the

---

[1] Gay, s.v. Michel.   [2] Texier, s.v. Affiquet.
[3] Laborde, *Ducs*, I, 181; they bought others on a second visit in 1425. ibid, I, 231.
[4] ibid., I, 465.   [5] *Vision of Piers Plowman*, I, 3543.
[6] Gay, s.v. Enseigne.
[7] See e.g. 1467 inventory of the Duke of Burgundy, Laborde, II, No. 3165.
[8] e.g. British Museum; Guildhall Museum; Cambridge Museum of Archaeology; Canterbury Museum; Musée de Cluny, Paris; Kunstgewerbe Museum, Cologne.

latter often have irregular silhouettes.[1] Other hat brooches, not perhaps of pilgrimage, but no less devotional in intention, are the 'Christofre' worn by Chaucer's Yeoman — a type of brooch represented by a silver gilt example in the British Museum — and the silver brooch with the Veronica and inscription JESVS NAZARENVS REX JVDAEORVM SALVE NOS in the Musée de Cluny.

The jewellery of the later Middle Ages may, then, be summed up as giving an increasing importance to gems in its design; though by the Flamboyant Gothic architectural details that often occur in it, it still clearly belongs to the Middle Ages.

---

[1] Even at the end of the sixteenth century such brooches were not unknown. The 1599 inventory of Gabrielle d'Estrées (Fréville, p. 169) includes 'Quinze petites enseignes d'or, taillées les unes de relief et les autres de basse taille, avec des petits saints dessus'.

CHAPTER FOUR

The Early Renaissance

The jewellery of the Renaissance was, like every kind of contemporary art, affected by that of classical antiquity. The influence was in general style and was derived from sculpture rather than from jewellery. Classical jewellery was little known and never imitated; only engraved gems formed any real link between the Roman past and the Renaissance present, and these, after all, were no new discovery, but had been appreciated all through the Middle Ages. By the middle of the fourteenth century they were not only appreciated but also imitated. As early as 1363 Jean le Bon, King of France, had as his privy seal a contemporary intaglio imitating a Greek original of great beauty.[1] The admirable portrait heads, also in intaglio, that appear as the seals of Bureau de la Rivière and a few other French courtiers may perhaps be by the same hand. In the High Renaissance the Italian amateurs could command cameo-cutters such as Domenico Compagni, Giovanni Bernardi, Valerio Vicentino and a score of others. Skill was more often employed on collectors' large pieces than on small medallions for jewels, but the gem-cutters also produced a certain number of portraits. In France cameo-cutters were engaged chiefly on small portrait cameos (Plate 44c); we do not know their names and can rarely identify their subjects.

Apart from the imitation of antique cameos there seems to have been little direct classical influence: neither the technique of filigree nor the style of jewels all of delicate gold were revived. The portraits by Piero della Francesca and other *quattrocento* artists show a different way of wearing jewels rather than jewels that differ greatly from those worn earlier. The portrait of Battista Sforza in the Uffizi (Plate 45) shows her wearing a collar of two rows of very large pearls linked by plaques of enamelled gold, alternately oval and lozenge shaped, themselves joined by similar pearls.[2] A festoon hangs in front, with another short row of pearls joining it from the centre of the necklace. A reliquary pendant hangs on a short chain below. The hair is plaited with ribbon to form a shell over the ears; this is centred by three jewelled clusters joined by threaded seed pearls.

[1] Babelon, *Histoire*, p. 103 pl. VII, 12.
[2] The necklace may be compared with that on a portrait in the Museo Poldi-Pezzoli at Milan. In this the lady wears pearls in her hair.

The ribbon that passes over the top of the head supports a flat cluster brooch at the summit, that is only seen in profile in the picture.

Another female portrait in the Uffizi, ascribed to Antonio Pollaiuolo,[1] shows a brooch similarly perched on the top of the head. The hair is elaborately wreathed with pearls; the lady wears a fine pendant with three pendant pearls, and a brooch with a large gem in a claw setting surrounded by golden leafage. Again, a portrait of a girl, in the Ambrosian Library at Milan, shows her wearing a hair net edged with pearls, a head ribbon studded with jewels in simple settings with pendant pearls, a necklace of large pearls, a simple pendant formed of one large gem and a pendant pearl, hanging from a gold chain, and a second pendant hardly less simple but formed of two stones and a pendant pearl. The portrait of Beatrice d'Este in the Pitti, sometimes ascribed to Lorenzo Costa and certainly of the last years of the fifteenth century, shows her wearing a pendant set with two huge stones, another at the neck, and a third not dissimilar hung over her left ear on the smooth bands of her hair.

Gradually, however, the new style crept in, both in subject and in design. Nymphs and satyrs (Plate 44d) and other classical subjects enter the iconography of jewels; the architectural frames have classical columns and pediments instead of Gothic crockets and pinnacles (Plate 37a, b). The illuminators learn to set cameos and medals in their borders[2] and a new monumental quality inspires even minute enamelled reliefs (Plate 47c).

This gradual influx of the new style into jewellery is not hard to explain. In the Italian Renaissance there existed a close link between the goldsmith's art and the arts of the painter and sculptor. The goldsmith's *bottega* was recognised as the best training school in accuracy of line and clarity of style even for those destined for greater art. Ghiberti (born in 1378) began as a goldsmith; Maso di Finiguerra, Antonio Pollaiuolo, Brunelleschi, Luca della Robbia, Andrea del Verocchio, Ambrogio Foppa called Caradosso, Botticelli, Ghirlandajo, Michelozzo and Lorenzo de Credi followed him. Francia, born in 1450, was a goldsmith rather than a painter until he was forty; Albert Dürer was the son of a goldsmith and his father's pupil. Even in the sixteenth century Andrea del Sarto and Baccio Bandinelli served the same apprenticeship.

Such a training had its results not only on the apprentices but also on the art they practised. They not only acquired a lifelong sense of exquisite linear beauty, and kept enough affection for the trade of their youth to design and paint practicable jewels for their Virgins and Virtues; but also by their linking, by practice and friendship, of the craft of jewellery with the great arts of painting and sculpture, they taught its practitioners to look beyond the traditional limits of their own art and to stretch their

[1] No. 3450. It has been much repainted but the painting of the jewels seems to be original.
[2] See Clifford Smith, p. 175; the fashion first appears about 1465.

familiar techniques to breaking-point in the attempt to rival artists in greater fields.

Botticelli thus paints the Graces of the *Primavera* with elegant pendants that could have been sold on the Ponte Vecchio; Piero Pollaiuolo gives his *Charity*[1] a fine cluster brooch with pearls round a central stone. In a Florentine Virgin and Child in the National Gallery the Virgin (Plate 48a) and one of the angels wear identical brooches, set with a table cut ruby between four pearls set 'à potences' with twelve enamelled blackberries or mulberries between and green leaves beyond. Lotto gives his *Lucrezia* a pendant which any skilled goldsmith could execute, with one large central ruby, a smaller one between and three sapphires set with two cornucopiae below and two baby fauns above (Plate 48b). Francia,[2] who sometimes signs his pictures OPVS FRANCIAE ;AVRIFICIS, remembers his youth when he paints the altarpiece of the Virgin of the Misericordia of Bologna, and paints above the Virgin's head a minute jeweller's picture of the votive jewel that his patron Francesco Felicini had dedicated at her shrine: a great round amethyst in an ornamental rim of gold enamelled in dark crimson with a hanging pearl.

Thus, too, certain Renaissance jewels are such *tours de force* of minute sculpture that they have passed the line that divides art from virtuosity. Such reliefs as that on a seal made for Cardinal de' Medici (Plate 49a) or the minute battle scene on a medallion for a cap brooch in the Fitzwilliam Museum (Plate 49b) demand judgment as pure sculpture, but can only receive it when they have been enlarged by scientific devices unknown to the age that produced them.

Benvenuto Cellini stands in the public eye as the type of the Renaissance jewellers who by sheer virtuosity attained the rank of artist. He was, indeed, originally apprenticed to the goldsmith Michelagnolo di Viviano, father of the sculptor Baccio Bandinelli;[3] both his autobiography and his *Treatises* shew him engaged not only on jewels but on the *lavori de oreficeria* — the church plate and table plate and other trappings of ecclesiastical and courtly ritual — that were a form of riches of which the Renaissance inherited the tradition from the Middle Ages. He describes himself[4] as making about 1519 a large silver belt clasp with antique foliage and *putti*; in 1523, when resetting diamonds for a lady, making a sculptor's model in wax of the little masks, animals and *amorini* that adorned the setting. He tells us that he made a cap-brooch in that year with Leda and the swan; another with four figures in 1524; and two others, with Hercules and the Nemean Lion, and Atlas bearing the world, in 1527. He even describes[5] the Atlas brooch in some detail: the golden figure on a ground of lapis lazuli, bearing a crystal engraved with the signs of the Zodiac, all framed in golden foliage with the motto (since his patron was in love with a lady of higher rank than himself) SUMMAM

---

[1] In the Uffizi. [2] See G. C. Williamson, *Francia*, 1901, p. 38.
[3] Clifford Smith, p. 171. [4] *Life*, ed. Cust, I, p. 67. [5] *Treatises*, trans. Ashbee, cap. XII.

TULISSE JUVAT. But there is no surviving jewel that can with probability be ascribed to him.

Cellini, indeed, makes his most significant contribution to the history of jewellery when he describes the fashion in 1524 for gold *enseignes* chased with the device of the wearer's choice,[1] and describes how he and Caradosso (the two most eminent in the art in his estimation) created these sculptural bas-reliefs.[2] The fashion, however, was already well established, and was a development of the mediaeval custom of wearing a brooch of livery or of devotion in the hat. The inventory of the jewels of Lucrezia Borgia drawn up in 1516 describes a medallion with the Sacrifice of Isaac and another with the figure of St. Roch as being on caps belonging to Don Ercole.[3] Another is listed as 'Una medaglia di oro cum San Francesco smaltato, di berettino, cum lettere di smalto

FIG. 2. Design for a belt-end. Albert Dürer

bianco in campo di smalto rosso et uno ritorto di oro intorno'.[4] Others in her possession were adorned with figures of the Virgin, of St. Louis, and of Daniel in the lions' den; one — a flame in a border of palms — was designed as an *impresa*.[5]

Similar medallions survive to illustrate the type in greater detail than does Lucrezia Borgia's inventory[5]. A superb example, traditionally said to have been made for Cosimo de' Medici by Ghiberti, but probably a little later, represents St. John the Baptist in the wilderness, in a border of pearls and diamonds in enamelled settings (Plate 52a). Another at Vienna (Plate 52b) shows the figure of St. John the Divine

---

[1] Such *enseignes* are often represented in the portraits by Bartolommeo Veneto, though it is not always easy to determine the subject.

[2] Cust, I, p. 115.

[3] Gay, s.v. Enseigne.

[4] ibid.

[5] Campori, p. 35.

mounted upon the eagle, and writing the first words of his gospel; it has a wreathed rim of enamelled gold, ornamented with vine leaves. A fine example in the Rosenborg Slott with a similar vine leaf edge is adorned with the figure of Perseus. Other hat medallions, a little later in date, are remarkable for the multiplicity of figures that are crowded into the space. One in the Waddesdon Bequest in the British Museum is enamelled in relief with the scene of the Conversion of St. Paul (Plate 46a). Round the edge is the inscription DVRVM EST COMTRA STIMVLVM CALCITRARE. An inscription on the back says that it once belonged to Don John of Austria, and that he himself set it in the cap of Camillo

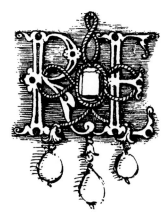

FIG. 3. Design for the back of a cross. Hans Holbein. *c.* 1530

FIG. 4. Design for a pendant with the initials RE. Holbein. *c.* 1530

Capizucchi. Another such ornament, possibly by the same hand, in the Bibliothèque Nationale, is enamelled with a battle scene,[1] that includes twelve men and eight horses in its tiny span: the figures are white, in golden armour, against a background of green. Yet more beautiful because of its composition, if less fantastically skilful, is a medallion in the Musée Condé at Chantilly that represents Apollo driving the horses of the Sun (Plate 46d). A fourth hat-medallion, now in the British Museum (Plate 46b), represents the Judgment of Paris within a border of garnets. Another in the Danish Royal Collection in the Rosenborg Slott represents St. George on a scale only little less minute. The dispersion of such jewels was greatly aided by Papal and royal gifts; even James V of

[1] It is probably identical with a cap-medallion described in the 1560 Inventory of the Château de Fontainebleau; 'une enseigne d'or, ovalle, à laquelle y a une bataille de petites figures montées sur petits chevaulx esmaillez de blanc . . .' Laborde, *Glossaire*. p. 286.

Scotland in 1539 owned 'the hatt that come fra the paip of gray velvett with the haly gaist sett all with orient perle'.[1]

The new style in jewellery was brought from Italy with the new style in painting, and often by the same artist. Dürer left some designs for the harness of belts that were later engraved by Hollar (Fig. 2)[2] and gave his wife, in his portrait of her, a charming necklace of irregularly-shaped gold links.[3] But the finest jewel designs by a great painter are those that Holbein drew after he came to England late in 1526. The finest and most delicate are for chains (Plate 51) and pendants (Plate 50 and Figs. 3 and 4): they show Holbein equally at home with such mediaeval motives as a lady holding a gem (here playfully inscribed *Well laydi well*), the newer styles of silhouette enamel in moresque designs, at that time called 'Spanish work', and those Renaissance *putti* which Henry VIII's clerks called 'antique boys'. Two designs for *imprese* or emblematic devices, such as were in great favour at the court of Henry VIII, were doubtless intended for hat jewels. One bears the inscription *Servar voglio quel che ho giurato*; the other, a trophy of dolphins, horns of abundance and a pair of compasses, is inscribed *Prudentement et par compas incontinent viendras*.[4]

Holbein himself was not a craftsman jeweller. It seems likely that jewels were made from his designs by his friend Hans of Antwerp, alias John Anwarpe. The fact of two foreigners thus working together on jewels in London illustrates the extreme difficulty of fixing the nationality of a Renaissance jewel. The difficulty is emphasised when we see how many of Henry VIII's jewellers have foreign names[5] — Robert Amadas, John Cryspyn, Cornelius Hays, John Cavalcant, Guillim Honyson, John of Utrecht, Allart Ploumyer, Jehan Lange, Baptist Leman, John Baptista de Consolavera, Alexander of Brussels, and the said Hans of Antwerp.[6] There was, too, a constant influx of transient merchants from abroad. Hall in his *Chronicles*[7] relates that the French King's ambassa-

---

[1] Thomson, p. 49.

[2] Other designs by him are three sketches for whistles in the Kunsthalle, Bremen; two for ring-shaped pendant whistles in the British Museum; four designs for brooches and clasps, in 1908 in a private collection at Karlsruhe; and a George pendant and a pomander etched by Hollar. See Clifford Smith, p. 190.

[3] In the Royal Gallery, Berlin.

[4] A third design for an *impresa enseigne* by Holbein, now in the American collection of Mr. and Mrs. Philip Hofer, represents Tantalus in a river trying to get apples from a tree just out of his reach. It may perhaps be compared with an entry in the French Royal accounts for 1529, of a gold *enseigne* chased with a man escaping from drowning by hanging on to a branch. Gay, s.v. Enseigne. Hans Eworth paints jewels as if he knew and understood them well, and his brother was a jeweller. Chamberlain, *Holbein*, 1913, II, p. 307.

[5] See Clifford Smith, p. 208.

[6] It is worth noting that as early as 1469 a hundred and twelve foreign master goldsmiths were recognised as denizens by the Goldsmiths' Company and were working in London. Herbert, *History of Twelve Great Livery Companies of London*, II p. 192.

[7] I, 168.

dors came to London in 1518, accompanied not only by gentlemen of the Court, but also by 'a great number of rascals and pedlars and juellers' who brought over 'diverse merchandise uncustomed, all under the colour of the Trussery of the Ambassadours'. Henry VIII, too, like every great man who was known to have a taste for jewels and the means to satisfy it, was constantly being approached by those who possessed particularly splendid examples and wished to sell them. In 1546 Vaughan, his agent in Antwerp, wrote to Paget in London[1] to tell him of a pendant formed of a large table diamond set in scrolls and masks, upheld by a satyr and a nymph, with a pendant pearl below. 'The time is unmeet', he writes, 'to pester the King with jewels, who already has more than most of the Princes of Christendom and therefore, although I told him (John Carolo, the owner of the jewel) that I would send the pattern to the King, I send it only to you'. The 'pattern' — a careful coloured drawing — remains, and serves to show the international character of the satyr and nymph motive in 1546 (Plate 44d).

Thus while it may exceptionally be possible to name the patron who ordered a Renaissance jewel, it is nearly always impossible to determine its nationality, except on purely stylistic grounds.

Yet it was a period when national character in dress was more marked than it had ever been before; and with dress the wearing of jewels varied from nation to nation. Four roughly contemporary portraits of great ladies shew a marked difference in the fashion of wearing jewels, though, perhaps, one less marked in their actual design. The portrait by Bernard Strigel (or one of his followers) of Bianca Maria Sforza, second wife of the Emperor Maximilian I (Plate 54) shews her wearing a jewelled necklace from which hangs an enormous pendant formed of a great oblong stone in a lobed setting, with a smaller stone above and a large pendant pearl below. She wears a cord and three chains disappearing inside her bodice; and over it a heavy cabled gold chain and a double row of pearls, each with groups of six pearls divided by a long enamelled bead. Her large toque-like hat surprisingly ends over her right shoulder in another enormous pendant with diamond sprays holding (like callipers) a pear-shaped pearl. Yet a portrait of Isabella of Austria by Jan Gossaert (Plate 55) depicts her most modestly jewelled. She wears a necklace of two rows of pearls set in enamelled gold, with a pendant cross of diamonds set lozenge-wise. Her hood is adorned with two rows of chain-like ornament of jewelled gold.

Eleanor of Austria, in a portrait painted not long before her marriage to Francis I in 1529 (Plate 56), is much more splendidly jewelled. Her beret, sewn with aglets and with a small brooch in front, is worn over a rich pearl circle: from which hangs a pendant of a large oblong jewel in a gold setting with a pendant pearl. She wears rather clumsy elliptical

---

[1] Gairdner, *Calendar of State Papers, Foreign and Domestic*, XXI, pt. 1, p. 55. The original is in Record Office SP 1/213.

earrings of gold, each set with two pearls, with three hanging pearls. She has a necklace of medallions of gold enamelled in black in arabesque designs, alternately large and small, the large in their turn set alternately with rubies and pearls. The tops of her sleeves are clasped with matching brooches. She also wears a rope of enormous pearls caught up in front by a brooch of a triangular diamond.

Finally Anne of Cleves, in the portrait painted by Holbein at the time of her marriage to Henry VIII in 1540 (Plate 58), wears an elegant *parure* of quite a different kind. Her coif is rimmed with jewels, in the usual northern fashion; a richly jewelled pendant is

FIG. 5. Engraved designs for belt-harness, Virgil Solis. *c.* 1540

pinned to it on the left side. She wears a necklace close about her throat formed of gem-centred flowers of white enamel; similar flowers stud the golden border of her square-cut *décolletage*. A long and heavy chain of square links goes twice round her neck and a ruby cross hangs from the necklace.

The difficulty of identifying the provenance of a jewel, even on stylistic grounds, is greatly increased from the middle of the sixteenth century by the multiplication of designs made by an artist or a master craftsman by means of engraving. Engravings for use in designing church plate had been produced a good deal earlier. The unknown master of 1466[1] published designs not specifically intended for jewels, but possibly adaptable to the design of gold work; the monogrammist WA of c. 1480, Martin Schongauer before his

[1] See Guilmard, p. 343.

death in 1499, Wenceslaus of Ollmutz in 1481 and Israel van Mecken between 1482 and 1498, all published designs for croziers and church plate.[1] In Italy such engravings were not needed, for there were many artists trained as goldsmiths;[2] in Spain very little engraving of any kind was done in the sixteenth century;[3] but in France, Germany and the Low Countries a constant stream of designs specifically designed for jewellers was produced alongside the main stream of pattern-books of Renaissance ornament, that could be applied to every art. Some of the earliest are the designs of Aldegrever,[4] who died in 1558. His patterns, however, are primarily intended for rich weapons: the buckles he includes are to match his daggers.[5] Brosamer's *Kunstbüchlein*, published between 1545 and 1548, is in its turn primarily occupied with cups and other table vessels, but includes four designs for pendants and four for ornamental whistles.

The most important of the early designers of engraved ornament for jewellers was Virgil Solis of Nuremberg, who was born in 1514 and died in 1562. He designed harness for belts engraved in moresques (Fig. 5), but his most characteristic engravings (Plate 59 and Fig. 6) are for pendants set with cabochon stones in high lobed settings, with caryatid figures and strapwork frames. He often includes the design of the back, decorated with champlevé enamel in a moresque pattern. He further includes designs for the links of the necklaces and chains from which the pendants are to hang, of complicated strap and scrollwork centred by table-cut or cabochon stones.

Virgil Solis' designs in the moresque style are paralleled in the first known book of engraved ornament published in England: the *Moryse and Damashin renewed and encreased, very profitable for Goldsmythes and Embroderars*, by Thomas Geminus at *London Anno* 1548. The author appears to have been a Fleming.[6]

By this time the tide of jewellers' pattern books had reached France. Étienne Delaune, who was born at Orleans in 1520 and was still working in Strasburg in 1590, made a great number of designs for jewels, of which many are now in the Ashmolean Museum[7] (Plates 60, 61; figs. 7, 8) from the collection of the antiquary Francis Douce. They

---

[1] Guilmard, pp. 343, 344, 345. Their tradition was continued in the early sixteenth century by Altdorfer of Ratisbon (d. 1538) and D. Hopfer who published engravings in 1527.

[2] Attention should be drawn, however, to the fifteenth-century prints made from nielli, though these are not strictly speaking jewels. Antonio Gentile's engravings (Guilmard, p. 294) are of church plate, not of jewels.

[3] Juan de Arphe in his *Varia commesuracion* cites only the church work in which Spanish goldsmiths excelled. See Davillier, p. 50.

[4] See Guilmard, p. 360.

[5] Theodore de Bry, born at Liège in 1528, who worked at Frankfort after c. 1560, was also primarily a designer of weapons and their belts rather than of jewels.

[6] The only known copy of the title page is in the Landesmuseum der Provinz Westfalen at Münster. Copies of the plates are in the Victoria and Albert Museum. See Campbell Dodgson in *Proc. Soc. Ants.*, 1917 (June 28), p. 210.

[7] My thanks are due to the Keeper and to Mr. John Woodward for drawing my attention to them.

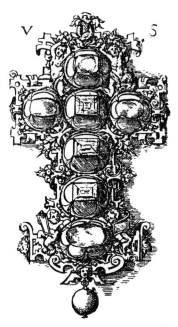

FIG. 6. Engraved design for a cross, Virgil Solis. *c.* 1540

FIGS. 7 and 8. Designs for pendants by Étienne Delaune. *c.* 1560

show a Mannerist version of High Renaissance style, with more elaborate use of masks and strapwork and Atlantid figures, and a fuller professional knowledge of technique.

Étienne Delaune, however, was not only a designer of jewels but also an engraver, and published a great quantity of engraved designs including a number for the enamelled backs of pendants[1] (figs. 7–8).

Delaune was a working goldsmith and his designs are not only practicable but conceived on the scale and in the relief of jewels. Other designers betray that they were accustomed to work on a larger scale. Pierre Woeiriot, born in Lorraine in 1532, settled at Lyons in 1555 and between that year and 1561 published a number of designs for swords, whistles and pendants. His designs for pendants (Fig. 9) show an increasing emphasis on figure work; they are so strongly sculptural that they could bear magnification into plaster or stone. Similarly the links for collars and bracelets designed by Matthias Zundt about 1560 (Fig. 10) are like cartouches in stone. This monumental character is yet more clearly evident, and with reason, in the designs for jewels published by the architect Jacques Androuet du Cerceau; his clasps and brooches, pendants and earrings, have heavy scrolls so architectural in character that they would look too massive for pleasure when translated into gold. Even his masks and Atlantid figures seem designed rather for stone than for enamel. Similarly René Boyvin tried without much success to bring the fantasies of his grotto sculptures into jewellery.[2]

The international dispersion of such engraved designs make it extremely difficult to attribute the jewels of the middle of the sixteenth century to any particular country. It is not even easy to determine which jewels are Italian and which not. Such a jewel as the splendid cap-brooch with St. George in the Waddesdon Bequest (Plate 62a) looks Italianate in its design, but technical tricks such as the setting of rubies to form the sleeve, and the diamond set in the horse's flank, suggest a German origin. The no less splendid oval cap brooch at Copenhagen (Plate 62b), representing a rather mature David with the head of Goliath, is given an Italian look by the use of a classical cameo for the head; but the rest of the mount looks on the whole Germanic. It finds, however, a close parallel in one described in the 1560 inventory of the jewels of Francis II of France, of David and Goliath, with the head, arms and legs of agate.[3]

The question of the provenance of these jewels using cameo heads and hands on a background of enamelled gold has never been satisfactorily decided. It is possible that

---

[1] See Guilmard, p. 18. One piece is dated 1561; the other dated pieces are later. Some of the pendants closely resemble the Ashmolean drawings but are modified in effect by the addition of optional side pieces to turn them into ornamental whistles. A. de Bruyn (c. 1538–1591) published imitations of some of Delaune's more popular designs for the backs of jewels.

[2] He worked at Angers, and may have been the son of a descendant of Robin Boyvin who worked as a metal founder at Moulins in 1453. Texier, s.v. Boyvin.

[3] Gay, s.v. Enseigne.

FIG. 9. Four engraved designs for pendants by Pierre Woeiriot. *c.* 1560

they are French, and perhaps all from one workshop. The most famous is the hat medallion with Leda and the Swan in the Imperial Collection at Vienna (Plate 63a): a jewel that because of its subject was long falsely attributed to Cellini, who is known to have made an *enseigne* with this theme. Its back is enamelled with the royal arms of France and with the salamander and FF that show it to have belonged to Francis I.[1] A pendant in New York (Plate 63b, c) with the figure of Prudence, the face and hands of chalcedony, has its back enamelled with Diana after a design by Étienne Delaune. His engraved pattern books were sometimes used outside France, but their use seems to confirm the possibliity of a French origin. The jewel may be compared with another figure of Prudence, with chalcedony face and hands but without background, in the

FIG. 10. Engraved designs by Matthias Zundt. *c.* 1560

Wallace Collection.[2] Confirmation of the French origin proposed for such jewels may perhaps be found in the number of them recorded in the French royal inventory of 1560,[3] such as an *enseigne* with a Julius Caesar of gold with a jacinth head. Often, too, if less characteristically, the method was counterchanged, and a figure of enamelled gold set against a background of semi-precious stone. Thus the same inventory includes an *enseigne* with Lucretia in gold on a background of lapis; another with Ceres with a silver body in a golden dress against agate, and a third with a man enamelled white, with a steel helmet, standing on a large sapphire on a ground of jet. Not dissimilar jewels are, however, known to have been made by Cellini.[4] Their artistic provenance, like that of the great majority of mounted cameos (Plate 64a, b), must remain uncertain.[5]

Iconography, again, is no certain guide. England had a particular liking for Old

[1] Arneth, p. 124.
[2] A cameo head of a woman, the head cornelian, the drapery amethyst, against a background of gold, is in the private collection of Her Majesty the Queen. Clifford Smith, Plate XXXI, 4.
[3] *Revue Universelle des Arts*, IV, 1856, p. 449.   [4] See above, p. 83.
[5] The most abundant collections will be found in Vienna and in the Cabinet des Médailles at Paris, but the great Museums have also fine examples.

Testament subjects. The portraits of Catherine Howard painted about 1521[1] show her wearing an oval gold pendant set with a sapphire, chased with the story of Tobit, and Princess Mary Tudor's inventory of 1542[2] lists brooches with the stories of the finding of Moses, Moses striking the rock, Susanna, Solomon, Abraham, David, Noah and Jacob's Dream, as well as subjects drawn from the New Testament.[3] The only recognisably secular subjects in her pictorial jewels, indeed, are a brooch with the history of Pyramus and Thisbe[4] and another with 'an Antike' and a French motto. On the fine portrait of her that has recently come to light[5] she wears a medallion with the scene of Ahasuerus touching Esther with his rod (Plate 76). An *enseigne* in the Wallace Collection with the story of Judith and Holofernes (Plate 64c) bears all the marks of English workmanship;[6] but a not dissimilar brooch, in the Cleveland Museum of Art in Ohio, with the Adoration of the Magi, has a French inscription, though this is hardly conclusive.[7]

The great 1560 inventory of the French royal jewels,[8] however, though it has a fairly high proportion of classical subjects, also includes *enseignes* with the stories of Susanna, Joachim, the Sacrifice of Isaac and David and Goliath. It must be remembered, indeed, that Aldegrever's engravings of 1540 include the subjects of Absalom, Susanna, Judith and Bathsheba, as well as such usual classical subjects as Hercules, Atlas and the Judgment of Paris.[9]

Henry VIII wore 'aglets' or golden points such as were used to finish laces, on his caps, as well as jewels; his inventory of 1526[10] includes a black Milan bonnet, double turfed, with seventeen pairs of rolls enamelled white, black and purple, and a brooch of a handful of feathers; and that for 1528[11] two crimson velvet bonnets, one with twelve pairs of aglets, the other with thirty-six pairs; and a Milan bonnet with five pairs of aglets and three of small buttons. Such ornaments, however, were also in fashion in Germany, if at a slightly later date; a portrait of Prince Albert of Bavaria of 1545[12] shows

---

[1] National Portrait Gallery No. 119; Toledo Museum, Ohio.

[2] Madden, p. 177, 182-4, 187; Evans, *English Jewellery*, p. 84.

[3] Christ healing a man of the palsy, the Passion and single figures of St. John and St. George.

[4] Also represented on a locket once in the collection of Sir Augustus Wollaston Franks (Evans, *English Jewellery*, p. 84) and in Aldegrever's pattern book. A jewel with the subject is listed in a manuscript inventory of the jewels of the House of Lorraine in 1599, Bibliothèque Nationale, MS Lorraine 183, f. 275.

[5] Bequeathed by Sir Bruce Ingram to the Fitzwilliam. See H. Clifford Smith in *Illustrated London News*, July 9, 1949, where the jewels are illustrated in detail.

[6] It appears to be by the same hand as the book-covers described *infra* p. 101.

[7] QVI . A . DIEV . VEVLT . CONPLAI(RE:H)ONNEVR LVY . DOVIT . FAIRE.

[8] *Revue Universelle des Arts*, IV, 1856, p. 449 *seq.*, p. 518 *seq.*

[9] Ducerceau's long series of 'fonds de coupes' used alike by the enamellers of the late school of Limoges and by silversmiths may also from their circular shape have been useful to *enseigne*-makers.

[10] Brewer, IV, pt. I, p. 846. The whole list is interesting as illustrating the variety of *enseigne* subjects.

[11] ibid, IV, pt. 2, p. 2244.　　[12] By H. Mielich. In the Alte Pinakothek, Munich; Röttger, p. 63.

him wearing a soft beret sewn with aglets; it bears as well a large round *enseigne* with the figure of an angel.

Exceptionally a particular technique may be associated with one country, and again, it would seem, with a single workshop. There is a group of enamels characterised by strong pictorial composition, great richness of colour and relief, and the use (to give sparkling detail) of a very narrow flat strip of gold goffered into ridges, technically known as crimped plate. One of the pieces — a circular *Adoration of the Magi* in the Victoria and Albert Museum — can be associated with a pax that once belonged to the abbey church of Halle and another made for Cardinal Albrecht of Brandenburg, and the group is attributable to a South German workshop of c. 1530. This also produced *enseignes*.[1] One in the private collection of Her Majesty the Queen (Colour Plate Va),* traditionally said to have belonged to Henry VIII, shows St. George and the Dragon; the horse and its trappings closely resemble those of the St. James relief. The crimped plate is used for the hem of the trappings and for the rim, and for the interlaced design on a green ground that adorns the back. The medallion from a second *enseigne* is in the Cabinet de Médailles of the Bibliothèque Nationale (Plate 65a). It represents the Adoration of the Magi, the subject that also adorns a third *enseigne*[2] that still keeps its rim of a close garland wreathed by a ribbon and studded with table diamonds, and has a back decorated like the Queen's *enseigne*.

Certain types of jewel are more often found in the non-Italian countries. One of the most characteristic is the enamelled portrait *enseigne* or pendant which was in favour in the years round 1520. Cameo portraits were already in fashion in Italy; Alessandro de' Medici sent his, cut by Domenico del Polo, to Francis I.[3] Francis I then imported his own cameo cutter from Italy and Matteo del Nassarro, who entered his service in 1515, made portrait cameos of his master which are still in the Cabinet des Médailles at Paris.[4] Richard Astyll who worked for Henry VIII[5] made portrait cameos of his master, one alone and one with his son as a little boy in a cap with a rattle, and others of Philip II of Spain and Queen Elizabeth, which are still in the private collection of Her Majesty the Queen; Jacopo di Trezzo cut cameos of Philip II of Spain and Don Carlos.[6] Even Martin Luther was cut in bloodstone.[7] The jewellers, not to be outdone, produced

---

[1] F. Steingräber, 'Süddeutsche Goldemailplastik der Frührenaissance', *Studien zur Geschichte der europäischer Plastik* (Festschrift Th. Müller), 1965, p. 223 ff. The Victoria and Albert Museum has a tablet representing St. James of Compostella at the Battle of Clavijos.

[2] Gibson Carmichael Collection, at one time lent to the Victoria and Albert Museum. See also Bonnaffé, *Spitzer Collection*, III, p. 124.

[3] It is in the Cabinet des Médailles of the Bibliothèque Nationale.

[4] See Babelon, *Histoire*, p. 129. He also practised as a lapidary; in 1531 he founded a watermill on boats in the Seine for cutting precious stones. Ibid., p. 132.

[5] See A. B. Tonnochy in *Connoisseur*, XCV, 1935, p. 275.

[6] Cabinet des Médailles, Bibliothèque Nationale.   [7] Waddesdon Bequest, British Museum, No. 175.

*In black and white in the Dover edition.

rival portraits in enamelled gold. The finest is that of the Emperor Charles V (Colour Plate IVa)*at Vienna, which is a real *tour de force* of the enameller's art. It has much of the quality of a picture; and this quality is again attempted in an enamelled portrait of Francis I.[1] Most of the medallions, however, are based on medals and keep the profile head in gold against a background of enamel or semi-precious stone. A fine example is that of the Emperor Charles V on a background of bloodstone with a rim of lapis lazuli (Plate 65b) in the Metropolitan Museum; it is based on a medal by Leone Leoni.

Another northern jewel that, like the portrait *enseignes* and pendants, laid emphasis on the individuality of the wearer, was formed of his initials. As early as 1467 the Duke of Burgundy had an ornament formed of two CC interlaced, set with table diamonds.[2] In 1494 the Este inventory includes one formed of an A, set with a diamond, a ruby and a pearl; it was presumably imported from France as it is described as 'a la Paresina'.[3] In 1515 Henry VIII gave the Dowager Queen of France, widow of Louis XII, a double A set with a diamond, a ruby and a pearl — possibly once the property of his brother Arthur — to be turned into an M.[4] Henry also owned a carcanet with EE, perhaps once his mother's.[5] Henry VIII himself greatly favoured the use of initials in jewellery, though his many marriages involved him in a certain amount of resetting. In 1528 he owned a carcanet with H and K, for himself and Katharine of Aragon,[6] and later Holbein designed him a pendant with H and I for himself and Jane Seymour. His daughter Mary inherited a number of jewels with H and H and K.[7] Other initial jewels are recorded in the inventories of Charles V[8] and James V of Scotland.[9] Their extremely personal character has prevented many of such jewels from surviving. A splendid pendant of a crowned C, set with rubies, on a background of enamelled scrolls and fruit, was found in the tomb of Caterina Jagellonica, Queen of Sweden, in Upsala Cathedral (Plate 66). A *putto* in white enamel disports himself in the arc of the C. The solid back is delicately enamelled in red and green in a design of fretwork and scrolls in Arabesque style.[10] A yet more splendid jewel by the same craftsman was before the War in the Green Vaults at Dresden[11] (Plate 67). It was made for Anna of Saxony and bears a double A — perhaps for Anna and August of Saxony — in table diamonds. The ruby

---

[1] Now in the Musée de Cluny; it may be that described in the King's inventory of 1519. Laborde, *Glossaire*, p. 108.

[2] Laborde, *Glossaire*, p. 213.
[3] Gay, s.v. A.
[4] Brewer, II, pt. i, p. 88.
[5] ibid., III, pt. i, p. 163.
[6] ibid., IV, pt. 2, p. 2243.
[7] MS Inventory, British Museum, Harl. MS. 611.
[8] See Gay, s.v. Bracelet.
[9] Thomson, p. 47. The 1551 inventory of Henry II includes an H enamelled red with a large diamond and a pendant ruby. Bapst, *Bijoux de la Couronne*, p. 67.
[10] See Upmark. It is shewn in a portrait of her by Lucas Cranach once in the Czartoryski palace at Cracow. She died in 1583. It was found in her tomb in 1833.
[11] Holzhausen, p. 180; Watzdorf, p. 52.   *In black and white in the Dover edition.

PLATE IV

(a) Hat medallion of enamelled gold with a portrait of the Emperor Charles V. 1520

(b) Hat medallion of enamelled gold with St George and the Dragon.
Middle of the sixteenth century

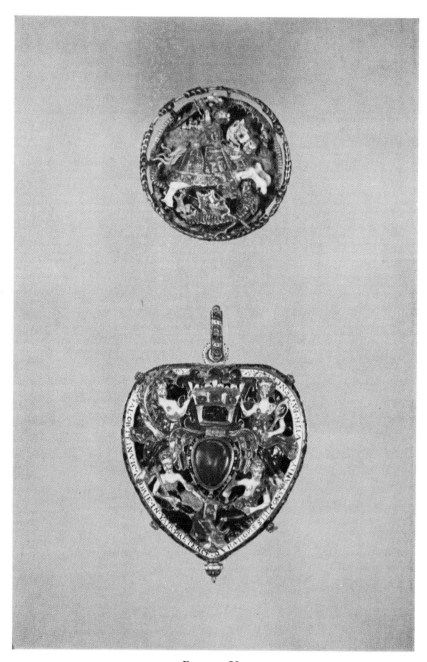

PLATE V

(*a*) Hat medallion of gold enamelled with St George and the Dragon.
German, *c.* 1540

(*b*) Front of the Lennox or Darnley Jewel. Enamelled gold set with sapphires

PLATE VI
(a) Back of the Lennox or Darnley Jewel. Enamelled gold
(b) Back of a pendant of enamelled gold with a medallion of Apollo and
Daphne. Italian, middle of the sixteenth century

PLATE VII

Pendant in enamelled gold set with rubies and emeralds. German, *c.* 1600

crown above is identical with that of the Upsala jewel; the fruit, scrolls and *putti* are by the same hand, and the back is enamelled in the same style, here in a design of terms and genii.[1] Before the last War Prince Czartoryski owned a third pendant of the kind, a crowned A with two *putti* resting along the gable of the letter.[2]

It is just possible that all these pendants were designed by Hans Mielich, a Munich man born in 1516, and a distinguished designer of jewels. A manuscript illuminated by him[3] has a D initial so heavily jewelled that it might well serve as a model for a pendant. His other jewel designs, however,[4] have less in common with the enamels of the Upsala and Dresden pendants.

A curious parallel with these initial pendants is afforded by those ornaments that bore the monogram IHS. An early example is the pendant in diamonds recorded in the 1480 inventory of Philibert of Savoy.[5] In 1519 Henry VIII had a similar pendant with three hanging pearls;[6] it is represented worn as a brooch on the portrait of Jane Seymour of about 1537 of the school of Holbein at Vienna.[7] The Gothic letters are set with table diamonds and appear against a background of golden leafage. Jewels of the kind continued in fashion all through the sixteenth century[8] (Plate 72). After that date they are chiefly found in Denmark;[9] one of the latest in precious materials is that in diamonds designed by Arnold Lulls for Anne of Denmark.[10]

Another kind of pendant characteristic of England and Denmark was the Tau Cross, which was considered to be prophylactic because of the text in the Vulgate version of Ezekiel[11] which says that the elect have 'signa Thau super frontes'. Such crosses are mentioned in English inventories and are shown on the brass of the four wives of Sir Richard Fitz-Lewes, dating from about 1528, in Ingrave Church, Essex. One set with rubies and sapphires is worn by Queen Mary Tudor in the portrait dated 1554 belonging to the Society of Antiquaries. A fine but bourgeois example in the National Museum

---

[1] A chain also formerly in the Green Vaults was formed of heart-shaped medallions with her initial. Watzdorf, p. 55.

[2] Bapst, *Joyaux de la Couronne, p. 15*.　　　　[3] Röttger, p. 31.

[4] See *infra*, p. 106.　　　　[5] Ménabréa, p. 282.

[6] Brewer, III, pt.i, 164; it is again recorded in Mary's inventory of 1542. Cf. the Jesus of diamonds set in gold mentioned in the 1537 will of Elizabeth Countess of Oxford. *Testamenta Vetusta*, p. 674.

[7] Kunsthistorisches Museum. Another version of it is in the collection of the Duke of Bedford. The pendant she wears in this picture may be compared with one in the author's possession. See Joan Evans in *Gazette des Beaux-Arts*, ser. 5, XIV, 1926, p. 357.

[8] One dated 1562 is now a morse in the Church of Santa Barbara at Mantua. The crowned IHS is surrounded by enamel figures of a secular kind. It appears to be of South German workmanship and may come from the same atelier as the A and C described above.

[9] A number of them in silver and silver gilt are in the National Museum, Copenhagen; one is dated 1574 but several look later.

[10] Drawing in the Victoria and Albert Museum: it closely resembles a jewel in the Cabinet des Médailles.

[11] Ezekiel, IX, 4.

of Copenhagen has the Crucifixion on one side and the Brazen Serpent with the sun and moon on the other.

Heart jewels, again, were more popular at the English Court than elsewhere. Henry VIII had no less than thirty-nine such pendants (one with the figure of St. Peter Martyr, two enamelled with pansies and gillyflowers, pierced through with arrows, and one with a man and woman under a hawthorn tree on one side and Our Lady and St. Anne on another, and another with Sts. George, Anthony and Sebastian) as well as one he gave to his daughter Mary, with a man and an antelope on one side and a lady on the other.[1]

Another widespread fashion was that for extremely heavy gold chains: about 1522, indeed, the chronicler Hall uses 'massye chenes and Curyous Collers' as the test of richness of attire.[2] The fashion, however, appears to have originated in Italy. A picture in the Brera of Ludovico il Moro and Beatrice d'Este kneeling before the Virgin, painted in 1494, shows him wearing a chain of immense gold links as his only jewel. In England and France such chains were chiefly worn by men.[3] In 1511 Henry VIII paid his goldsmith Roy £199 — then a very large sum — for a chain of gold weighing 98 ounces.[4] Holbein's portrait of Sir Brian Tuke[5] shows him wearing a heavy plain gold chain with a cross hanging from it; and the contemporary portrait of Sir Percival Hart[6] portrays him wearing an incredibly massive gold chain, each link as big as a wedding ring;[7] it may be compared with the 'chesne d'or a anneletz, façon de chesne de puis, à crochet', in the 1554 inventory of Emard de Nicolay.[8] In Tudor England, indeed, heavy gold chains were used, as snuff-boxes were at a later date, as the common present to the suites of ambassadors and to any gentleman who had rendered the King a service.

In Flanders and Germany, however, such chains were chiefly worn by women. They appear in almost all the female portraits of Lucas Cranach the Elder after 1506. Chains with wreathed links as heavy as fetters appear on his portrait of a Saxon Princess of 1516–18,[9] and on the portrait of Anna Buchner of 1518.[10] A portrait of 1526 in the

[1] Brewer, IV, pt. 2, p. 2243 and IV, pt. 3, p. 3069. He had twenty-one hands holding hearts, but these may well have been badges: cf. a carcanet of hearts with a hand at each end, ibid, III, pt. i. p. 163.

[2] e.g. *Chronicles*, I. 20.

[3] The wearing of official collars continued. In 1523 Henry VIII ordered that the collar of the Garter should be worn on state occasions and the collar of SS continued in official use. The Lord Mayor of London has a fine collar of SS given by Sir John Alleyn in 1546. Other surviving official collars of the period are those of the Beverley Waits, the Exeter Waits, and the civic minstrels of Norwich and Bristol. See Joan Evans, *English Jewellery*, 80, n. 3.

[4] Clifford Smith, p. 237.   [5] Burlington Fine Arts Club Exhibition, 1909, No. 43.

[6] In the collection of Sir Oliver Hart-Dyke, Bart.

[7] As late as 1588 Elizabeth was given as a New Year's gift a chain weighing 161 oz., but this may have been merely a delicate way of giving a present of specie.

[8] Gay, s.v. Chaîne. Twelve heavy chains are recorded in the 1539 inventory of James V of Scotland. Thomson, p. 49.

[9] In the Booth Collection, Detroit.   [10] In the Hohenzollern-Sigmaringen Collection.

Hermitage shows a lady wearing a heavy dog-collar of jewelled gold round the throat and a quadruple chain of immense weight. A similar chain appears on the bridal portrait of Sibylle of Cleves of the same year.[1] The portrait of Cranach's own wife (Plate 68) illustrates his use of a chain with large reeded links twisted with half a turn, like a vine stem. The triptych painted by Barend van Orley for the Hanneton family about 1525[2] portrays the wife of the head of the family wearing a massive chain of plain links; her elder daughter wears a lighter chain of the same design to support a beautiful pendant set with three gems and three pearls in floriated gold work round a central stone.[3] Holbein's portrait of Dame Alice More,[4] probably painted in 1527, shows her wearing a gold chain twice close round the neck and once down in front, and a second triple chain with a crucifix hanging to the waist.

Besides these chains of plain links the monarchs of Northern Europe usually had at least one immensely rich jewelled collar which remained their classic jewel for state occasions. The type, glorified by the fancy of the artist, may be illustrated from a Flemish picture of the Magi dating from the early years of the sixteenth century in the Uffizi. One king wears a collar of enormous rubies, some square and some oval, in scrolled settings of gold. Great pearls project above and below the medallion links and a matching pendant set with an immense oblong ruby hangs below.

Henry VIII's legendary collar of balases was hardly less magnificent. It appears in a number of his portraits, notably in that now in the National Gallery of Rome (Plate 69). It was composed of a number of flat cut balas rubies, some square and some oval, in petalled settings, linked by ornaments of richly foliated gold, each studded with two enormous pearls.[5] The whole was hinged together to give a flexible ribbon-like effect. In the Rome portrait the king's coat is clasped by four matching rubies down the front and the sleeves show eighteen more: others are presumably on the parts of them hidden in the picture. Hall gives a description of the King in 1539 which corresponds fairly closely with the array shown in the portrait. 'His persone was apparelled in a coate of purple velvet . . . the sleves and brest were cut, lined with clothe of golde, and tied together with great buttons of Diamondes, Rubyes and Orient Perle . . . his night cappe garnished with stone, but his bonnet was so ryche of juels that fewe men coulde value them. Besyde all this he ware in baudrike wyse a coller of such Balistes and Perle that

---

[1] In the Schloss Museum of Weimar.   [2] Now in the Brussels Museum.
[3] The younger daughter wears a cross pendant of five stones and three pearls in the same style.
[4] In the collection of Lord Methuen.
[5] The differently set rubies and pearls on the collar depicted on the early portrait (c. 1516) of Henry VIII in the collection of Mr. Clifford Smith (*Illustrated London News*, Dec. 9, 1933) suggest that many of these jewels were inherited from his father and reset later in his reign. A great collar of balas rubies is shewn in a portrait of Henry VII in Lord Brownlow's Collection; Burlington Fine Arts Club Exhibition of English Portraits, 1907, No. 10.

few men ever sawe the lyke.'[1] Besides this great collar Henry had a second one, with nine balases standing between angels and thirty-six pearls.[2] A second series of portraits[3] shows Henry wearing the same great collar and ruby clasps and a set of at least twelve strap-like clasps, each centring in a huge sapphire, with two lesser sapphires on either side, all set in golden scrolling foliage like that of the great collar.

Henry VIII was not alone in magnificence. In 1530[4] Francis I, who had a taste for diamonds, had a great collar of eleven notable stones, some table cut and some pointed, joined by friars' knots of pearls, an A-shaped pendant mounted with the diamond *Prant-Poincte*, and two diamond brooches, a table and the *Pointe de Bretagne*[5]. In his cap he wore the great diamond of the House of Dunois, cut mirrorwise, with three hanging ruby drops. He instituted the crown jewels of France as a permanent collection. When he married Eleanor of Austria she had the usufruct of them only; and Mary Stuart, after her first husband's death, handed back to the King of France the great diamond with a hanging pearl that Francis I had bought for sixty-five thousand crowns and had given her to wear.[6] His goldsmith, Jean Duvet, who died about 1562, mounted them in 'classic' jewels that stayed in fashion for a long time. When Catherine de Médicis came to France to marry Henry Duke of Orléans in 1532 she brought with her the finest pearls ever seen in France.[7] At his coronation in 1548 Henry no longer wore the traditional fleur-de-lis clasp for his mantle, but a cross of nine great diamonds, five table stones for the cross and a round stone and three lance-shaped ones for the foot, set in gold with coloured enamels, that Francis I had had made.[8] A portrait of Henry dated 1555[9] shows him wearing a great swag of pearls held together by enamelled ribbons, with an oval medallion in a scrolled setting below.

The High Renaissance was a time when the wealth of the courts of England, France and Spain was vastly increased. In England, at least, the vast treasures of the Church were at the royal use; from the shrine of St. Thomas Becket alone two great chests, so heavy that six or eight men could hardly move them, were filled with gold and jewels of inestimable value for the King's use. Moreover the countries of the old world began to

---

[1] Hall's *Chronicles* II, 298.

[2] Brewer, III, pt. i, 163; the collar with sixteen balases and forty-four pearls is probably that represented in the picture.

[3] e.g. at Warwick Castle and Castle Howard; see *Illustrated London News*, Oct. 14, 1933.

[4] Bapst, p. 4.   [5] Cérémonial de France, 1515; cited Gay, s.v. Bague.

[6] Laborde, *Glossaire*, p. 504. She herself owned an 'accoustrement de gros diamens' of seven pieces. Robertson, p. 75.

[7] Brantôme, VII, 330. She later gave them to Mary Stuart: six strings of large pearls strung rosary-wise, and twenty-five still larger pearls. After Mary's death they were bought by Elizabeth, at a bargain price.

[8] Bapst, *Bijoux de la Couronne*, p. 44. It was later borrowed by Diane de Poitiers.

[9] Museum of Le Puy.

be enriched by the treasures of the new; the Spanish plate-ships brought their yearly burden of gold and silver, pearls and stones from the Americas to join the riches of the older Indies. Yet it is worthy of remark that magnificence in the first half of the sixteenth century lay less in an immense multiplication of rich jewels, than in the possession of two or three splendid *parures*. Hat jewels are an exception; it is in these that fancy ruled, and with fancy's changes its expression was numberless. But there was, in the earlier part of the century, a less abundant proliferation of elegant trifles than there had been, for instance, in the late fourteenth century.

There were, however, pomanders, generally worn hanging at the girdle. The 1514 inventory of Charlotte d'Albret[1] mentions one of gold shaped like a pomegranate, with pierced sides; one, half like a chestnut and half like rose-branches, and another made like a sphere with the world inside are listed in the 1561 inventory of the Château de Pau[2] and forty-four of one kind and another occur in the French royal inventory of 1560.[3] The surviving examples are mostly of silver; an exception is a pomander case of closely coiled gold wire, ornamented with pearls, found by a bargeman in the mud on the south side of the Thames.[4]

Little prayer books of jewelled and enamelled gold were also worn at the girdle end. A design for one in nielloed gold was offered by Lucas de Salamanca as his *épreuve de maîtrise* to the goldsmiths' guild of Barcelona about 1520.[5] Holbein's jewel designs include one for such a book, enamelled in arabesques on a ground of two colours, with the initals T. W.: probably for Thomas Wyatt the poet, clerk of the King's jewels. The inventory of Henry VIII's jewels in the secret Jewel-House[6] includes a book of the kind, with a diamond cross and other jewels on one side, hanging from a chain of emeralds. Queen Elizabeth wore a book containing a copy of the last prayer of Edward VI, in golden covers decorated with black champlevé enamel in arabesque designs and white enamel rosettes. One side is set with a shell cameo, and the other with a boss of translucent enamel in red and green.[7] It passed by Elizabeth's cousin, Lord Hunsdon, into the Berkeley family, where it is still preserved.

A golden book cover in the British Museum (Plate 70) is decorated with pictorial reliefs picked out in white enamel; the slightly clumsy proportion suggests English workmanship. On one side is the worship of the brazen serpent with the inscription: MAKE THE A FYRYE SERPENT AN SET IT VP FOR A SIGNE THAT AS MANY AS ARE BYTTE MAYE LOKE VPON IT AN LYVE. On the other is the Judgment of Solomon, with the inscription: THEN THE KING ANSVERED AN SAYD GYVE HER THE LYVING CHILD

---

[1] Gay, s.v. Pomme de Musc.
[3] *Revue Universelle des Arts*, IV, 1856, p. 520-3.
[4] In the British Museum.
[6] British Museum, Stowe MS 560.

[2] Gay, s.v. Pomme de Musc.
[5] Davillier, Plate III, Fig. 3.
[7] Clifford Smith, Plate XXXV, 7; p. 274.

AN SLAYE ET NOT FOR SHE IS THE MOTHER THEREOF. A second set of book covers, now unmounted, in the same Museum, is similarly enamelled with the Judgment of Solomon in two scenes; it must be by the same hand. A particularly splendid example of foreign workmanship (Plate 71) has its central medallions enamelled with the Creation of Eve and a scene of nymphs surprised while bathing. The angles are filled by seated figures among scrolls and foliage; the whole is a masterpiece in its kind.[1]

The first half of the sixteenth century may be thought of as the age in which jewellery was most strongly linked with the great arts of sculpture and painting. The resources of the jewellers' technique were stretched to the utmost to maintain the link; and sometimes it must be admitted that the result was mere virtuosity. Yet it suffices to look at such designs as those of Holbein to realise that the classical *misura* was not often lost, and that the jewels of the early sixteenth century have their own qualities of splendour, nobleness and serenity.

[1] Some very fine early seventeenth-century book covers of enamelled gold are in the Rosenborg Slott at Copenhagen and in the Myntkabinett at Stockholm. They no longer have the loop for hanging and have thus ceased to be personal ornaments.

CHAPTER FIVE

The Later Renaissance

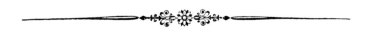

It had taken some twenty years for the influence of the early Renaissance in sculpture and painting fully to infiltrate into the design of jewels. By about 1540 this early phase had in the great arts given way to that of mannerism: the phase of elaboration and virtuosity, of smaller scale, more violent movement, of ornate splendour rather than noble simplicity. Once again it was some twenty years before the full impact of the new style was felt upon jewellery design, but about 1560 the new spirit makes itself clearly felt in the minor art.

There is no definable break; it is hard even to find an exact criterion of change, for the change is one rather of spirit and of sense of values than of form. But there can be no question that after 1560 a fresh element of display comes into jewellery, and quickly becomes a dominant factor, at the expense of the rather severe and almost architectural magnificence of the first half of the century.

The emphasis was tending to shift from architectural magnificence to mere profusion; and it corresponded with a transference of the centres of jewel design from Italy and (to a lesser degree) from France to the great cities of Germany and Austria. In Italy itself the tradition of monumental elegance was maintained. The many Bronzinos of Eleanor of Toledo always show her in a plain dress of the most splendid brocade imaginable, with a short string and a long rope of enormous pearls. The only jeweller's work about her attire is a simple pendant of a large stone with a pearl drop and a belt of jewels in enamelled settings. A splendid pendant (Colour Plate VIb)[*]in the private collection of H.M. the Queen is more elaborate in its *entassement* of cupids and warriors and sirens round its central medallion of Apollo and Daphne, but it has an ordered richness with an architectonic line.[1]

In France style developed more rapidly than in Italy, but the Wars of Religion led to a wave of royal borrowing on a large scale with jewels as security, and for a time after 1577 the credit of France was exhausted[2] and the demand for splendid jewels came

---

[1] We know comparatively little of the Italian jewellers of the period, though Garzoni in *La piazza universale* (cap. 58, p. 516), second ed. 1587, says that Paolo Rizzio was then the best jeweller in Venice.

[2] See Bapst, *Rôle économique*.

*In black and white in the Dover edition.   103

almost to an end. The *Discours sur les causes de l'extrême cherté qui est aujourd'hui en France,* published at Paris in 1574, states that Francis I loved jewels and that in consequence everyone wore them during his reign, whereas Henri II disliked them, and they were little worn in his time. This, however, was the result rather of penury than of personal taste. The splendid diamonds and pearls of Francis I, reset by Francis II in 1559 as a short necklace, a bandeau for the forehead and a long shoulder collar of friars' knots, all in gold enhanced with red enamel, were usually in pawn.[1] Only two years after the resetting one of the most important diamonds was offered to Elizabeth as an indemnity for Calais; and then for years they became things no longer of pleasure but of security

Fig. 11. Drawing for a diamond jewel belonging to the Duke of Lorraine in 1592

on which money could be borrowed.[2] Such use, however, did not necessarily lead to destruction, though they might hardly be seen for years. Exceptionally the records of gift or pawning add to our knowledge of such jewels. A careful drawing survives of a diamond ornament[3] (Fig. 11) which was given by the Duke of Lorraine in 1592 to the Duchess of Elbeuf to help pay her husband's ransom.

In the German lands Augsburg continued to be an important centre, and Prague rose to distinction between about 1570 and 1612 in the time of the Emperor Rudolf, King of Hungary and Bohemia; then the Thirty Years' War brought its prosperity to an end. England and Spain were great centres of jewellery in the time of the rivalry of Elizabeth

[1] Bapst, *Couronne,* p. 55. [2] ibid., p. 61.
[3] Bibliothèque Nationale MS fonds Lorraine, 183, fol. 253.

and Philip II; but England at least sank into a secondary position with the Civil War.

The varying fortunes of the European sovereigns and their courts did much to further the international trade in jewels that was already organised on a considerable scale. It is little easier to pin a national label to a jewel of the late sixteenth century than it is to do so for a jewel of the first half of the century. Catherine de Médicis' jewellers were French — Dujardin, Mathurin Lussaut, Hérondelle;[1] Elizabeth employed many Englishmen, though her chief jeweller, Master Spilman, was 'an High Germaine';[2] but all were influenced by engraved designs and jewels imported from other centres.

One of the influences which may have helped to bring about a love of profusion rather than of severer elegance at this time was the gradual concentration of jewels as women's wear. Up till now they had been worn in as great profusion by men as by women; Henry VIII wore more jewels, and more splendid jewels, than any of his wives. But in the second half of the century, though men still wore embroidered garments of great luxury, they were rarely sewn and strewn with jewels as they once had been.[3] The portraits of the duc d'Alençon,[4] for example, show him dandiacal enough, but wearing only a long collar formed of three rows of large pearls linked by large square plaques, each set with a single jewel in an enamelled frame, with a hat band to match. The full-length portrait of Henri III in the Louvre, dating from about 1580, shows him wearing an immense tress of pearls about a dozen rows thick; twelve brooch-like aglets down the front of his coat, and a large hat jewel serving as the base to an aigrette of heron's feathers.[5] It is a splendid enough array, but elegant rather than profuse. Yet contemporary portraits of Catherine de Médicis[6] and Elisabeth of Austria, Queen of France, show the upper parts of their dress as a trellis of pearls, with jewels at the intersections. Their coifs are richly jewelled; they wear short necklaces, and long chains to match fixed as borders to the bodice, with lesser chains and a great pendant below (Plate 74). That these are jewels that actually existed can be proved by a comparison between the portrait of Elisabeth of Austria and the bills for resetting what remained of the French crown jewels, and other documents.[7] The lower chain of rubies, emeralds and diamonds, with the pendant formed of a great diamond with a ruby above and a pendant pearl, was

[1] Bapst, *Couronne*, p. 114.
[2] Nichols p. II, p. 592: he came from the free town of Lindau on Lake Constance.
[3] The ornaments were usually restricted to buttons; Prince Ranuccio Farnese in 1587 had twelve of gold with a crowned eagle in the middle (Campori, p. 48) and the King of France in 1591 one hundred and forty-three in sets of varying sizes. Bapst, *Couronne*, p. 237.
[4] e.g. in the Musée Condé, Chantilly.
[5] His inventory, quoted Gay, s.v. Pendants d'oreille, includes a pair of diamond earrings.
[6] A good instance is that by Pourbus in the Uffizi, which shows the entire dress trellised with pearls. It dates from about 1559.
[7] Bapst, *Couronne*, p. 114.

her wedding present from Catherine de Médicis;[1] the necklace-like ornament in her hair appears to be that given her by the bridegroom. Her caskets, indeed, held five complete *parures*, with diamonds, emeralds, sapphires, pearls or rubies predominating in each, and each including *carcan* or short necklace, collar for the shoulders, *cotière* or chain with pendant, and *bordure* for the head; the diamond one had a belt as well.[2] Similarly the Duchess of Lorraine had a *carcan* and a collar of table-cut diamonds, a *cotière*, cross and *touret* to match.[3] The *cotière* had to be pawned in 1610, when a fuller description[4] was made; it had forty links enamelled in white, red and green, that at the end larger, and shaped like a crowned heart; the whole was set on one side with sixty-four diamonds and on the other with sixty-two rubies.

Yet more splendid jewels of the same kind may be seen on portraits of the Austrian House at Vienna, and it would seem not impossible that the idea of such *parures* was evolved at the court of Maximilian. The portrait of Elisabeth of Valois,[5] Queen of Spain, painted by Alonzo Sanchez Coello in the early 1560's, shows that by then it had reached Spain. Her *carcan, cotière* (here worn square) belt and head-dress are all *en suite* and are composed of plaques of richly chased and enamelled gold set alternately with tiers of large pearls and with single enormous table-cut rubies. The portraits of the Infantas of Spain of Philip II's family in the Prado show similar jewels adapted for another kind of dress (Plate 75).[6] The carcanet is worn at the base of a high collar; there is no shoulder necklace but a no less rich belt takes its place. The front of the dress and the shoulder pieces are sewn with splendid brooch-like aglets. The fashion for these belts soon spread to France; a fine portrait of a lady of about 1570 in the Museum of Lille, shews her wearing carcanet, belt and bracelets all formed of medallions of a central stone surrounded by eight daisies of pearls. The drawings of Hans Mielich of Munich,[7] made to illustrate an inventory of the jewels of Duke Albert V of Bavaria and Anne of Austria, admirably illustrate such jewels (Plate 73). They are particularly interesting as depicting the elaborate backs of the carcanets, enamelled in delicate moresque designs. A superb chain in the Schatzkammer at Munich, known as the Collar of the Order of St. George, survives to show the kind of work lavished upon such jewels.[8]

---

[1] V. von Klarwill, *Fugger Newsletters*, II, 1925, p. 11.

[2] Bapst, *Couronne*, p. 117. In 1588 Queen Margot sold some of her jewels; the Grand Duke of Tuscany bought the diamonds and the Duke of Mantua the rubies. ibid, p. 153.

[3] Bibliothèque Nationale MS Lorraine, 183, fol. 15.   [4] Roy, p. 336.   [5] At Vienna.

[6] A like *parure* of slightly different design may be seen in Coello's portrait of the Infanta Caterina Michela in the same gallery.

[7] Some are in the Royal Library at Munich, some in the Bavarian National Museum, and some are (or were till recently) in the Hefner-Altneck Collection at Munich. See von Hefner Altneck, *Deutsche Goldschmiede-werke des sechzehnten Jahrhunderts*, Frankfurt, 1890.

[8] A pendant formerly in the Figdor Collection at Vienna (Rosenberg, *Figdor*, Fig. 80) had a back enamelled in the same style as that shown in Mielich's drawing.

Elsewhere in Germany such ordered splendour was more slowly achieved. A picture of Kurfürstin Anna of Saxony by Lucas Cranach the younger, dated 1564,[1] shows her wearing splendid but disparate ornaments. Two more or less triangular pendants are hung one below the other, and below them again is one set with four great jewels under a crown. She has an immense double chain and a rich carcanet and bracelets. Her dress is sewn with aglets. The splendour is no less, but it is not integrated.

In Britain the achievement of a *parure* was more slowly conquered by women. Henry VIII had had at least two sets of jewels on the grandest scale intended to be worn together, but his daughter Mary Tudor did not attempt to rival such magnificence.[2] Her portrait, belonging to the Society of Antiquaries of London, depicts her as wearing a pearl and sapphire necklace with a Tau Cross, a pendant of a huge diamond (probably the legendary 'Mirror of France') surrounded by figures of satyrs in enamelled gold,[3] with a round pendant hanging from her waist set with a crosslet of diamonds with enamelled figures between the limbs. Mary Queen of Scots naturally followed the French fashion, and by 1561 had an 'acoustrement de gros diamens' with two *bordures*, carcanet, *cotière*, belt and two chaplets, as well as smaller *parures* of diamonds, one in white and one in black enamel, four of large rubies and pearls and two in threaded pearls.[4]

Queen Elizabeth, however, shows better than anyone the shift of jewellery between the sexes in a century when much of European sovereignty lay in women's hands. It is worth remembering, too, that Elizabeth's household included a man — Nicholas Hilliard — who in the best Renaissance tradition was both painter and jeweller.[5] Hilliard's grandfather John Wall had been a London goldsmith; his father practised the same trade at Exeter and Hilliard seems to have received his preliminary training in the craft. In his *Arte of Limning* he gives instructions on how to paint precious stones in some detail. For him gems are the archetypes of colour, and he writes of the patience that graphic art demands in terms of the patience of the lapidary and the jeweller.

The portrait of Elizabeth in the National Portrait Gallery (Plate 77) shows her wearing a superb carcanet and collar, the second centred with a great sapphire, still in the rose

---

[1] Now in the Staatliches Historisches Museum of Dresden. Watzdorf, p. 51.

[2] She appears to have shared in the family passion for jewels; it is noteworthy that her New Year's gifts include many though, of course, she received other sorts of gifts, dress, plate etc. Nichols, I, p. XXXIV *seq.*

[3] The same jewel is represented in her portrait by Anthonis Mor in the collection of Lord Northampton.

[4] Robertson, p. 75. A jewelled *cotière* with snake links in green enamel given by her to Mary Seton is now divided between the royal collection at Windsor (to which it was added by H.M. Queen Mary, to whom Lady Bathurst had given it on the occasion of the silver Jubilee in 1935) and that of Mr. Hays, the heir of the Setons, at Duns Castle.

[5] See P. Norman, 'Nicholas Hilliard's Treatise concerning "The Arte of Limning",' in *Walpole Society Transactions*, vol. I, 1911–2, p. 13. In his paean to the diamond (p. 43) he takes it for granted that it should be set 'on his black feyntor' or foil.

setting in which her father had worn it. The carcanet is made of groups of four, the collar of groups of five, pearls in settings of gold enamelled in black, divided by medallions alternately of a large diamond in a setting of red enamel and of a ruby in a setting of black. She does not wear a *cotière*, but a large pendant of a phoenix (one of her badges) hangs at her breast. Her head ornament matches her necklace. Her belt is of large pearls and her dress is sewn with pearls[1] and small square cut gems in enamelled settings. By 1584 the Queen's most accomplished courtiers were giving her *parures en suite*. On New Year's day in that year Sir Christopher Hatton gave her an attire for the head of seven pieces, three formed as crowns imperial and four as victories, all set with diamonds, rubies, pearls and opals. On the next New Year's day he gave her an 'upper and nether abillement' — that is a head-dress and a collar — the former of links formed as crowns imperial and hearts.[2] As ruffs grew bigger a carcanet was no longer wearable, but on her portrait of 1588 in the National Maritime Museum at Greenwich the pearl clusters of her carcanet and collar, detached, are sewn down the front of her dress.

Profusion came into the jewellers' art not only in such displays as these but also by the exploiting of new fields of decoration.[3] The first portable timekeeper is said to have been made by Peter Henlein of Nuremberg soon after 1500, and the inventory of the jewels given to Catherine Howard by Henry VIII[4] includes three 'tabletts' of gold 'wherein is a clocke' and a gold pomander containing another. The portrait of Mary of Lorraine in the National Portrait Gallery[5] depicts her as wearing two watches, one hanging from her bodice on a rich *cotière* and the other at the end of the long pendant of her golden chain belt.[6] They were soon richly ornamented. Marguerite de Valois in 1579 had a little watch set with diamonds and rubies,[7] but the best idea of the variety of sixteenth-century watches can be obtained from the lists of Queen Elizabeth's jewels. In 1572, for example,[8] she was given an 'armlet or skakell of golde, all over fairely garnishedd with rubyes and dyamondes, haveing in the closing thearof a clocke'. Her 1587 inventory[9] has a section entirely devoted to watches. Eight were of gold or crystal; one was adorned with a frog and a lion; and two 'flowers' were set with watches. Watches, indeed, had not yet achieved a form of their own, but imitated that of other jewels. A crystal watch in a setting of enamelled gold that is said to have belonged to Elizabeth is

---

[1] Not all of these were real; a bill of 1569 is for 520 'pearles for the Quene's use' at a penny apiece. Nichols, I, p. 271.

[2] Nichols, II, pp. 419, 426.

[3] Even ear-picks were jewelled; see Joan Evans, *English Jewellery*, p. 81.

[4] British Museum Stowe MS 559.

[5] Once called the Fraser-Tytler portrait of Mary Queen of Scots.

[6] Even as late as 1610 watches are included in the section 'pendans à porter à la ceinture' in the inventory of Marie de Médicis. Bruel, p. 200.

[7] Gay, s.v. Montre. [8] Nichols, I, p. 294.

[9] British Museum MS Royal Append. 68.

FIG. 12. Engraved designs for jewels by Erasmus Hornick. 1562

now in the possession of the Royal Institution; it is very much like a reliquary pendant in shape. Others were formed as crosses, pomanders and miniature cases;[1] a few were turned into *memento mori* pendants — a fit shape for things that record the passing of time — by being shaped as death's heads.[2]

The portraits of the period show that every possible object of attire was jewelled. A picture of Queen Elizabeth[3] shows her holding an ostrich feather fan in a jewelled handle, and many such fans are recorded in her inventories. Such handles occur in the engraved designs of Erasmus Hornick of Nuremberg published in 1562 (Fig. 12) together with others for jewelled heads and claws for sable skins, such as are found in some of the inventories of the period,[4] and for pendants formed of dragons and sea-horses, *enseignes* with the figures of lovers,[5] and ornamental watches. A list of jewels stolen from two Antwerp goldsmiths in London in 1561[6] affords a remarkably exact parallel with Hornick's designs, and shows how closely he followed fashion: it includes a splendid fan, 'with figures of divers beasts set in diamonds and rubies', brooches 'of gold and figures' richly jewelled, and a jewelled sable.

The most important of Hornick's designs, however, are those for the large figured pendants which were beginning to take the place of cap-brooches as a field of display for the virtuosity of jeweller and enameller alike. They were sometimes worn hanging close to the throat, as in the portrait of Anne of Habsburg, Queen of Spain, painted by Anthonis Mor about 1570;[7] sometimes on the *cotière* on the breast, as on a portrait of Lady Willoughby, dated 1573, in the collection of Lord Middleton;[8] but more often pinned to swing from the stiff sleeve, as in many portraits of Queen Elizabeth. They were often extremely large; one with the subject of the Annunciation in the Louvre[9] is, with the little chains from which it hangs, five and a quarter inches long.

Erasmus Hornick's designs for pendants are formed of dragons and seahorses (Fig. 13). They are paralleled by a whole series of such pendants, most of which exploit the possibilities of using the baroque pearls that had lately come into fashion in the expression of monstrous forms. A typical example is a great sea dragon pendant in the

---

[1] See Williamson, *Catalogue of the Pierpont Morgan Collection of Watches.*

[2] See Véron in *L'Art*, XXIX, 1882, p. 217.

[3] National Portrait Gallery No. 2471; the portrait is remarkable for the size and number of the jewels with which the Queen's dress is sewn.

[4] e.g. Inventory of Lady Arabella Stuart, 1608, in *Reliquary*, I, 1860-1, p. 118. 'A Fiche Sable, the head and clawes of Goldsmith worke enamelled and set with diamonds and rubies.' One is represented in the Sidney Sussex College portrait of the foundress, Lady Frances Sidney. A surviving example belongs to Mr. John Hunt.

[5] cf. charming pendants with this subject in the Waddesdon Bequest at the British Museum and in the Sauvageot Collection at the Louvre.

[6] British Museum MS, Harl., 286, item 3.   [7] In the Kunsthistorisches Museum, Vienna.

[8] She wears a pendant on the left breast, of a mermaid in a ship.

[9] Adolphe Rothschild Bequest; probably Augsburg work.

FIG. 13. Two engraved designs for pendants by Erasmus Hornick. 1562

Waddesdon Bequest (Plate 82a) of which one side is all in baroque pearls and enamelled gold, and the other is of enamelled gold set with emeralds. Another in the same collection (Plate 82c) yet more closely resembles Hornick's designs in that the nereid it represents is mounted by a little figure in enamelled gold.[1] Winged terrestrial dragons, evidently by the same hand, are splendidly represented in the Victoria and Albert

[1] cf. The jewel of a mermaid with a maiden on her back given to Queen Elizabeth on New Year's day 1574. Nichols I, p. 379, and that with a dolphin with a man riding on his back in her inventory of 1587. British Museum MS Royal Append. 68 Sect.

Museum and in the Wernher Collection at Luton Hoo. Another pendant, that looks as if it came from the same workshop, represents a mermaid (Plate 82b), a subject also represented, with a baroque pearl body, in a pendant belonging to H.M. the Queen,[1] and in smaller jewels in the Danish Royal collection and in the Wernher Collection at Luton Hoo. A merman monster is represented in the famous jewel (Plate 81a) brought from India by Lord Canning,[2] on a fine jewel recently in New York,[3] and in a Spanish pendant in the Davillier bequest in the Louvre (Plate 83). A Spanish pendant (Plate 81b) shows no monster, but a lizard. In Spain, indeed, the fashion was as much, or more, for natural creatures as for monsters. A number of Spanish pendants represent birds (Plate 84): there are a crowned eagle and a little dove in the Wallace Collection, parrots from the treasure of the Virgen del Pilar in the Victoria and Albert Museum and in the Waddesdon Bequest;[4] a swan in the Metropolitan Museum of New York; while among four-footed creatures there is a hind and a lamb, a little dog and a rabbit in the Waddesdon Bequest.

Lord Fairhaven[5] owns a remarkable jewel with a baroque pearl set to represent a lion's face; its enamelled back is in the style of Corvinianus Saur, the Bavarian who was court goldsmith to Christian IV of Denmark. He also made the fine bird with a baroque pearl body that is still in the Danish Royal Collection, and published designs for engraved ornament between 1591 and 1597. The *Monilium bullarum in aurumque icones* published by Hans Collaert of Antwerp in 1581 includes similar monster pendants to those of Hornick's (Fig. 14), with rather more emphasis laid on the figures riding on the backs of the monsters. Such subjects, indeed, were in fashion in many countries. Prince Ranuccio Farnese in 1587[6] had a hat jewel with the Chariot of Fortune drawn by four horses with a dolphin below; the Pierpont Morgan Collection[7] included a pendant formed of a baroque pearl dolphin on which stands Fortune waving a scarf; and both are evidently in relation with one of Collaert's designs.[8] So too is the jewel 'being a fishe called a bull of the sea' with a man kneeling on it, set with diamonds and rubies, with a pear-shaped pendant, and hung by three small chains set with the same stones, which belonged to Queen Elizabeth in 1572.[9]

A more important change of taste, however, is shown by the inclusion in the design

---

[1] Unfortunately defaced by a top that does not belong to it.
[2] The carved ruby on the body and the ruby medallion above the pendant pearl appear to have been added when the jewel was in India.
[3] Lent by Messrs. Duveen Bros. to the Cleveland Museum of Art, Cleveland, Ohio, in 1947. Another was in the Pierpont Morgan Collection, catalogue No. 24.
[4] Another is in the Louvre. Jewels with a parrot, a salamander, a falcon, a dolphin and an eagle were given to Queen Elizabeth on New Year's Day, 1574. Nichols I, p. 379.
[5] See Beard in *Connoisseur*, CI, 1938, p. 72.   [6] Campori, p. 49.
[7] Catalogue No. 25.   [8] Victoria and Albert Museum, Engraving 2210-1911.
[9] Nichols I, p. 295.

FIG. 14. Engraved design for a pendant by Hans Collaert. 1581

of pendants of architectural elements[1] expressed in lines of square-cut stones. Architectural frames thus set are, indeed, the characteristic of many pendants of the last
quarter of the century, that, if they do not achieve the mannerist elegance of Collaert's
engraved architectural frames[2] (Fig. 15) are none the less expressions of the same
trend in taste. A fine example in the Waddesdon Bequest (Plate 85) with the figure of

[1] The tendency had been shown a little earlier in the designs for jewels published by Adrien Hubert
in 1576. Guilmard, p. 26.
[2] Notably the 'Architecture' pendant, Fig. 12 of his series, Bibliothèque Nationale.

113

FIG. 15. Engraved design for a pendant by Hans Collaert. 1581

Charity in the centre and Faith and Fortitude standing on either side, not only has the figures on the front framed in pilasters and an arch of diamonds and rubies, but also has the back enamelled with an architectural arcade.[1] In other instances — for example in a pendant with the Adoration of the Magi in the same collection (Plate 86) — the architectural lines are heavily stressed on the jewelled front, and the enamelled back is more lightly treated.

The subjects of these pendants fall roughly into three series: Biblical subjects, such as the *Noli me Tangere* in the Wallace Collection (Plate 87b) and the Adoration of the Magi already illustrated (Plate 86); Virtues, such as the Charity in the Waddesdon Bequest, the Justice in New York (Plate 87a) and, rather more rarely, classical subjects such as the Venus rising from the sea in the Waddesdon Bequest[2]. The style,

[1] A bronze maquette for a jewel apparently by the same hand was in the collection of the late Sir Robert Witt.

[2] cf. a pendant with the figures of *Pax* and *Justicia* embracing, formerly in the Green Vaults at Dresden. Holzhausen, p. 174.

however, is reasonably constant, though the variety in technique suggests that the jewels come from more than one workshop. The stylistic impression that they are of German origin is confirmed by references in contemporary inventories. In 1593, for example, Claude de France[1] owned 'une bague d'or à pendre façon d'Allemaigne représentant la figure de Jésus-Christ mis au Sépulchre'.

The repetition of certain themes makes it clear that the same drawing or engraving was used, not always by the same man. Mr. Clifford Smith has pointed out,[2] for instance, the similarities between a pendant with Antony and Cleopatra standing in a ship, sold at Christie's in 1903,[3] and one in the Vienna Museum with an identical ship, rowers and mandoline players, but hung by three chains instead of from a ring, and differently jewelled. A third with similar figures but a fish instead of a ship is in the Bavarian National Museum at Munich; a fourth with Cleopatra is recorded in the 1587 inventory of Queen Elizabeth.[4] Even when the fronts resemble each other the backs are often adorned in quite different style.

The great majority of these pendants are of German make, but exceptionally they may have been imitated in other countries. Sometimes the background is completely solid, as in an Annunciation pendant (Plate 88a) in the Waddesdon Bequest, which hardly looks German; sometimes the whole is of fretwork delicacy, as in the charming pendant of Hercules and the daughters of Atlas in the Victoria and Albert Museum (Plate 88b).

Exceptionally other jewels were designed to match such pendants. Jeanne de Bourdeille, Dame de Sainte-Aulaire, in 1595[5] owned a *chene* formed of eighteen oval medallions enamelled with the story of Venus, surrounded by pearls; and Gabrielle d'Estrées four years later[6] had a carcanet of sixteen pieces, eight simply jewelled, seven decorated with the seven planets, and one, in the centre, with Jupiter. A magnificent necklace and pendant survives in the Louvre (Plate 89) formed of eleven medallions most delicately enamelled with scenes of the Passion. It supports a pendant of the Crucifixion surrounded by a collar of the golden Fleece and a crown, which suggests that it was made for the Emperor Rudolf II. It may be compared with a more richly jewelled necklace recorded in the 1610 inventory of Marie de Médicis,[7] formed of eight medallions with the emblems of the Passion — lantern, cock, crown of thorns, and so on — ending with an IHS monogram and a cross, the whole set with diamonds. The chain to match[8] was formed of crowns of thorns and crosses linked by knots, all similarly jewelled.

[1] Bapst, *Couronne*, p. 119, n. 1.   [2] p. 247.
[3] Formerly in the collection of Mr. Charles Wertheimer.
[4] British Museum MS Royal Append. 68 Sect. 1.
[5] Montégut, p. 238. It was probably a girdle.
[6] Fréville, p. 166.   [7] Bruel, p. 197.   [8] ibid., p. 191.

In England the jewels with subjects of Virtues and the personages of classical myth-ology were developed under the influence of the taste for emblems and *imprese*. Such devices had been especially characteristic of the jousts and pageants of the strange late-flowering chivalry fostered by Henry VIII, and continued in fashion in these islands all through the sixteenth century. The decorative arts such as plasterwork, wood carving and embroidery drew much on the illustrated emblem books[1] of Alciatus, Paradin and the rest, but the more restricted field of jewels could hardly compass such designs. Yet jewellery, in Great Britain at least, was profoundly influenced by the fashion.

One of the most famous sixteenth-century jewels in Great Britain is the Lennox or Darnley jewel, once in Horace Walpole's possession and now in the collection of H.M. the Queen[2] (Colour Plates Vb, VIa).* It was made by the order of Lady Margaret Douglas in memory of her husband Matthew Stuart, Earl of Lennox, who was killed in 1571; its emblems trace the story of her eventful and unhappy life. The jewel itself is a gold pendant two and a half inches long shaped as a heart, the cognizance of the house of Douglas. One side is set with a large heart-shaped cabochon sapphire between wings enamelled in red, blue and green, beneath a jewelled crown. Round this are figures of Faith with her cross and lamb, Hope with her anchor, Victory with the olive branch, and Truth with a mirror. The crown opens to disclose two hearts united by a gold knot with a motto and cipher of M.S.L. The sapphire heart opens also to show two clasped hands and other emblems and another motto. Round the pendant runs the legend

QVHA HOPIS STIL CONSTANLY VITH PATIENCE SAL OBTEIN VICTORIE IN YAIR PRETENCE

The reverse of the pendant is enamelled with the sun in glory and the moon, a crowned salamander in flames, a pelican in her piety, a phoenix, and the figure of a man between a sunflower and a laurel bush. The inner meaning of all these emblems is lost to us with the secret history of Margaret Lennox's intrigues for her son Darnley. It is not made clear by the inscription:

MY STAIT TO YIR I MAY COMPAER
FOR ZOU QHA IS OF BONTES RAIR

The locket opens; it once held a miniature, presumably of the Regent Lennox. The inside of the lid is enamelled with a series of no less abstruse emblems, with enigmatic inscriptions which at least show that they have personal reference to Lady Margaret Douglas and her husband.

---

[1] See Evans, *Pattern*, I, p. 154.
[2] It was described by Mr. Combe of the Society of Antiquaries on April 18, 1782, and later by P. Fraser Tytler and was exhibited at the Winter Exhibition at the Royal Academy in 1934.
*In black and white in the Dover edition.

The Darnley jewel is unique in its abstruseness and complexity, but the various lists of Elizabeth's jewels show that the 'conceits' of the literature of her age were no less freely expressed in jewellery. Among her New Year's gifts in 1574 was a jewel with the story of Neptune, with verses at the back making an acrostic of ELIZABETH;[1] in 1575 one with a woman holding a ship upon her knee;[2] and another with *Sapientia Victrix*. In 1578 she was given a jewel enamelled with the figure of Virtue standing on a rainbow, holding compasses and a green garland;[3] another 'being a lampe with a harte in a flame of fyer . . . and a sarpent of ophall'; and a third of a dog leading a blind man over a bridge, with 'certayne verces written' on the back.[4] As late as 1586[5] Sir Christopher Hatton gave her a head ornament formed of Gordian knots with alphas and omegas; but by this time Elizabethan emblems were lapsing into a petty and purposeless naturalism. Even in 1572[6] the Earl of Warwick had given her a New Year's gift of a jewel formed of a branch of bay leaves, with one white rose and six red roses of enamelled gold on it, a spider and a bee; in 1576[7] she was given jewels with a squirrel and two cherries with an opal butterfly; while the list for 1583[8] includes a number of such stupid and ugly subjects as a honeysuckle, a warming-pan, a trumpet and a castle. An elegantly fretted and enamelled mousetrap in the National Museum of Stockholm remains to show the exquisite workmanship lavished even on such subjects as these. The inventories of Anne of Denmark[9] are full of such jewels, and her portraits usually show her wearing a disparate collection of little brooches of commonplace design.

In France emblems were much less widely used in jewellery; even the emblematic inscriptions seem to appear only on jewels designed for Queen Elizabeth. In 1582[10] Anjou gave her a padlocked bracelet inscribed SERVIET ETERNVM DVLCIS QVEM TORQVET ELIZA. A miniature case[11] exquisitely enamelled with the lilies of France and the roses of England, with the inscription GRACE DEDANS LE LIS HA (itself containing a pun on ELIZA) may well have been made as a similar gift. Occasionally gifts between lovers were decorated with emblems of a simple kind. Etienne Delaune's designs for jewels in the Ashmolean include one for a bracelet of jewelled plaques formed of pansies and marigolds — *pensées* and *soucis* — and Gabrielle d'Estrées in 1599 owned a chain of crystal fleurs-de-lis and other motifs surrounded by golden flames, joined by knots, that must have been a gift from her royal lover.[12]

The sixteenth century was a time when maritime supremacy took on a new importance and the powers that claimed it, notably Venice and England, favoured jewels in the

[1] Nichols I, p. 380.
[2] ibid., I, p. 412.
[3] Nichols II, p. 79, p.74.
[4] ibid., II, p. 74.
[5] ibid., II, p. 451.
[6] ibid., I, p. 294.
[7] ibid., II, p. 1.
[8] ibid., II, p. 396.
[9] Joan Evans, *English Jewellery*, p. 114.
[10] Nichols II, p. 387.
[11] Now in the Sauvageot Collection at the Louvre.
[12] Gay, s.v. Chaîne.

form of ships. Two Venetian pendants, one in the Louvre and one in the Victoria and Albert Museum (Plate 91b), are evidently from the same workshop. A rather heavier and less stylised three-masted ship pendant is in the Metropolitan Museum (Plate 91a); the hull is of crystal, the keel, decks and rigging are of gold partly enamelled. A smaller caïque in the Luton Hoo Collection has its hull of coral; it is on a small enough scale for the little gold figures of rowers to play a lively part in the design. A little crystal ship in the Victoria and Albert Museum (Plate 91c) is less realistic; decorative scrolls adorn the poop and there are no figures in it.

In England ship jewels were in fashion from the beginning of the sixteenth century; by 1519 Henry VIII already had one of diamonds with a hanging pearl.[1] Queen Elizabeth is said[2] to have received a ship jewel from Sir Francis Drake, and to have given it to Lord Hunsdon; it is now among the heirlooms at Berkeley Castle. The hull is of ebony, set with a table diamond; the masts and rigging are of enamelled gold set with pearls. An enamelled Victory stands on deck, blowing a horn, while Cupid crowns her. A little dinghy hangs below the ship.

The mediaeval fashion for scented jewellery continued in a century in which it was needed at least as much as in the Middle Ages. Mary Queen of Scots had two complete *accoustrements de senteurs*,[3] comprising a double head ornament, carcanet, *cotière* and belt, besides bracelets, rosaries and chains of pomander beads. She went to her death wearing a chain of pomander beads from which hung an Agnus Dei.[4] The Pierpont Morgan collection included[5] a pendant typical of the genre. It is formed of ambergris in mounts of gold and represents the familiar subject of Charity with three children, accompanied by four musicians, all of ambergris.

Cap brooches, as has been said, were passing out of fashion; one of the last clearly meant to be so worn is that presented by Queen Elizabeth to Sir Francis Drake about 1579.[6] It is set with a central ruby carved with the orb and cross, surrounded by eight opals — which were much in fashion in England in the years after 1573[7] — in an outer rim of alternate opals and diamonds. Beyond this project rays, alternately straight and waved, set with table-cut rubies. In 1599 Gabrielle d'Estrées owned an *enseigne* of Peace in a triumphal chariot, with a great diamond above, and three pearls below,

---

[1] Brewer, III, pt. i, p. 164.   [2] Clifford Smith, p. 253; Plate XXXV, 2.

[3] Bannatyne Club, *Inventaire de Marie Stouart Royne d'Escosse*, 1566. The fashion was, I think, rather French than English. cf. the 1632 inventory of the Marquis de Rémoville which includes a chain of gold beads filled with scent between sixteen large wheels of pearls, and another of vases and olives of crystal divided by pomander beads. Gay, s.v. Chaîne.

[4] Gay, s.v. Agnus Dei. Her inventories reveal that the Agnus Dei was ornamented with a figure of Neptune.

[5] Catalogue No. 7; I have not been able to discover its present whereabouts. It was formerly in the Spitzer Collection.

[6] Clifford Smith, Plates XXXIV, 3 and XXX, 2.   [7] See for instance Nichols I, p. 380.

suspended from a diamond-set chain with a large diamond and pear-pearl at the top. Yet though *enseignes* were hardly worn both antique gems and portrait cameos continued to be mounted in enamelled gold, sometimes merely for display. The Vienna Cabinet and the Cabinet des Médailles at Paris both have admirable collections of such jewels, mounted as *enseignes* but hardly intended for wear (Plate 90). A superb series of royal portrait cameos can also be made up from the two collections; every great sovereign of the age is represented,[1] though most of the cameos have lost their mounts.

An interesting series of portrait cameos of Mary Queen of Scots can be brought together: perhaps the most authentic portraits of her that exist. Three at least have retained their mounts. One in the Bibliothèque Nationale has still its original rim of enamelled gold enhanced with rubies (Plate 92b). Another given by her to the Duke of Norfolk and now in the collection of the Duke of Portland is mounted as a pendant, with delicate tendrils of enamelled gold between table-cut rubies (Plate 92a) and a third is set in a heart-shaped jewel of enamelled gold (Plate 92c). The rather heavy style of the third pendant suggests that it may be of Scottish manufacture; it is comparable with the Penicuik locket in the National Museum of Antiquities of Scotland, which contains tiny portraits of the Queen and James VI and probably dates from between 1576 and 1579.

The cameos of Queen Elizabeth are even more numerous and their history is often known. The accounts of the court of Navarre for 1587[2] include a payment to Thomas Papillon for an onyx cut with the portrait 'au vif' of Queen Elizabeth, set in gold and diamonds; and in 1596 Julien de Fontenay, cameo cutter to Henri IV, was sent for to England to cut her portrait.[3] It is tempting to associate these with the two cameos with her profile in the Cabinet des Médailles,[4] but there is no precise evidence for the identification. Cameos of the Queen are to be found in several English collections.[5] There is in the British Museum a charming small oval pendant with a minute cameo of the Queen in a rim of white enamel set with rubies. It may be compared with the Barbor jewel, now in the Victoria and Albert Museum, which is said to have been made in commemoration of the deliverance of William Barbor from the stake at Smithfield in consequence of the Queen's accession. Yet more elegant is the Wild jewel, at present lent by the Wild family to the Victoria and Albert Museum, in which the Queen's portrait is cut not in sardonyx but in turquoise; it is said to have been a christening present from the Queen to a member of the family. In 1579 she gave Sir Francis Drake a splendid cameo of a negro's head with a second head in the white layer behind, mounted in enamelled and jewelled gold and backed by a miniature of her by Hilliard dated 1575.[6] Drake wears

[1] Fréville, p. 166. See J. Arneth for Vienna and E. Babelon for Paris.
[2] Gay, s.v. Camahieu.   [3] Babelon, *Histoire*, p. 139.   [4] Babelon, IX, 15 and X, 7.
[5] Several are illustrated in Joan Evans, *English Jewellery*, Plate XIX.
[6] Illustrated Clifford Smith, Plate XXXIV, 3. It is in the possession of Sir Francis Fuller-Elliot Drake.

it at his belt in a portrait by Marc Gheerardts the Elder.[1] Her gifts were more usually of a form based upon her medals, as is the Phoenix Jewel bequeathed to the British Museum by Sir Hans Sloane in 1753. It shows a bust of the Queen cut from the Phoenix medal of 1574,[2] framed in a wreath of particoloured Tudor roses most delicately executed in enamelled gold. Similarly a miniature case in the Poldi-Pezzoli Museum at Milan[3] is formed of a mother-of-pearl plaque based on the Naval Award Medal of 1588, with a border of rubies set in enamelled gold.

The most splendid of these gifts is undoubtedly the Heneage Jewel (Plate 93) now in the Victoria and Albert Museum, allegedly given by the Queen to Sir Thomas Heneage, of Copt Hall, Essex,[4] in recognition of his services as Treasurer at War of the armies levied to resist invasion at the time of the Armada. The front of the jewel displays a bust of the Queen from the Personal or Garter badge of 1582, on a ground of translucent blue enamel. The rim, as often in English jewels of the time, stands a little away from the central medallion; it is of white enamel picked out in red and green and set with rubies and diamonds.[5] The back is enamelled with an 'emblem' of the storm-tossed ark with the legend SAEVAS TRANQVILLA PER VNDAS: the motto that appears on the Naval Award medal of 1588. This lifts up to reveal a miniature of the Queen by Nicholas Hilliard within. The inside of the lid is enamelled with a rose within a wreath of rose leaves and the motto *Hei mihi quod tanto virtus perfusa decore non habet eternos inuiolata dies*: the motto which appears on the reverse of the Phoenix Badge of 1574.

The German princes followed the same custom in simpler fashion. A number of pendants exist[6] formed of gold medals set within scrolled rims of enamelled gold, hanging from little chains and ending in pendant pearls. They are often duplicated and triplicated and were probably given, like the Elizabethan jewels, for services rendered to the sovereign.

The profusion and fantasy of Elizabethan jewels was represented in the Jacobean period by a miscellany of decadent little ornaments such as appear in the portraits of Anne of Denmark: such as initials of her brother and herself, anchors and snakes, rather plainly set with diamonds and emeralds, and lacking either elegance or meaning. A similar pettiness of design and want of invention is evident in the hoard from a jeweller's shop of about 1615 found beneath the floor of a cellar between St. Paul's and

---

[1] *Illustrated London News*, July 16, 1932.

[2] See Helen Farquhar, 'John Rutlinger and the Phoenix Badge of Queen Elizabeth', in *Numismatic Chronicle*, fifth series, III, 1923, p. 270.

[3] Illustrated Clifford Smith, Plate XXXV, 3.

[4] It remained in the family until 1902, when it was bought for the Pierpont Morgan collection. When this was dispersed it was bought by Lord Wakefield and given to the Victoria and Albert Museum.

[5] It is tempting to say that it and the British Museum Jewel are both by Nicholas Hilliard.

[6] See Clifford Smith, p. 247.

FIG. 16. Engraved design for a pendant by Paul Birckenhulz. 1617

the London Central Post Office in 1912.[1] The chandelier-like earrings, the flowered chains, the bracelets and so on are more elegant than Anne of Denmark's jewels, but wholly lacking in the quality of great art that inspires the finest of Renaissance jewels. It would not be unfair to call them dainty.

The sumptuary laws promulgated by Philip III of Spain in 1600[2] permitted a woman to wear any amount of pearls, and a man chain and belt of gold and ornaments of cameo and pearl, but forbade the manufacture of jewels with reliefs and figures except for church use. It is never easy to say how strictly such sumptuary laws were enforced; but these at least coincided with a definite change in style in Spain.

In Germany, however, the more classical pendants of the late Renaissance continued in fashion with less figure work, greater lightness and a more symmetrical design. The rich and varied colour of such jewels (Colour Plate VII)[*] makes up in some degree for the impoverishment of their design; they are perfect accompaniments for the Italian brocades of the time — dove grey or sea green or carnation or soft blue — powdered with small repeating sprigs of golden leafage.

A certain number are more or less globular (Plate 95a) and seem designed to be worn as girdle ends.[3] The designer of engraved ornament whose work is closest to such jewels

[1] Now in the London Museum and the Victoria and Albert Museum. Some of the motives used—for example a caduceus and bunches of grapes in carved amethyst — recur in the designs of Arnold Lulls.
[2] Davillier, p. 124.
[3] Others are in the Musée Jacquemart André and in the Rothschild collection.
*In black and white in the Dover edition.   121

is Paul Birckenhulz, who published a set of plates at Frankfort on the Main in 1617 (Fig. 16). One of his designs for a trophy of arms finds a parallel in an aigrette in the Waddesdon Bequest and in a splendid ruby-set jewel in the Soane Museum (Plate 96b), which Charles I is said to have lost on the field of Naseby. It shows a knight armed with sword and shield surrounded by a trophy of arms. A flag bears the St. Andrew's Cross, and a lion crouches at his feet; it may well have been to the order of the King of Denmark as a present to James I.[1]

A new beauty in the lighter and more symmetrical style was achieved in the designs of Daniel Mignot, a Huguenot Frenchman who worked at Augsburg early in the seventeenth century. The designs for jewels which he published between 1596 and 1616 show a strict symmetry of design and a curious stylisation of form. Each is composed of a back plate (Fig. 17a) pierced in elegant formal strapwork, and a design for the next stratum of the ornament (Fig. 17b), of jewels to be pinned through holes marked in the back plate. Separate designs for a central rosette complete the third stratum of the ornament. The designs are good; the effect is elegant; yet the whole system marks the decline of the sculptured feeling of the Renaissance jewellers: a decline that was not only marked but also in some degree caused by the constant use of such engraved designs as these. Mignot's other designs include some for the enamelled backs of figure pendants of a pictorial kind (Fig. 18); one or two survive to show the end of a long-lived genre.

Others of his designs are for aigrettes, with feathers set with square-cut gems; a kind of ornament much in fashion in the years about the turn of the century. 'Bodkins' for the hair had been the mode about 1580; five were given to Queen Elizabeth on New Year's Day 1580 and six more in 1583.[2] They had a natural tendency to develop in size and height, and the French royal accounts of 1591[3] include 'une enseigne d'or faicte en pannache', set with diamonds. A good example shaped rather like the Prince of Wales' feathers is in the Wallace Collection; it must date from the closing years of the century. Several very handsome aigrettes are included in the book of jewellery designs made between 1593 and 1602 by Jakob Mores of Hamburg,[4] and a fine example was found in the tomb of Otto Heinrich Count Palatine of Neuburg, who died in 1604.[5] It rises from an openwork heart that holds the initials of his wife Dorothea Maria in rubies. So strong was the fashion that it affected even jewels of state; the crown of Christian IV

---

[1] It was exhibited at the Society of Antiquaries on April 17, 1755, by Mr. Lock. It then passed to Mr. Whitehead of Hambrook near Bristol and his sister Mrs. Barnes of Redland Hall. It was sold after her death in 1833.

[2] Nichols, II, p. 289, p. 397.

[3] Gay, s.v. Enseigne. A finer one of the same kind occurs in Marie de Médicis's inventory of 1609–10. Bruel, p. 194.

[4] In the Hamburg City Library; see Stettiner.

[5] In the Bavarian National Museum at Munich.

FIG. 17. Engraved designs for the back and front of an aigrette by Daniel Mignot. 1616

FIG. 18. Engraved design for the back of a pendant by Daniel Mignot. 1616

of Denmark, made by Didrik Fiuren in 1595, has its fleurons formed like aigrettes, alternately large and small.[1] His sister, Anne of Denmark, introduced the fashion into England; designs for four or five aigrettes probably for her are among the drawings left by her Dutch jeweller, Arnold Lulls[2] (Plate 99). Aigrettes of hanging pear-shaped

[1] In the Rosenborg Slott, Copenhagen.   [2] In the Victoria and Albert Museum.

pearls are worn in the seventeenth century by such jewel-loving women as Maria Capponi[1] and the Archduchess Isabella Clara Eugenia[2] and by various Austrian and Spanish princesses painted by Coello (Plates 100, 101, and 102).

It is perhaps significant that this account of the jewellery of the second half of the sixteenth century and the beginning of the seventeenth has been confined to the jewels of royal personages and their courtiers. Theirs was the wealth that could order them; theirs the dress — still magnificent and unpractical — on which they could be displayed. It was the age when dress was distinctive not only of nationality but also of class; it was not enough for Hollar to give engravings of an English lady; he had also to illustrate the dress of a gentlewoman, a citizen's wife and a countrywoman. The same distinctions were evident in the other countries of Europe, and were as valid for jewels as for dress. For all but the people of the court the traditions of the early part of the sixteenth century were continued until its close, and beyond. The inventory of the jewels of Isabeau Bonnefoy, a bourgeoise of Le Puy en Velay, drawn up in 1601,[3] describes a handsome collection of jewellery of the modest kind: three head ornaments, one of enamelled gold, a chain of golden stars, three plain gold chains, a collar of stamped gold, four gold and two coral bracelets, two gold rosaries, a pendant with a painting of Susanna under crystal, another of two rubies, a diamond and a pendant pearl, a cameo pendant, a pearl necklace with three gold pendants and another with garnets, a gold girdle, two silver ones, and one of garnets and gold beads — all jewels that read more as if they were characteristic of 1500 than of 1600. The same characteristic is evident in the remarkable *bourgeois* jewels in the Copenhagen Museum.[4] A very fine silver belt, for instance (Plate 94), of close-linked chain with plaques embossed with heads in the style of the early Renaissance, is inscribed MAREN KNVDSDATTER, 1608. An interesting series of gold chains and bracelets of about 1612 are in the Germanic Museum at Nuremberg;[5] they all belonged to the Holtzendorff family and were buried in the Thirty Years' War and recovered in 1893.

The jewels of the second half of the sixteenth century reveal themselves, like its literature, astonishingly disparate, full of conceits and fancies, of great richness and technical skill. In their characteristic form they are the products of the courts of kings and queens who were seeking power and wealth rather than the cultivation of the things of the spirit. Their jewels lack the proportion and line of great art, and only achieve characterisation by a want of style. Yet such work of the closing years of the century as the Heneage jewel — probably designed by Nicholas Hilliard himself — suggests in its *misura* the elegance of the succeeding age.

---

[1] Portrait in the Uffizi.   [2] Portrait at Versailles.

[3] Rouchon in *Bull. Arch.* 1914, p. 556.

[4] See also the collection in the Musée du Cinquantenaire at Brussels and the Clemens Collection at Cologne.

[5] See Bösch.

CHAPTER SIX

The Seventeenth Century

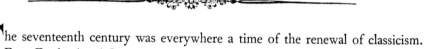

The seventeenth century was everywhere a time of the renewal of classicism. Even England and Germany attempted a new purity of style in architecture, as France and England did in literature. The Age of Taste had dawned in North-Western Europe.

The new fastidiousness was quickly reflected in the design of jewels. The fantasy and profusion of the Mannerist period was succeeded by the majestic dignity of the Baroque. Figure work went out of fashion; and emphasis gradually shifted from the varicoloured brightness of enamelled gold to the glow and glitter of gems. Yet alongside such jewels — jewels in the strictest sense of the word — other things, such as watches and miniature cases, received the most delicate ornament in enamel that a craftsman has ever achieved.

The severe outlines of miniature cases and watches exactly met the new wish for a regular and almost architectural field. Miniature cases, that had long been a field for ornamentation,[1] took on a new importance in the years round 1600. As early as 1580 Brantôme[2] complained that widows no longer wore mourning jewels but such 'petites gentillesses' as portraits of their husbands at their breasts. The fashion no doubt prospered at the hands of men such as Hilliard who were both goldsmiths and miniature painters. The inventory of the jewels of Gabrielle d'Estrées drawn up after her death in 1599,[3] includes a vast number of portraits of her royal lover in jewelled and enamelled frames, including one set in the base of a feather-shaped hat-jewel of diamonds. Marie de Médicis again, in 1610[4] had a large bracelet formed of six medallions, each holding a miniature under a lid enamelled with devices set with diamonds, the medallions linked by knots of white enamel with arrows and flames.[5]

---

[1] A miniature of Mrs. Pemberton by Holbein in the Victoria and Albert Museum, dating from about 1535, is in an enamelled frame with her arms on the back. Princess Mary had two enamelled miniature cases as early as 1542. Madden, p. 178.

[2] Quoted Laborde, *Glossaire*, p. 246.

[3] Fréville, p. 168. [4] Bruel, p. 199.

[5] Ashmole records in his *Institution of the Order of the Garter* that Charles I's onyx Lesser George had his Queen's miniature under a lid at the back.

126

Such devices find a parallel on two miniature cases in the Fitzwilliam Museum (Plate 103). One, which contains a miniature of Anne of Denmark attributed to Hilliard, is in a case enamelled in a lovely tawny shade of red. The back is decorated in white with two interlaced AA, crowned, and the S device which she also wore as a brooch;[1] the lid has similar initials in diamonds, with two linked CC added, perhaps for her brother or her younger son. The second case holds a miniature of an unknown man by John Hoskins. The back is enamelled solid in translucent dark blue over an engraved ground. The lid is fretted, so as to half-show the miniature beneath. The centre is occupied by a double knot in rubies, within a band of white enamel with golden letters FAST THOVGH VNTIED, which is joined to the edge by diamonds and rubies in elaborate settings. The back of the fretted lid is delightfully enamelled in bright red and green, with tiny beads of blue enamel to give relief. The whole is a little masterpiece of the jeweller's art.

A number of engraved designs were produced for such miniature cases about 1610 by engravers such as Daniel Mignot, who published designs at Augsburg between 1590 and 1616, Nicolas Rouillart, the engraver P.R.K., and Etienne Carteron, 1615 (Fig. 19). A miniature case with a portrait of Queen Elizabeth in the Victoria and Albert Museum (Plate 104), with a fretted lid set with diamonds, has its back enamelled in many colours after a design by Mignot; and like influences may be deciphered in many of the other beautiful miniature cases that survive.[2] Another example in the same Museum (Plate 105a) formerly in the Pierpont Morgan collection, has both sides enamelled in a light design of birds and leafage in the manner of Mignot. Another in the Waddesdon Bequest (Plate 105b) is enamelled in silhouette strapwork in a style that recalls the designs of Nicolas Rouillart. An effective design in white and gold on a black ground (Plate 106a) is evidently in relation with the engraved designs of Jean Toutin of Châteaudun (Plate 106b).

The normal technique for the decoration of such miniature cases was champlevé enamelling, in which remarkable purity of line could be achieved. Exceptionally, however, miniature cases were adorned with enamel of another kind, known as *émail en résille sur verre*: a technique so difficult that it was only practised for a decade or so, and probably only by one or two exceptionally skilled enamellers, who seemed to have worked in France. The only engraved designs that are recognisably intended for it are, however, those published by Valentin Sezenius[3] between 1619 and 1624. It consisted in

[1] See p. 120.
[2] Noteworthy examples are Nos. 168, 169 and 170 in the Waddesdon Bequest; several in the Victoria and Albert Museum; and others (illustrated by Clifford Smith) in the collection of H.M. the Queen. Some fine examples were in the Pierpont Morgan Collection: see Williamson's Catalogue.
[3] See C. C. Oman in *Apollo*, VI, 1927, p. 149; he illustrates a plaque in the Victoria and Albert Museum after a design by Sezenius.

FIG. 19. Engraved designs for the backs of miniature cases by Étienne Carteron. 1615

taking a medallion of glass, usually dark blue or blue green, and engraving the design in it in low intaglio. The hollow reliefs thus formed were then lined with extremely thin gold foil, and filled with powdered enamel which would fuse at a lower temperature than the glass ground. One of the most ambitious works in the genre is a plaque with Apollo and Daphne within a wreath (Plate 107b). A more usual type of design is represented by the cover of an engraved silver portrait of Princess Mary of Austria, daughter of Philip III of Spain, formerly in the Pierpont Morgan Collection.

Similar work was used for contemporary watch cases[1] for which such engravers as

---

[1] Exceptionally watch and miniature case were combined, as they were in a watch of about 1620 given by James I to the first Lord Brooke. G. C. Williamson, *Catalogue of Watches in the Pierpont Morgan Collection*, No. 131.

THE SEVENTEENTH CENTURY

Jacques Hurtu and Michel le Blon[1] provided convenient models.[2] The study of watches forms a separate subject,[3] but at this time their cases formed so definite a part of jewellery that they can hardly be altogether omitted. Mention has already been made of the elaborate watch pendants of the sixteenth century. Just before 1600 smoother shapes were in fashion, often delicately fretted and engraved[4] (Plate 108a). The fashion then turned to watches shaped as shells, flowers and fruit; the Clockmakers' Company's collection in the Guildhall Museum contains a silver watch shaped as a cockle shell; the British Museum, one made by John Willow between 1630 and 1640, shaped as a scallop shell; and the same Museum also owns a delightful watch made about 1620 by Edward Bysse shaped as a fritillary, with silver petals chequered in niello.

Another fashion was for watch cases of crystal held together by delicate rims of gold; one in the Nelthropp Collection at the Guildhall[5] is notable for the elegance of the engraving on the face and rims. Exceptionally the system was followed in more precious material; the Post Office hoard[6] includes a watch case cut out of a block of emerald with the dial enamelled in translucent green to match. A particularly beautiful watch in the British Museum (Plate 109) has its back formed of a large sapphire and its lid set with another surrounded by eight smaller stones surrounded by delicate scrolling leafage in enamel. The inside of the lid and the face are enamelled with bird and insects.

The geometrical shapes of miniature cases and watches offered quasi-architectural fields for the new style of design. In other kinds of jewels a new formal massiveness was added to ornaments of a traditional kind. Spain still produced bird pendants (Plate 110), but produced them with a new weight.[7] The Spanish devotional jewels of about 1630, too, have a magnificently architectural line (Plate 111).

The shift of emphasis from enamel to gems may be illustrated from the designs for jewels of Arnold Lulls, the Dutch jeweller who worked in England for Anne of Denmark.[8] His pendants — a cabochon ruby surrounded by a snake enamelled green; three table-cut emeralds held by a jewelled wreath of olive branches; an enormous table-cut emerald linked with an oval of rubies by snakes of black-speckled white enamel and

---

[1] A Frankfort man (probably a Huguenot refugee) who worked at the court of Queen Christina of Sweden and died at Amsterdam in 1656. His designs were published in 1605 and onwards.

[2] One or two belts were also made of plaques of *émail en résille sur verre*; examples with hunting scenes may be seen in the Victoria and Albert Museum and the Wallace Collection.

[3] See Britten.

[4] A magnificent series of these may be seen in the Garnier Collection in the Louvre. For other seventeenth-century watches the J. F. Mallett Collection in the Ashmolean Museum.

[5] No. 14. A number of these watches were made at Geneva; see e. 8, Nos. 27 and 50 in the same collection.

[6] See p. 120-1. The watch is in the London Museum.

[7] A similar formality is evident in the eagle brooch (probably German) in the Louvre.

[8] His designs are in the Victoria and Albert Museum. He was working for the King in 1605; Devon, *Issues of the Exchequer*, James I (Pells), p. 49.

formal arrangements of table-cut stones (Plate 112) — all illustrate the new balance of interest. His square-cut diamonds are displayed with the slightest possible background of enamelled scrolls. The increased stress on gems owed something to the development of the art of jewel-cutting.[1] More varied styles of cutting come to be mentioned in the inventories. The great wedding necklace of Marie de Médicis,[2] made in 1600, was formed of eight pieces, each set with a large diamond surrounded by lesser stones, linked by lesser medallions of pearls surrounded by diamonds; six of the large stones were table cut, but two were 'à facettes' or rose-cut.[3] Arnold Lull's designs similarly include rose-cut as well as table diamonds. A list of diamonds pawned by James I with John Spilman in 1614[4] includes one 'cut like the quarre of a glass window' and two rose-cut briolette drops, perhaps from India, for it must be remembered that the Golconda diamond mines in Hyderabad were opened up in the seventeenth century. Then, between 1640 and 1645, the 'taille à facettes' was improved into the 'taille en seize'. Similar improvements were made in the cutting of coloured stones, and cabochon gems of any kind are rarely found after about 1640.

The revived interest in gems for their own sakes caused the survivors of the great Burgundian stones of the fifteenth century to come into their own again. A typical jewel of the turn of the century is that bought by Nicolas Harlay de Sancy in 1593.[5] Its central stone was an enormous diamond, some said that lost by Charles the Bold on the field of Grandson, lately recut as a rose, in a simple gold setting with a hanging pearl. The great rubies known as the Three Brothers, which Henry VIII had acquired just before his death, were reset for Charles Prince of Wales to wear on his embassy to Spain in 1623. The jewels that were lent him for the journey[6] included a hat-band adorned with 'twentie faire dyamondes, sett in buttons of gould, in manner of Spanish worke,[7] wherof eight are fower square table dyamondes, two large sixe square table dyamondes, two eight square table dyamondes, two fower square table dyamondes, cutt with fawcettes, two large pointed dyamondes, one faire hart dyamond, and three triangle dyamondes.' He took with him another famous diamond called 'The Mirror of France', and the Portugal diamond with the Cobham Pearl hanging at it, the Three Brothers, newly set; four diamond crosses, as well as for the Infanta a great Lorraine Cross of diamonds,[8] a

---

[1] See Bapst, *Couronne*, p. 16.   [2] Bruel, p. 188.

[3] cf. the *enseigne* given her by the King at the New Year 1608, with a table diamond in the centre and four faceted diamonds and thirty-two table cut stones round it. Bruel, p. 194.

[4] British Museum Stowe MS 560; Evans, *English Jewellery*, p. 111.

[5] For its full history see Bapst, *Couronne*, p. 184. James I bought it in 1604; Henrietta Maria pawned it in Paris in 1647 and Mazarin acquired it in 1657. He left it, with his other diamonds, to the French Crown.

[6] Rymer, *Foedera*, XVII, 509; Evans, *English Jewellery*, p. 111.

[7] i.e. the gold was ornamented with champlevé enamel in black.

[8] See *Archaeologia*, XXI, 1827, p. 150.

set of pear-pearls and a quantity of other jewels.[1] In all of them the emphasis is laid on the size and splendour of the stones rather than on the design or setting.[2] Yet Charles himself was accustomed to show a Frenchified elegance in his use of jewels; his most usual ornament was a single pear-pearl earring which was rescued from the scaffold by a faithful follower for his daughter.[3]

His own tastes, indeed, lay less in actual jewels than in engraved gems. The portrait of the Keeper of his jewels, Thomas Chiffinch, in the National Portrait Gallery, shows him surrounded by coins and gems of the kind. Some of the gems are in good enamelled

FIG. 20. Engraved designs for the backs of jewels by Guillaume de la Quewellerie. 1611

settings; a few survive in the Royal Collection. The letters of Dorothy Osborne to her lover Sir William Temple show that the fashion for antique gems was undiminished in 1653. She asks him to get her some set as seals, reminds him that the best come from Italy, and tells him that Mrs. Smith 'wears twenty strung upon a ribbon, like the nuts boys play withal'.

The portraits of the first half of the century show at once an increasing simplicity and an increasing magnificence of jewels. The Sustermans portrait of Claudia de'Medici[4]

[1] See Nichols, *Progresses of James I*, IV, pp. 831 and 845.
[2] The same tendency is evident in the 1614 inventory of the jewels of Henry Howard, Earl of Nottingham; *Archaeologia*, XLII, pt. 2, 1869, p. 348.
[3] Queen Mary II gave it to the first Earl of Portland, and it has descended to the present Duke.
[4] In the Uffizi; another portrait there, full length in a light coloured dress, shows identical jewels.

(Plate 115) shows much the same kind of jewels as a lady of 1590 would have worn: a *cotière*, a rope of pearls, aglets on sleeve and dress, a pendant hanging at the shoulder and another at the breast; but all are set with large stones in relatively simple designs. The jewels of the kind that survive show little but gems in front, but their backs are still elaborately enamelled. Even their imitations in less precious gems such as crystal and paste (Plate 127a) show enamel, usually in pale blue or white, with judicious touches, like pen strokes, of black.

FIG. 21. Engraved designs for the backs of jewels by Jacques Hurtu. 1614

The moresque designs of the sixteenth century were developed *en silhouette*, and a considerable number of engravings in the style were produced to serve as models between 1602 and 1620.[1] They are among the most elegant of engraved jewel designs (Figs. 20 and 21). Such silhouette ornament adorns many jewels of Spanish origin

[1] The beginnings of the style may be traced in the work of Hans van Ghemert, 1557. Other engravings are those of Daniel Mignot, 1590; Hans de Bull (Prague), 1590 and 1592; Corvinianus Saur, 1597; Hieronymus Berkhausen, 1592; the German Master A.C. 1598; Hans Hensel, 1599; Jean Vovert, 1602 and 1604; Daniel Hailler, 1604; Michel le Blon (Amsterdam) 1605; A.D., 1608; Guillaume de la Quewellerie, 1611; Jacques Hurtu, 1614–19; Nicholas Drusse, 1607 and 1614; P.R.K., 1609; Étienne Carteron (Châtillon) 1615; Paul Birckenhulz, 1617; Mathias Grundler (Augsburg) 1617; Jean Toutin (Châteaudun) 1618 and 1619; Esaias van Hulsen (Stuttgart) 1617; P. Kolin 1620; Giovanni Battista Costantino (Rome) 1622.

FIG. 22. Engraved design for an aigrette by P. Symony. 1621

(Colour Plate VIII[*]: Plate 116), usually on a ground of black or white.[1] Tiny patches of it may be found in many less obvious places, for example in the details of Charles I's trophy jewel (Plate 96b). A distinguished English example of its use is the case containing a miniature of James I given by him to Thomas Lyte of Lyte's Cary[2] (Plate 117a).

The rival style was a development into an equally stylised kind of naturalism. A certain number of the large pendants in fashion about 1620 (Plates 114, 115) show an increasing tendency to develop the gold settings that enclose the gems into leaf-shaped forms. Such forms, and others of a more pod-like kind, were the bases of a particular style of ornament that was used alike for the settings of jewels and for the enamel that adorned their backs. One of the earliest dateable examples of settings in the style is the sconce[3] given to Marie de Médici on her marriage in 1600; it is set with cameos and plain agates, held by settings of typical pea-pod form.

The style was propagated in its turn by a whole series of engraved designs of which the most important date from 1619 to 1635[4] (Figs. 22–24); but its most charming manifestations are in jewels themselves. The style was admirably fitted to the backs of miniature cases[5] (Plate 118a), to the frames of cameos (Plate 118b), and yet more beautifully to the cases of watches (Plate 119).

The gradual tendency of *cosse de pois* design was towards naturalism. Such designs as those of François Le Febvre show naturalistic flowers only slightly and subtly distorted by the conventional style (Fig. 25). Naturalism of a flowery kind was, indeed, an inevitable development in an age in which a vivid interest in flowers was felt in most of the countries of Europe.[6] At the end of the sixteenth century an intelligent French gardener, Jean Robin, opened a garden with hothouses in Paris, partly in order that his plants might serve as models for designers of embroidery. A few years later Henri IV bought the establishment, and as the Jardin du Roi (later the Jardin des Plantes) it continued to be a centre of interest and study in rare and beautiful blossoms. The intensification of

---

[1] The style is perpetuated in the late seventeenth-century reliquaries of opaque enamel on gilt copper, that were probably made at Barcelona. Davillier, p. 76.

[2] See Waddesdon Bequest No. 167, and Evans, *English Jewellery*, p. 120. I have not seen the similar back of the case of a miniature by Peter Oliver, 1626, formerly in the Pierpont Morgan Collection, but suspect it to be a modern copy.

[3] In the Louvre.

[4] W. Dietterlin (Lyons) 1614; J. Toutin (Châteaudun) 1619; Jacques Hurtu, 1619; P. Symony, (Strasbourg) 1621; Pierre Marchant (Paris) 1623; Antoine Hedouyns, (Paris) 1623 and 1633; Vivot, 1623; Balthasar Lemersier, 1625 and 1626; Honervogt (Holland) 1625; Gédéon Légaré (Paris) 1625; Hans Georg Mosbach (Strasbourg) 1626; Bruckh, 1626; Jacques Caillart, 1627; Pierre de la Barre, 1630; Pierre Firens, 1632; Pierre Boucquet, 1634. No date: I.M. (perhaps Jean Morien) and Assuerus van Londerseel.

An exceptionally late instance of its use occurs on a crown made by Leonardo di Montalbano and Michele Castellani dedicated at Enna in 1652. See Maria Accàscina in *Dedalo*, XI, pts. 1-2, 1930, p. 161.

[5] An admirable design by Pierre Firens has inspired the case of a miniature probably of the second Duke of Hamilton, in the Salting Collection in the Victoria and Albert Museum.

[6] See Evans, *Pattern*, I, p. 78.

*In black and white in the Dover edition. 134

FIG. 23. Engraved design by Balthasar Lemersier. 1626

FIG. 24. Engraved design by Balthasar Lemersier. 1626

PLATE VIII

Front and back of a pendant formed of the letters MARIA of lapis lazuli ornamented and set in enamelled gold, the back enamelled in black and white. Spanish, *c.* 1620

PLATE IX

(a) Locket of *émail en résille sur verre*. French, *c.* 1610

(b) Miniature case of *émail en résille sur verre*. English or French, *c.* 1630

(c) Miniature of champlevé enamel on gold. English, *c.* 1600

trade with the Levant brought such flowers as the crown imperial and fritillary into European gardens; and Gesner saw the first tulip in flower in Augsburg in 1559 and published the first picture of it in 1561. It took seventy-five years for the flower to conquer Europe; 1634 was the year of tulipomania.

In England, it may fairly be said, the mediaeval tradition of naturalistic flower ornament had never been broken. Any Tudor inventory shows it to be still living in an England of oak-woods and fern-brakes, of orchards and walled gardens, in which men still loved the flowers that had figured in fifteenth-century illuminations. An enamelled miniature case of about 1600 (Colour Plate IXb)*which its central Tudor rose suggests may have been intended for a portrait of Elizabeth herself, is delicately enamelled in colours in the champlevé technique with roses, pansies, corn-flowers and pinks in the mediaeval tradition. A miniature case of some twenty-five or thirty years later (Colour Plate IXc)*still has a rose in the centre and other flowers round it, but it is worked out in the difficult technique of *émail en résille sur verre*. The fashion lingered on past the middle years of the century; just before the Restoration Lady Warwick owned a 'fair knott of gold enamelled with Tulipps and set with diamonds'.[1]

The engravers of ornament were quick to exploit the horticultural style. The earliest engravings were of sprays and garlands and vases of flowers intended rather for painting and embroidery than for jewels. The earliest flower designs intended for jewellers seem to be those published by Jean Vovert in 1602. There was then a pause, while silhouette and pea-pod designs predominated, until about 1620, when the engraver F.S. published a design for the back of a miniature case enamelled with lilies, roses, tulips and other flowers. François Lefebvre followed with his *Livre des fleurs* of 1635, in which a few *cosse de pois* designs are accompanied by many of lilies and roses and tulips intended for enamel (Fig. 25). In 1650 J. P. Hauer of Nuremberg published designs of flowers for the backs of cross pendants, small *étuis* and miniature cases, and was followed by Heinrich Raab (Fig. 26), and J. Heel. Moncornet, who had engraved most of the earlier French flower designs, produced a repertory of his own about 1665, and there were various reprints even later. New life was given to the style by the publication in 1663 of Gilles Légaré's *Livre des Ouvrages d'Orfèvrerie*, in which flower designs played no small part, for Légaré was himself a jeweller and enameller of the first order.[2] The creative impulse of the style ended with the publication of Jean Vauquer's extremely accomplished *Livre de Fleurs propre pour Orfèvres et Graveurs* at Blois in 1680. He too belonged to one of the seventeenth-century dynasties of French goldsmiths, and his designs, though difficult of execution, were made by a man with a thorough understanding of the technique of enamelling.

[1] *Verney Memoirs*, III, p. 428.
[2] See Joan Evans, 'Gilles Légaré and his Work', in *Burlington Magazine*, XXX, April 1917, p. 140.
*In black and white in the Dover edition. **137**

FIG. 25. Engraved design for the back of a miniature case by François Le Febvre

FIG. 26. Engraved design for the back of a bow jewel by Heinrich Raab

It is perhaps because of the impracticability of some of the earlier designs that most of the surviving jewels in the style belong to the middle or the second half of the century. A rather crude flower pattern in champlevé enamel on a white ground adorns the case of an enamelled miniature of Oliver Cromwell in the Ashmolean Museum, that must date from about 1645;[1] but the style could only achieve elegance in other techniques than champlevé.[2] An exquisite watch in the British Museum (Plate 120a, b) is enamelled in the raised technique, of which the invention is usually attributed to the Toutin family, with varicoloured flowers on a black ground. The lid has a wreath fitted in between the rim and the central rosette, both set with rose diamonds; the back has a flowing bunch of roses, tulips, lilies, fritillaries, pansies and other flowers, that closely resembles Légaré's designs of 1663 (Fig. 27). It may be compared with a slightly later work by Nicolaus Rugendas the Younger, formerly in the Pierpont Morgan Collection, which has a similar if less exquisite wreath of enamelled flowers set among emeralds. A second watch (Plate 120c) has a rather more formal arrangement of flowers most

[1] A miniature case apparently by the same hand contains a miniature of Thomas Egerton in the collection of the Duke of Buccleuch.
[2] A later watch in the Victoria and Albert Museum is more successful.

139

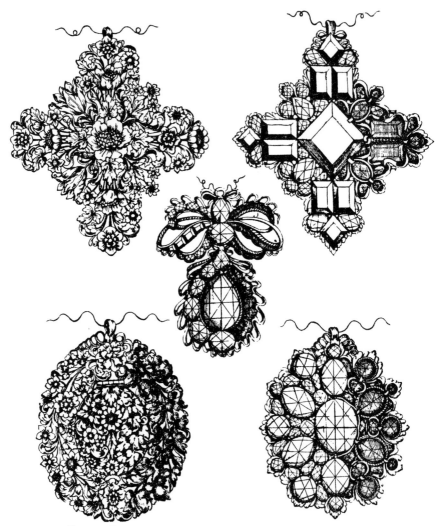

FIG. 27. Engraved designs for the fronts and backs of pendants by
Gilles Légaré. 1663

exquisitely wrought in fretted enamel in relief. More often flower designs were executed
in painted enamel, as in the delightful watch by Jacques Huon of Paris painted with
roses, lilies, columbines, tulips and daffodils in pinkish grisaille on a black ground
(Plate 121a, b). Similar subjects, much less well painted on a white ground, adorn two
cases by Christopher Morlière of Blois, formerly in the Pierpont Morgan Collection.[1]

[1] Williamson, *Catalogue*, Nos. 77 and 78.

Finally the style was made more widely available by its use in pierced and engraved silver for the backs of more ordinary watches in the second half of the century.[1]

The later versions of the style, indeed, are less elegant. There is a whole series of small oval miniature cases (Plate 126a) of the second half of the century, English or Dutch in manufacture, with conventional bouquets in rather hot colours. That illustrated is enamelled with tulips in orange, mauve and blue; the inside of the lid is decorated in painted enamel with a charming wooded landscape — a decoration not uncommon in the lids of watches of the same date. A few frames of cameos, notably one in the Bibliothèque Nationale (Plate 121c) and some portrait cameos in the Rosenborg Slott, and some detailed work accompanying figure designs, are remaining examples of the achievements of flower enamel. A little later the same designs were used as models not for enamel, but for engraving on metal, which in the second half of the seventeenth century was practised with remarkable delicacy, especially in France. An enamelled miniature of a lady, in the style of Mignard, has the back of its gold case (Plate 126c) engraved on a minutely and almost imperceptibly matted ground with her initials within a wreath of roses and other flowers in the style of the engraved designs of Gilles Légaré (Fig. 27).

The women who ruled fashion in the years following 1625 reacted against the contorted dresses and the multitudinous ornaments that had pleased their mothers. Henrietta Maria and her generation loved soft and flowing draperies, and their jewels were modified to match. The lovely portrait of Beatrice de Cusance by Vandyck[2] shows her wearing no other jewels than a quantity of pearls at neck and wrists. Vittoria della Rovere, wife of Ferdinando II dei Medici, in her portrait by Sustermans[3] also wears few jewels but pearls, though she wears them in greater profusion: a short necklace of very large ones, a long rope wound round the shoulders, nine diminishing rows down her stomacher, four strings round each wrist, and five great brooches each formed of a large jewel surrounded by eight enormous pearls, with a pear-shaped pearl pendant. Henrietta Maria used her jewels with greater discretion: her draperies are usually clasped with large stones and pearls, and sometimes by a cross of five large table-cut diamonds with three pendant pearls. One portrait[4] shows her with her dress fastened by gold ornaments shaped as doves, with diamonds in their breasts. Sometimes, too, a rich chain is slung from her shoulder: it may be that which she pawned in Paris in 1646, of heavy gold set

---

[1] e.g. those by Louis Arthaud of Lyons and Etienne Hubert of Rouen in the Victoria and Albert Museum.

[2] In the Louvre. The inventory made after her death in 1663 (Gauthier, p. 134) records her necklace and bracelets of pearls, as well as a number of fine diamonds, a diamond-set watch, very rich diamond and emerald bracelets, as well as others of rubies, turquoises, sapphires and jacinths, a Maria and a Jesus in diamonds, and miniatures in jewelled settings.

[3] In the Uffizi.   [4] In the collection of the Duke of Northumberland.

with a hundred and sixty pearls of about three carats each, every sixteen divided by a large ruby. Van Dyck's portrait of Lady Rich,[1] painted about 1635 (Plate 122) shows her dress fastened by simple and massive jewelled clasps of great magnificence. A portrait of the Duchesse de Longueville painted a few years later (Plate 123) shows her *décolletage* and sleeves edged with swags of pearls held together by jewelled clasps, with lines of pearls divided by jewels marking the seams of the bodice.

In Spain the fashion was rather for one enormous jewel of great splendour, sometimes accompanied by earrings to match. A *demi-parure* of the kind (Plate 128) is ornamented with tawny orange topazes, very flatly faceted, set in gold, and small table-cut diamonds that seem to merge into the silver scrolls they adorn; the back is of gold delicately engraved in a floral pattern. The jewel of Maria of Austria, Queen of Spain, long preserved in the convent of Salesas Reales in Madrid,[2] of which she became Abbess on the death of her husband, is set entirely with diamonds. The back is adorned with white enamel, with touches of black, on a green ground.

In the second half of the sixteenth century, in the Europe of the Counter Reformation and of Calvinism, a constant preoccupation with death became once more a fashionable devotional trend, and appears in jewellery designs. Even in 1533 Holbein had painted Jean de Dinteville in his picture of *The Ambassadors* wearing an *enseigne* enamelled with a skull, and Pierre Woeiriot had included a pendant surmounted by a death's head among the engravings he published at Lyons in 1559. An enamelled jewel of the early seventeenth century in the Clemens Collection[3] represents a skull with a Cupid standing over it with his bow and a crown over all.

The sixteenth century, too, had been a period when people wore mourning in the grand style. Brantôme in 1580 wrote of the death's head jewels that widows had used to wear in cameo or relief, and of the tears of jet or enamelled gold. The 1596 inventory of the Duchess of Lorraine[4] mentions a little *carcan* for mourning wear enamelled in white and black with lovers' knots and set with pearls; and other contemporary inventories of her house[5] show its princesses buying *cotières* of faceted jet and carcans of jet tears to wear when they were in mourning. The 1632 inventory of the Marquis de Rémoville includes a chain of ambergris beads — themselves black — divided by nine death's heads, each set with fifteen diamonds,[6] and a pair of diamond death's head earrings to match.

Such mourning jewellery was complemented, especially in England, by *memento mori* jewels of a yet more gloomy kind. A small coffin-shaped pendant of plain gold of about 1600[7] bears the legend *Cogita mori ut vivas,* and another (Plate 125f) is enamelled

---

[1] In the collection of Lady Lucas, who has kindly allowed me to have it photographed.
[2] Now in a private collection.   [3] In the Kunstgewerbe Museum, Cologne.
[4] Bibliothèque Nationale MS Lorraine 183 fol. 15.   [5] Roy, p. 335 and 337.
[6] Quoted Gay, s.v. Chaîne.   [7] In the British Museum.

with death's heads, hangs from a chain of crossbones and has a skull and crossbones hanging below. Another coffin pendant (Plate 124a) found at Torre Abbey, the cover delicately ornamented with champlevé enamel in black, contains a skeleton enamelled white that is a masterpiece of craftsmanship. Round the sides is the inscription *Through the Resurrection of Christe we be all sanctified.*

The general tendency in England was for *memento mori* jewellery to be transmuted into memorials of the death of specific people. A considerable number of jewels of a modest kind were made to commemorate the execution of Charles I; most of them are slides to be worn on a ribbon at neck or wrist, with the CR minutely executed in fine twisted wire on a silk ground, under a flattish faceted crystal. Others of the same sort, commemorating less illustrious dead, had the initials set on a ground of finely woven hair.[1] One Scottish family still owns a necklace made of thirty-one such medallions, each of crystal over hair with initials of gold wire, made as a set to be worn together.[2] They all have the setting characteristic of the period, with a minute serrated saw-like ornament running round the base. Other memorial jewels of the time are decorated with enamel; one has in front a fret of gold over hair enamelled with four skulls round a winged hour glass, and the back (Plate 125d) enamelled with a skull and crossbones on a black ground. Other enamelled ornaments of the time were evidently intended to be worn secretly by Royalists: one (Plate 125b) has two rather crude oval pictures of Charles I and the young Charles II, both wearing the George of the Garter on its blue ribbon. The back is enamelled with flowers in colour on a white ground. The only other characteristic fashion of Commonwealth jewellery was one for filigree (Plate 125c); a fashion which was perhaps introduced here from the Low Countries.

Louis XIV loved jewels, but his wife Marie-Thérèse was not interested in them.[3] It was he who wore the great diamonds of the Crown Jewels, and set the standard of luxury in them for his Court. After his assumption of power in 1661 he introduced the fashion of a richly jewelled watch hanging at the waist[4] and gave up wearing the traditional cross pendant.[5] At the fêtes at Fontainebleau held in 1677[6] he wore a coat of gold tissue embroidered in silver and gold, the jewels arranged 'en boucles de baudrier'. On the same occasion the Duke of Orleans wore a coat 'tout couvert de pierreries arrangées comme le sont les longues boutonnières des casaques à la Brandebourg'. These

---

[1] A number are illustrated in Clifford Smith, Plate XLIV.
[2] See Sharp, in *Proc. Soc. Ants. Scotland*, LVII, 1923, p. 226.
[3] Bapst, *Couronne*, p. 346.
[4] Bapst, *Couronne*, p. 351.
[5] Gold chains had altogether gone out of fashion for royal use though kings sometimes gave them as presents, perhaps because of their easily realisable value. The Ashmolean Museum still possesses two gold chains, one given to Elias Ashmole by Christian V, King of Denmark in 1674, and the other by Frederick William, Elector of Brandenburg, in 1678.
[6] Bapst, *Couronne*, p. 353.

FIG. 28. Engraved design for a *Sévigné* by Gilles Légaré. 1663

Brandebourgs or frogs of diamonds, invented for masculine use, soon spread to feminine wear. The portraits of Marie-Thérèse[1] show her with her long triangular bodice-front covered with diamond and pearl clasps of diminishing size, and similar ornaments all of diamonds are worn by the Duchess of Orleans (Plate 129) with brooches and sleeve-clasps to match.[2]

The jewels of the latter part of the century show no great change of style but a gradual lightening of design. The general climate of professional taste in jewellery is well expressed in the advice to apprentices which Berquen prefaced to his jewel designs in 1661. He came of a Bruges family; he worked for some time in Madrid, and was now established as one of the great jewellers of Paris, so he spoke with authority. 'Le solide fondement de l'art d'Orfèurerie est d'apprendre à bien portraire. Puis à ébaucher en cire ou en terre, et en suitte à tailler.' He still assumes that enamelling is an essential part of gem-setting, and continues: 'Sur tout vous prendrez garde auparavant que d'esmailler, que les couleurs de vostre esmail puissent embellir les Pierres et ayent un bon rapport

[1] ibid., p. 350.
[2] Designs for Brandebourgs and clasps of the kind will be found in the engraved designs for jewels published by Le Juge at Paris in 1678.

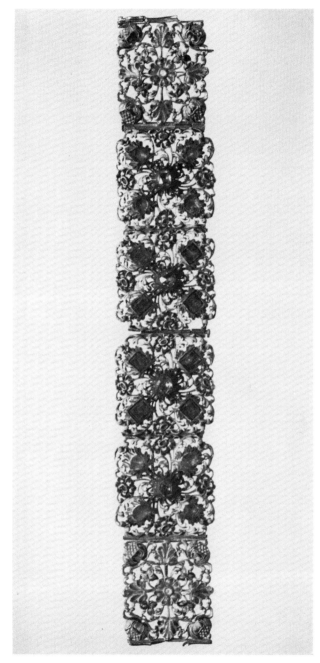

PLATE X

Bracelet with diamonds, emeralds and rubies set in enamelled gold.
Probably by Gilles Légaré, *c.* 1665

avec elles. Car si les Diamans demandent le noir, les Pierres de couleur au contraire veulent le blanc et la diuersité des couleurs.' He advises foiling and setting to give the maximum colour and size to the stone, choosing the colour of the foil with care and setting it in a rim just deep enough for safety and not too deep to hide any appreciable part of the jewel.

The general style of jewels at the middle of the century is best seen in the engraved designs published by Gilles Légaré in 1663 (Figs. 27–29). He came of a dynasty of Champenois jewellers, and reached such eminence in the profession of jeweller that he was lodged in the Louvre. His designs show jewellery at a transitional stage, with the chief interest of colour focused on the gems with which it was set, but every possible *nuance* of design and technique lavished on the enamelling and engraving of the settings. The designs are essentially those of a practising jeweller; even the flower patterns are produced in a form that could serve without modification as models for enamellers, while the black silhouette designs for watches and miniature cases are no less practical, and are found with little modification in contemporary work (Plate 126b). A bracelet (Colour Plate X)* set with rubies, emeralds and diamonds in floral settings of enamelled gold has all its elements so closely modelled upon his designs that it is tempting to ascribe it to Légaré himself: at all events it admirably illustrates the transitional style of the 1660's. A new flexibility is evident in Légaré's designs for necklaces; almost all of them are formed of plaques with a double narrow tube at the back through which two fine cords could be threaded so that they should form a ribbon-like band.[1] The other novelty is the emphasis on bow-shaped ornaments (Fig. 28) of the kind later known as *Sévignés,* and on *girandole* earrings to match with three (and sometimes five) pear-shaped pendants[2] (Fig. 29). The ribbon-like impression must have been enhanced when the necklaces were fastened (as they were originally) with a bow of ribbon tied through the two loops set for the purpose at the end. This preoccupation with ribbons and bows is evident in the design of necklace-links (Plate 131b) and of larger ornaments; one (Plate 131a), dedicated by the Marquis de Navarens at the Shrine of the Virgen del Pilar at Saragossa in 1679,[3] is formed as a bow from which hangs a lace-edged jabot in gold enamelled white and set with diamonds, itself ornamented with three bows in white enamel. Madame d'Aulnoy, in her *Relation d'un Voyage en Espagne,* describes how the Spanish ladies wear a great

---

[1] An existing necklace of this kind in the British Museum is set with diamonds, with a sapphire pendant; the back is enamelled in scrolls and rosettes in white enamel picked out in black. See Y. Hackenbroch, in *Antiquaries Journal,* XXI, 1941, p. 342. Two diamond bracelets of the kind, now rethreaded as a necklace are illustrated in *Proc. Soc. Ants. Scotland,* LVII, 1923, p. 226. They display the characteristic English saw-toothed edge to the collets.

[2] Some good examples set with garnets, amethysts and pearls, survive in the Myntkabinett at Stockholm.

[3] Now in the Victoria and Albert Museum.

*In black and white in the Dover edition.

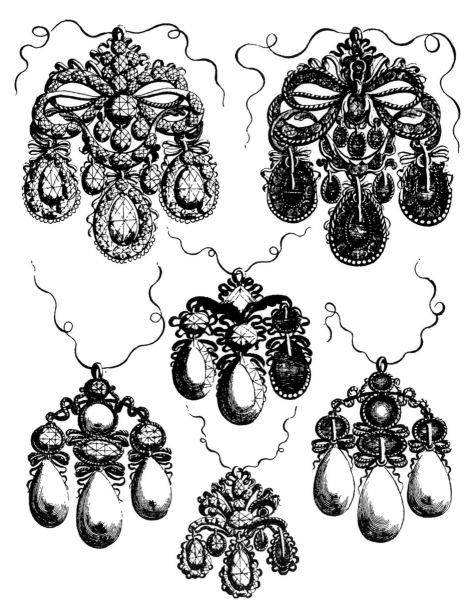

FIG. 29. Engraved designs for *girandole* earrings by Gilles Légaré. 1663

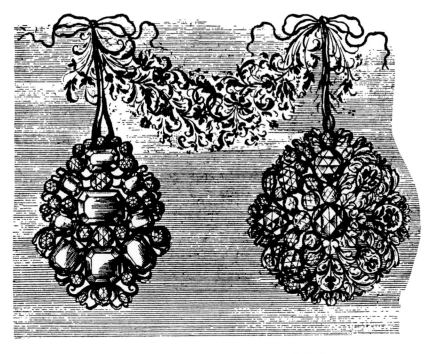

FIG. 30. Engraved designs for miniature cases by J. Le Juge. 1678

brooch high on the dress with chains of pearls or diamonds hanging from it; she notices that they rarely wear necklaces, but have many bracelets and earrings longer than one's hand. She draws a distinction between the French custom of having one splendid *parure* and the Spanish habit of having eight or ten in different colours, all rather heavily set in gold.

The marriage of Catherine of Braganza to Charles II in 1662 brought the Portuguese fashion of wearing a knot brooch on the shoulder to England; but by the time Mary of Modena had succeeded her as Queen Consort it had gone out, and Mary wore her dress fastened with *girandole* brooches on either shoulder.

The designs of Gilles Légaré and Le Juge (Fig. 30) show how much faceted gems had come to encroach on the enamelled field of miniature cases. A historical instance is that sent by the King of Spain to Mademoiselle d'Orléans in 1679,[1] lozenge-shaped, all of diamonds, hanging from seven loops of diamonds in a knot. They were sometimes set with diamonds of great size; one recorded in the inventory of the Maréchal de la Meilleraye[2] drawn up in 1664 was set with twenty-six diamonds worth thirty thousand livres.

[1] Havard, *Orfèvrerie*, p. 389.   [2] ibid.

Because of the diamonds with which they were set, comparatively few of these survive. The Duke of Portland owns one set with triangular diamonds round a square-cut stone, that was bequeathed as an heirloom by his ancestor James Dallas in 1683.[1] More often the diamonds have been reset and the enamelled back of the frame alone survives (Plate 132a) usually enamelled in black and white on a ground of opaque blue. Some, however, survive intact that are set with less precious stones: an instance (Plate 127a) is adorned with three concentric circles of emeralds, all divided by symmetrical and formal leafage enamelled white with touches of black. The end of the series is represented by another in the Queen's private collection (Plate 137) which is set with beautifully-cut crystals. It is no longer a miniature case with a lid; an enamelled portrait of William of Orange is set to form the central ornament of the back.

Towards the end of the century the enamel scroll work of such jewels became more luxuriant and architectural (Plate 132): a style represented in engraved ornament by the designs of Louis Roupert of Metz. Coloured gems were still much in fashion, especially rubies, emeralds and topazes, and they were combined with courage in ensembles of subdued brilliance that matched the brocades of the time (Plate 135). These jewels, too, were beginning to be set without any visible enamel and with backs of matted or slightly engraved gold. The Renaissance had inherited the mediaeval tradition of enamelling and had enriched it anew; but at last the potentialities of the tradition had been exhausted, and a new age demanded jewels of another kind.

[1] See Joan Evans, *English Jewellery*, Plate XXV, 7, 9.

CHAPTER SEVEN

The Eighteenth Century

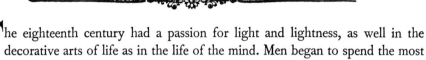

The eighteenth century had a passion for light and lightness, as well in the decorative arts of life as in the life of the mind. Men began to spend the most enjoyable part of their lives by candlelight. The fact had a repercussion, of which the importance cannot be over-emphasised, on the style of jewellery. Moreover, the development, both in England and France, of country-house life, which was sharply divided between relatively simple outdoor pursuits by day and the elegance of salon life by night, established a distinction hitherto unknown between jewels intended for daytime wear and those intended for display by candlelight.

The shift to the new way of life began a little before the turn of the century. The rather theatrical elegance of Versailles at the end of the seventeenth century was a candlelight elegance; its quality is reflected in Louis XIV's own jewels. In 1691[1] he owned for his own use two complete *parures* of diamonds for the ornament of his *justaucorps* and *veste*. One comprised a hundred and twenty-three buttons, three hundred buttonholes and nineteen 'fleurons' or Brandebourgs for the *justaucorps*, and forty-eight buttons and ninety-six buttonholes for the *veste*. The other consisted in a hundred and sixty-eight buttons and twice the number of buttonholes and nineteen 'fleurons' for the *justaucorps*, and forty-eight buttons and a corresponding series of buttonholes for the *veste*. Both *parures* included a loop for cocking the hat, garters, the cross of the Saint Esprit and a diamond hilted sword.[2] Such splendours were shared, too, by the weaker sex; Queen Mary on her death in 1694 owed Mr. Richard Beauvoir, jeweller of London, for diamond tags, buckles, sleeve clasps, loops, stars and a breast jewel.[3] Evelyn's *Mundus Muliebris*, published in 1690, lists the fashionable items:

> *Diamond buckles too,*
> *For garters, and as rich for shoo . . .*
> *A manteau girdle, ruby buckle,*
> *And brilliant diamond rings for knuckle . . .*

[1] Bapst, *Couronne*, p. 354.
[2] James II attempted a similar magnificence. In 1702 he sold a diamond girdle and buckle for £21,000 and a pair of diamond shoe buckles for £3,000. Evans, *English Jewellery*, p. 132.
[3] BM. MS Roy. 5751A, fol. 144.

THE EIGHTEENTH CENTURY

A sapphire bodkin for the hair,
Or sparkling facet diamonds there;
Then turquois, ruby, emrauld rings
For fingers, and such pretty things
As diamond pendants for the ears
Must needs be had, or two pearl pears,
Pearl necklace, large and oriental
And diamond, and of amber pale.[1]

A surviving *parure* of considerable interest is that which adorns the funeral effigy of Frances Stuart, Duchess of Richmond, in Westminster Abbey, which must either have been taken from her own jewels or bought expressly at the time of her death in 1702. It consists of a necklace with two loops in front which give something of the effect of a triple chain; a pair of drop earrings, a pair of sleeve-clasps and handsome oval ornament of the fashionable Brandebourg type (Plate 136). All are set with well faceted crystals; the necklace and earrings have their backs rather coarsely enamelled, but the large clasp is more fashionable in having its back engraved in a design of leafy scrolls.

The next stage is represented by the paste jewels on the waxen effigy of Queen Mary; she died in 1694, but the effigy does not seem to have been dressed so early.[2] They comprise three matching brooch-like ornaments, each fixed on a strong hook-like pin: the 'French croshet' mentioned in Evelyn's *Mundus Muliebris*.[3] The whole design is lighter and less geometrical, and the foliation of the scrolling design is more evident on the front than on the back, which is not enamelled and is only roughly engraved.

Enamel, indeed, was at last being divorced from jewel-setting. The engraved designs published at Augsburg by Friedrich Jacob Morisson, who worked at Vienna, in the last years of the seventeenth century, are, perhaps, the last to offer designs for painted enamel for the backs of jewels, though even he offers alternate designs for engraved gold.

Only in conservative Spain (Plate 134) do the jewels of the early eighteenth century continue to be enhanced by the contrast between the glitter of gems and the pure colour of enamel: and even there it was not long before a new balance was evolved that gave to chiselled gold the rôle of enhancing the brilliance of diamonds (Plate 138).

Elsewhere the decadence of enamel was felt at an earlier date. Even the 1679 inventory of the jewels of the House of Savoy[4] makes little mention of enamel, though it dis-

---

[1] The list may be compared with the inventory of Sarah Duchess of Marlborough recording jewels bought a few years later. (BM. Add. 29316 fol. 9.) It includes a number of diamond earrings, six loops of rose diamonds, other diamond buttons and loops, diamond stay buckles and a ruby cross.
[2] See *Illustrated London News*, October 5, 1935.
[3] A pair of 'croshetts' in brilliants from George Wickes cost Mrs. Fuller £440 in 1743. Garrard, p. 87.
[4] Promis, p. 214.

tinguishes between the diamonds that are 'a facette perfette' and those that are not. The divorce between the two arts reduced the jeweller's art to a craft of setting diamonds and coloured stones to the best effect, and made jewels themselves little more than a kind of *passementerie*. As a consequence of the conception of them as the high-lights of dress, they became subject to all the changes of fashion. As early as 1672 the *Mercure de France* had declared:[1] 'Les personnes de qualité ne gardent les pierreries jamais deux ou trois ans, sans les faire changer de figure.' In the book of designs which Jean Bourget published in Paris in 1712, he only gave designs for a miniature case and its back, a clasp, two crosses, and two pairs of earrings for 'cela me paroit inutile d'autant que les modes changent, et de plus c'est que les dessins se forment selon la quantité, la grandeur des Diamants qu'on a à mettre en oeuvre'.

For those who had not a quantity of diamonds to set, there was an immense production of paste jewellery. As early as 1657 Villiers, in his *Journal d'un voyageur à Paris*, had said[2] that a Sieur d'Arre living in the Temple quarter of Paris, who had learned to counterfeit diamonds, emeralds, topazes and rubies, had made so much money at his trade that he had built two houses and kept his coach. In 1676 George Ravenscroft, the proprietor of the Savoy Glass House in London, found that the addition of oxide of lead to flint-glass would produce a paste that when skilfully cut would glitter plausibly in candlelight. Stras, who gave his name to paste jewellery in France,[3] was received as 'maître orfèvre et joaillier privilégié du Roi' in 1734. He invented an improved flint-glass and a method of colouring foils for tinting diamonds. In 1767 a corporation of three hundred and fourteen 'joailliers-fausetiers' was established in Paris.[4]

From the first the designs of paste jewels approximated — with a surprisingly small time-lag — to those of diamonds. Queen Mary, in her picture in the National Portrait Gallery, presumably of about 1690, wears a large diamond rosette brooch with an oblong central stone surrounded by six petals, and a similar design is frequent in paste jewellery of about 1720. It must be remembered that such men as Stras were distinguished jewellers dealing in jewels of diamonds as well as of paste. In England, again, Messrs. Wickes and Netherton — the predecessors of Garrards' and also distinguished jewellers — in the 1750s advertised on their trade card that they had 'Variety of False-stone work in Aigrettes, Earrings, Buckles, etc.'[5]

The early paste is often rose-cut, like the diamonds it imitated. So too are the crystals from Bristol — 'the Bristowes brave and bright' — that adorn English and Flemish

---

[1] Ann. III, p. 294.　　　　　　　　　　[2] p. 45.
[3] See Bapst, *Couronne*, p. 419. He was born at Strasbourg in 1700. He retired from business in 1752 in favour of his son-in-law, Georges-Michel Bapst.
[4] Clifford Smith, p. 314.
[5] Garrard, p. 87. George Wickes had established the business in 1721 in the Haymarket, that was rapidly succeeding Cheapside as the jewellers' quarter of London.

FIG. 31. Engraved designs for rose-cut gems. Noe Pauwels, 1710

jewels of the early eighteenth century.[1] A stomacher (Plate 139) combines the bow and cross designs which are to be found in such engraved designs as those which Noe Pauwels published in Brussels in 1710 (Fig. 31) into an impressive ornament. It differs from the diamond jewellery of its time chiefly in the relatively rough finish of the back. Both diamonds and crystals show a gradual transition from what are essentially cluster settings. Such a jewel as the Duchess of Richmond's clasp (Plate 136) which in front appears more or less geometrical in plan, has the setting at the back transformed into a flowing foliate design. The stomacher (Plate 139) shows the front similarly designed; and such floral and foliate designs, sometimes accompanied by ribbon bows, are the basis of most gem-set jewels from the seventy years between 1710 and 1780 (Plate 140).

The tendency in such designs was always towards lightness. Just as jewels in the seventeenth century had shared in the glowing colour of brocades, and had echoed the branching curves of damask design, so in the eighteenth they were married in scale and delicacy to the leafy fantasy of point lace. The one added a focus of enhanced colour to the glow of brocaded silk, the other a point of sparkling light to a ruffle of Argentan or Point de France.

The brilliant-cutting of diamonds was invented by the Venetian Vicenzo Peruzzi about 1700, and added a new quality to diamonds which made them (and their imitations) the dominant jewel. Auguste Duflos, in the preface to his *Dessins de Joaillerie* published soon after 1722, declares that coloured stones are altogether out of fashion, and that in

---

[1] Similar crystals called 'Bagshot diamonds' were exploited between about 1770 and 1800. In France crystals of the kind from Châtellerault and Alençon were used.

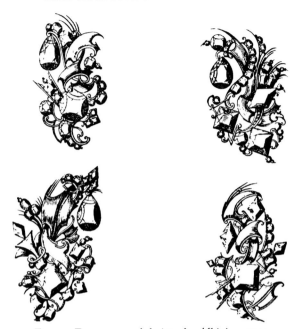

FIG. 32. Four engraved designs by Albini. *c.* 1744

consequence the field of design is restricted. He indicates two changes that were to have a profound effect on the development of jewels. First, he says that design and execution are becoming divorced, and that the design is more and more often executed by other hands, with bad results. Second, he declares that 'Les Dames sont le principal objet de l'art du joaillier'. He expresses the hope that his designs (which strike the present-day beholder as rather banal) may fall into their hands and recall them to the liking for noble simplicity, which is better fitted to set off their natural beauty than the 'étalage papillotant' which has been in fashion recently. Monsieur Duflos had missed the tide of fashion, which was running towards a rocaille elegance.

The drawings for brooches by Girolamo Venturi,[1] some of which are dated 1739, show a rocaille asymmetry; and the same tendency is evident in the engraved designs by Thomas Flach published in London in 1736, in those by Albini published in 1744 (Fig. 32) and in those by J. C. Mallia of about the same date. The same irregularity is evident in a few jewels that seem for the most part to be Italian, Spanish or Portuguese in origin (Plate 141). Yet, except for ornaments formed as more or less naturalistic flowers, rocaille asymmetry had a remarkably short period of influence over the design

[1] They form part of the most important series of some 600 drawings of jewellery of the eighteenth and nineteenth centuries in the Cooper Union Museum for the Arts of Decoration, New York.

of jewels; its real influence lay in the curving of jewels like sculpture in three dimensions, and in the universal adoption of a flowing line.

By the middle of the century the drawings of Christian Taute[1] show a preponderance of perfectly regular *Sévignés*, and the engraved designs published by de la Cour at about the same time show the asymmetrical rocaille designs all reserved for snuffboxes; his jewels are of the most symmetrical and regular kind. Only in the Peninsula did the style remain in fashion until about 1765, and there chiefly in designs in which asymmetry is given a naturalistic justification by the use of flower and feather motives.

The *corbeille de mariage* given to Marie-Josèphe de Saxe for her wedding to the son of the King of France in 1746[2] included earrings with additional 'pendeloques', knots, and a large pendant to match from her father, and a pair of large *girandole* earrings and a pair of bracelets from the King of France, all of diamonds. She also had a pair of pearl bracelets with diamond-surrounded portraits of Louis and the Dauphin, and a 'croix de brillants à la dévote', which soon went out of fashion and was reset.[3] Her jewel casket eventually included a diamond *parure* comprising stomacher, side pieces, ornaments for the back, 'deux trousses-côtés' and a 'trousse-queue', shoe buckles, earrings, 'pompons' or cuff-ornaments, sleeve-knots, collar and pendant and brooches.[4] Diamonds were at this time relatively cheap,[5] for both Brazil and Golconda were at the height of their productivity. Never, probably, have jewels of greater intrinsic magnificence been produced. Each court had its famous pieces, of which few now survive. Augustus III of Saxony (father of Marie-Josèphe) had a magnificent ornament (Plate 142) with which to cock his hat, set with brilliants and a legendary green diamond,[6] which was made in Dresden in 1740. It is most accomplished in its contrast between smooth rivers of diamonds and the exquisitely delicate leafage that surrounds the great green stone. The same jeweller made an Order of the Golden Fleece for his master (Plate 143) that is far more an ornament than a badge, and shows the same delicacy in the setting of large stones. In France, too, some of the largest diamonds in the Royal Collection were employed for a Golden Fleece of unparalleled splendour. It has long since disappeared.[7]

[1] Victoria and Albert Museum, E.2041.1914.   [2] Bapst, *Inventaire de Marie-Josèphe de Saxe*, p. 183.

[3] A number of crosses are included in the designs published by S. H. Dinglinger in London in 1751, but they then went out of fashion for some thirty or forty years.

[4] Bapst, *Inventaire de Marie-Josèphe de Saxe*, p. 182. A not dissimilar *parure* belonging to the Duchess of Parma in 1771 is recorded by J. Chepy in a manuscript at the Victoria and Albert Museum, 86 ZZ 149.

[5] ibid., p. 187, n. 1.

[6] It was in the Green Vaults at Dresden until 1944; its present whereabouts are unknown.

[7] Some of its stones are said to be reset in the pendant illustrated in Plate 181. Even the comparatively ordinary Golden Fleece made in Spain about 1770, set with rose diamonds and later presented by the Princess de Chinchona to the Duke of Wellington, strikes a modern observer as magnificent. It has recently been presented to the Victoria and Albert Museum by the present Duke.

Augustus of Saxony's other daughter, Maria Amalia Christina, married Charles III of Spain and was no less interested in jewels than her father. In 1759 Louis XV of France wished for political reasons to placate her, for she was no Francophile. The most delicate negotiations with her maid of honour resulted in the gift of a pair of bracelets each with an enormous diamond in the clasp.[1] A portrait of the Queen by Raphael Mengs in the Louvre (Plate 144) shows her copiously yet elegantly jewelled. She has five diamond stars in her hair; enormous *girandole* earrings of diamonds; a close necklace to match with a bow and drop centre, laid on black velvet; a bow *en suite* to fix the cross of an order at her breast, and a pair of bracelets each of four strands of large pearls clasped with a miniature framed in diamonds.

All the Courts of Europe displayed a similar magnificence. A portrait of the Electress Anna Maria Ludovica de' Medici[2] painted about 1730 shows her wearing a very handsome aigrette and a wide stomacher, both set with large diamonds and hung with pear pearls, as well as bracelets and armlets of diamonds. A portrait of Queen Charlotte of Mecklenburg-Strelitz, painted in the studio of Allan Ramsay at the time of her coronation in 1762[3] (Plate 145), shows her yet more magnificently, if less elegantly, jewelled, with a great stomacher of diamonds in a flowered design covering the whole triangular front of her bodice. Her necklace of very large diamonds is worn high on the throat; she wears no earrings. A mezzotint of her published in the same year by Thomas Frye shows her in less official dress wearing four strings of pearls and a diamond *suite* of tiara, *girandole* earrings in seven sections, *Sévigné* brooch and pendant. Her most splendid diamonds were those given to her by the Nabob of Arcot; contemporary drawings of them are in the Victoria and Albert Museum.[4]

Yet the splendours of London, Dresden and Madrid were eclipsed in the middle of the century by those of Petersburg: splendours which were partially revealed by the sale of a part of them in London in 1927.[5] The major portion of them is still in Russia. They comprise complete sets of little diamond flower sprays for sewing on dresses, to mimic the bright tinsel flowers of brocade; diamond bracelets, chiefly of flower and ribbon design and always in pairs; not only magnificent diamond necklaces, but also whole borders for dresses closely set with large brilliants, and any number of flower sprays (Plate 146b) and *girandole* earrings, each *suite* more splendid than the last. They include some remarkable examples of diamond-set watches and chatelaines, of a kind

---

[1] Bourguet, p. 441. The maid of honour received two French snuff-boxes, very elegant but without diamonds, for acting as intermediary.
[2] In the collection of the Marchese Peruzzi de' Medici.
[3] In the National Portrait Gallery.
[4] V. and A.M. Drawing D.401, 99.
[5] See the illustrated catalogue prepared by Messrs. Christie, Manson and Woods, for the sale on Wednesday, March 16.

rarely represented nowadays even in royal collections.[1] One of gold and agates set with brilliants in a formal floral pattern is signed by Charles Cabrier at London, and has the hallmark for 1752–3; another, a few years later in date, with slightly asymmetrical flower and scroll ornament in brilliants on a ground of green enamel, was made in St. Petersburg itself.

A few of the splendid diamond jewels of the age survive. In this country the Cory bequest in the Victoria and Albert Museum, for example, includes a set of leaf or shuttle-shaped diamond ornaments, probably made for Russia and intended to be sewn to the dress; and a suite of one large and two small bow-brooches (Plate 154) of great elegance. The majority of the great mass of eighteenth-century diamond jewels have, however, been reset; their design can often be most easily studied in the *parures* of less precious stones that exactly imitated them (Plates 148, 149, 151).

The Russian Imperial jewels show, as do other sources, that a fresh wave of naturalism invaded design about 1760. They include a nosegay of narcissus in gold, green enamel and diamonds of about that date, and another of pinks in diamonds and rubies. The recent bequest of Lady Cory to the Victoria and Albert Museum includes a delightful bouquet of this kind, with narcissus, pinks and other flowers in diamonds and rubies with green enamelled stems. A Spanish bouquet of the kind was dedicated by Doña Juana Ravasa to the Virgen del Pilar of Saragossa, and is also in the Victoria and Albert Museum (Plate 147). It was probably these naturalistic influences that served to bring back colour into jewellery. The comedy of the *Clandestine Marriage*,[2] published in 1766, describes a varicoloured jewel of the kind. The rich bride declares:

'I have a bouquet to come home tomorrow, made up of diamonds and rubies, and emeralds and topazes, and amethysts — jewels of all colours, green, red, blue, yellow, intermixt — the prettiest thing you ever saw in your life.'

In Spain, indeed, colour had never been so completely out of fashion as in France; many *parures* were produced there in the middle of the century in which the glitter of diamonds was enhanced by the glow of topazes (Plate 149) and some jewels are orchestrated in all the gamut of purples and pinks and oranges and yellows that can be achieved with foiled amethyst and topaz (Plate 150). Even in France a measure of discreet colour was admitted in the middle of the century, and diamonds were warmed by topazes (Plate 151) or white sapphires enhanced with blue[3] (Plates 152, 153). The

---

[1] A magnificent example of about 1770 is in the Danish Royal Collection at the Rosenborg Slott. Designs for such chatelaines were published in London by Thomas Flach in 1736.

[2] By Colman and Garrick, Act I, Scene 2.

[3] The *Sévigné*, neck-slide, girandole earrings and aigrette are all set with very brilliant lemon-hued sapphires bordered with others in pale steely blue. The gold setting is elegantly worked at the back with leafy sprays for strength where the design demands it.

inventory of Marie-Josèphe de Saxe, drawn up after her death in 1767,[1] includes a bouquet set with white and yellow diamonds and rubies, and a knot for a dressing-gown in diamonds and emeralds.

In nearly all these French *parures* a fairly naturalistic treatment of flowers is given form and shape by a formal frame of ribbons or a use of the traditional *Sévigné* form.[2] In France, too, experiments were made in the setting of coloured stones to give all the delicate variety of the hues of brocade. Such jewels, meant for the salon rather than the Court, may well stand for the *finesse* of the eighteenth century in France (Colour Plate XI).[*] It was in France too, then as now, that women excelled in giving jewels a fresh significance by wearing them in an unusual way: so a lady in a portrait called 'La Frileuse',[3] wrapped in the velvets and furs of winter, enhances her beauty by wearing a diamond and pearl pendant on the hood.

The same elegance is evident in such minor jewels as a pair of bracelet clasps (Plate 155c) with Marie Antoinette's initials and the turtle-doves and hymeneal torches that were her device at the time of her marriage, each under the simple wreath that stood at Trianon for the splendours of the Crown of France. In the same spirit of elegant — and expensive — simplicity, the Queen in 1788 ordered her jeweller Bapst to make her a bouquet in diamonds of wild roses and hawthorn blossom.[4]

The Queen is more tragically represented by the diamond necklace, the 'Collier de la Reine', which she did *not* receive.[5] It was originally ordered by Louis XV for Madame du Barry from his jewellers Boehmer and Bassanges, but it was not completed when he died in 1774, and when it was finished Louis XVI considered it too expensive for him to take it over. A plot was laid by a woman called Jeanne de Saint Rémy, wife of an officer named Lamotte, who made the Cardinal de Rohan her tool. She told him that the Queen needed money for charity, and he provided it. Then she persuaded him, by forged letters, that the Queen wished to buy the necklace without the King's knowledge and desired the Cardinal to negotiate the purchase. He did so, and the jewel was handed over to a man who represented himself as the Queen's servant. When the fraud was discovered the Queen refused to settle the bill quietly; she said nothing to the Cardinal but had him watched. He meanwhile was calm in the belief that the Queen had received it and that all was well. Finally the whole story came out; Lamotte was arrested and Cagliostro, the cabalistic adviser of the Cardinal, seriously implicated. In May 1786 the Cardinal was found not guilty, but had to resign his Court post and retire to his titular abbey of

[1] Bapst, p. 184. A golden monstrance in the Treasury of Prague Cathedral made in 1766 incorporates a whole secular *parure* of diamonds and rubies of great magnificence. Podlaha and Sittler, p. 153.

[2] The rather ill-drawn designs published by Pouget in 1762 give a répertoire of flowers, feathers and bows. The designs published by van de Cruycen in 1770 are more accomplished but not very practical.

[3] In the Museum of Marseilles.

[4] Bapst, *Joyaux*, p. 434.   [5] See Barrera, p. 80.

[*]In black and white in the Dover edition.   157

La Chaise Dieu. Lamotte was flogged, branded and imprisoned; but his wife organised an elaborate system of blackmail and he was soon released. Unhappily the memory of the scandal survived to blacken the reputation of the perfectly innocent Marie Antoinette, and undoubtedly helped to bring about the downfall of the monarchy. An engraving of the necklace[1] shows it to have been an ostentatious affair consisting in a *tour de cou* of seventeen large brilliants from which hung three festoons and four pendants of diamonds, and a longer necklace consisting of a double *rivière* of diamonds with four tassels of the same stones.[2] Marie Antoinette's own diamond necklace, a *rivière* of thirty brilliants with thirteen pear-shaped brilliant pendants spaced round it, was far less ostentatious.[3] Her splendid *parure* of large sapphires rimmed in diamonds and linked by hanging leafy tassels of diamonds was bequeathed by Queen Marie Amélie to the Comtesse de Paris and is still in the possession of the Bourbons.

Such jewels were meant to be worn with Court dress and to be seen by candlelight. The broadcloth and doeskin, the taffetas and frilled muslin of the daylight hours demanded jewels of quite another kind. In them, quite as much as in the showier *parures* of candlelight, the exquisite and reasonable taste of the eighteenth century found its expression. Fashion played so large a part in the design of these jewels that the women's papers of the time advise what is to be worn. The *Lady's Magazine* of March 1774 advises the wearing of small drop earrings, but by July it is so important to wear no earrings at all that the news is put into capitals.[4]

Jewels of semi-precious stones might be all the gentlewoman of modest means possessed; but even Empresses owned them too. The Russian State Jewels included a number of suites dating from between 1770 and 1790 in smoked crystals, garnets, river-pearls and agates, and other semi-precious stones, intended for daytime use; and few of our eighteenth-century ancestresses but had their *parure* of garnets or agates or cornelians.

[1] Published at Paris by M. Taunay, rue de l'Enfer, Place Saint Michel; a copy is in the Bibliothèque Nationale.

[2] The general design may be compared with that of jewels worn by Queen Charlotte in 1800. The *Lady's Magazine* for June states:
'Her Majesty was magnificently attired in a lilac crape petticoat . . . with five superb diamond bands, composed of collets, and fifteen large brilliant roses and stars, at equal distances on the bands; these bands were terminated at the bottom with four very magnificent bows and tassels of diamonds and large pearls, from which were also suspended festoons of beautiful pearls in wreathes; over the left side flowed two corners of lilac crape, caged with diamond chains and pearls, with pearl tassels at bottom, and fastened at the pocket holes with a superb diamond and pearl bands and chains.' The ensemble was completed by a diamond stomacher, necklace, bouquet and bandeau.

[3] It was sold at Sotheby's on July 1, 1937, by the Archduchess Blanca of Austria and her sister Beatrix Princess of Massimo, who had jointly inherited it. The forty-three stones weighed 180 carats. See *Illustrated London News*, June 19, 1937.

[4] It is perhaps worth recording that a French edict of 1720 forbade the wearing of diamonds, pearls and precious stones and ordered jewellers to export what they had in stock. It was only in force for six months. Havard, *Orfèvrerie*, p. 393.

PLATE XI
Suite set with coloured gems. French, c. 1760

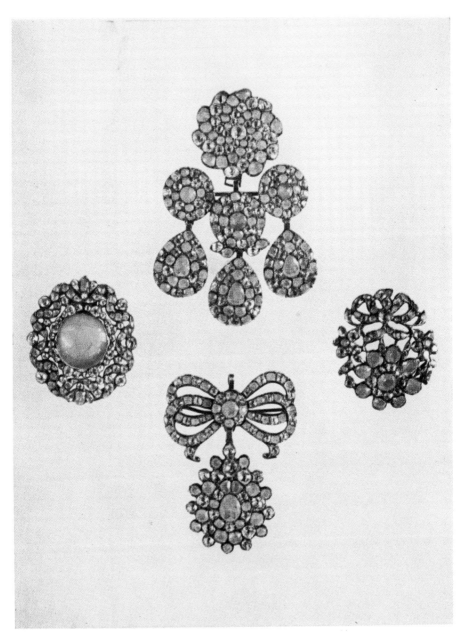

PLATE XII
Jewels in opal paste. English, second half of the eighteenth century

THE EIGHTEENTH CENTURY

The fashion for these day-time jewels began at the end of the seventeenth century, when some pretty *parures* were made in the Low Countries of amber set in silver over red foil to give a rose-coloured effect. Garnets came into fashion early in the eighteenth century; Sarah Duchess of Marlborough owned a pair of garnet earrings and a necklace, as well as a necklace of French — that is, imitation — pearls and turquoises.[1] The garnet necklaces were set in the flower and ribbon designs of the designers of diamond jewellery, with cluster and pear-drop earrings; the stones were cut thin and mounted over foil to give them brilliance. After about 1770 garnet jewellery was usually more simple and geometrical in design; it looks as though the *genre* has passed into the hands of one or two workshops who had approached mass-production.

The function of paste had primarily been to imitate diamonds cheaply; but it was not long before the jewellers created *genres* of paste that had little relation with real stones. Aventurine paste in brown was apt to be even brighter than its natural prototype, and was soon made (as nature had omitted to do) with a bright blue base on which its golden flecks made a brilliant effect. In France, again, and to a less degree in England, opal paste was produced, of a pinkish milky kind that derived a novel beauty from the rose-coloured foil over which it was set (Colour Plate XII).* It is not in the least like opals, but it is quite charming.

Similarly marcasites — faceted crystals of iron pyrites — were used in Switzerland, England and France, at first to imitate diamonds, and then to create schemes of a steely brilliance of their own. They were often set over plaques of blue or red glass, following *longo intervallo*, but with little intention of mimicry, the diamond-set enamels of the rich.

The *parures* of precious stones quickly acquired a style of their own, that varied, it is true, but only within narrow limits. The ornaments of a less valuable kind were far quicker to reflect the changes of decorative taste of a more general kind. The taste in the early years of the century for delicate decoration in gold on a coloured ground is represented in engraved ornament by the designs for chased and engraved gold of such engravers as Morisson and Briceau,[2] and by the very delicate and charming watch-cases produced in France and England. One may be cited, inlaid with curved plates of lapis lazuli held in place by a fretwork of exquisitely engraved gold set with diamonds and rubies;[3] another, in the British Museum, has its outer case of pierced and engraved gold set with curved plates of cornelian, with a cornelian cameo in the middle. The chatelaines that accompanied such watches were no less delicate. A watch and chatelaine in the Fitzwilliam Museum (Plate 156), made by Thuilst for Queen Anne about 1705, are of

[1] British Museum Add. MS 29316, fol. 9.
[2] 'Maître orfèvre de Paris'; he published designs in 1701. Other engravings in the same style were published in London by J. Herbst and S. Gribelin.
[3] Formerly in the collection of Mr. C. W. Dyson Perrins; Joan Evans, *English Jewellery*, Plate XXVI, No. 6.
*In black and white in the Dover edition. 159

pierced and chased gold, inlaid with mother of pearl, which in its turn is set with garnets in a border of gold enamelled in black, picked out in red.

Most of our knowledge of such early chatelaines, however, is derived from examples not in gold but in such imitations as pinchbeck.[1] These pinchbeck chatelaines of the early eighteenth century are exquisitely finished, but since their elements were cast they show an element of standardisation in their design. The Victoria and Albert Museum, the London Museum and a private collection all include examples of which the hook-plate represents Cleopatra dissolving the pearl for Antony, though the hanging plaques below are of different patterns.

In the second decade of the century the fashion changed to classical subjects in relief in solid gold. At the same time the chatelaine was made to support not only (or always) a watch but also an *étui* or pendant case containing an assortment of sewing and designing necessaries, such as scissors, thimble, a ruler, a pencil and a minute pair of compasses. Such an adornment — then called 'an equipage' — is described in Lady Mary Wortley Montagu's fourth *Town Eclogue*.[2]

> *Behold this equipage, by Mathers wrought,*
> *With fifty guineas (a great penn'orth!) bought.*
> *See on the tooth pick Mars and Cupid strive,*
> *And both the struggling figures seem to live.*
> *Upon the bottom see the Queen's bright face,*
> *A myrtle foliage round the thimble case;*
> *Jove, Jove himself does on the scissors shine,*
> *The metal and the workmanship divine.*

Gastrell, Manby and Moser were hardly less famous as gold chasers than Mathers, and work by them and by other craftsmen shows a remarkably high standard of skill. A watch in the Nelthropp Collection[3] is chased by Manby with the Choice of Hercules; another by Isaac Duhamel bears the figures of Esther and Ahasuerus. A watch and chatelaine in the Fitzwilliam Museum[4] are chased with scenes from the story of Alexander (Plate 157). Nearest, perhaps, to Lady Mary Wortley Montagu's description is an *étui* and chatelaine of gold, the hook-plate chased with a seated figure of Britannia, and the *étui* with Mars and Venus framed in asymmetrical scrolls and leafage on a matted ground. The *étui* contains a tiny gold spoon, pencil, scissors, bodkin, tweezers and a little ivory writing tablet (Plate 158). It is interesting to compare this 'equipage' with one in pinchbeck in the Victoria and Albert Museum. The hook-plate has a head of

[1] An alloy of copper and zinc, so called after its inventor, Christopher Pinchbeck, a Fleet Street watchmaker who died in 1732. A somewhat similar alloy was also used in Holland.
[2] Dating from 1716. Dodsley's *Collection*, I, 96.
[3] No. 281; Guildhall Museum.　　　　[4] By James Rowe. Hall Mark 1753.

Britannia framed in architectural scrolls; the pierced links of the chain are not dissimilar; and the *étui* mimics the golden one fairly closely, thought it has neither the elegant serpentine shape nor the precision of finish.

About 1760 the taste for *chinoiseries*, that otherwise seems not to have influenced the design of jewels, was reflected in a few chatelaines in base metal. One in pierced copper gilt[1] has a Chinese lady with a parasol on the hook-plate and a Chinese dancer on the hanging plaque; another (Plate 159a) shows lute-players and dancers under a palm tree. It was a popular design, and is to be found both gilt all over and with gilt figures on a silvered ground.

At this time, indeed, an effect of solid gold was felt to be a little unrefined. Chased gold had never been so popular in France as in England: even in 1747 the seven watches in the *corbeille de mariage* of Marie-Josèphe de Saxe had not included a single one in chased gold: four were enamelled in red, blue, green and 'verd lac', one was engine-turned, and two were plain.[2] In England, the revulsion of taste against chased gold made itself felt in the decade after 1760. Many of the gilt metal chatelaines of about 1770 (Plate 159b) have rayed designs picked out in silver, while others have decoration in silver and gold of two colours on a ground of bright blued steel, giving an unusual gamut of metallic hues. Some gold watches and chatelaines have colour added by *taille d'épargne* — that is, by a pattern chiselled out of the gold and filled in with enamel flush with the ground. A good example in the Fitzwilliam Museum is thus adorned with a flower pattern in dark blue.[3] More usually the 'equipages' of precious materials have a ground of agate to set off their delicately worked garlands of golden flowers[4] (Plate 160).

After about 1775 the most usual decoration for watches and their matching chatelaines of high quality was painted enamel on gold. George Michael Moser, a Swiss working in London, was described by Reynolds as the first gold-chaser in the kingdom; but about 1770 he had to transfer his skill to the production of figure compositions in enamel because of the change of fashion. Such watches and chatelaines, especially those of French manufacture, tend to be in close relation in design and technique with the snuffboxes of the time. They were often enamelled with hunting scenes, and even more often with classical or sentimental subjects (Plate 161). About 1780 a number were adorned with classical figures in the manner of Angelica Kauffmann. About 1772 the Macaroni or hookless chatelaine came into fashion, to be worn as a handkerchief might be with two ends hanging down from a close-fitting belt. At one end hung the watch, at

[1] Illustrated, Joan Evans, *English Jewellery*, Plate No. 5.
[2] Bapst, *Inventaire de Marie-Josèphe de Saxe*, p. 214.
[3] Illustrated, Joan Evans, *English Jewellery*, Plate XXVIII, 1. The watch is by Francis Périgal of London.
[4] A long watch-chatelaine in the same style with a moss agate base is in the Rosenborg Slott at Copenhagen.

FIG. 33. Engraved designs for buckles. Jean Quien

the other usually a seal or tassel; occasionally, however, a second sham watch or *fausse-montre* balanced the real one. These hookless chatelaines, all of gold, were usually formed of delicately enamelled chains linked by plaques, enamelled to match, and often studded with diamonds or rimmed with pearls, and made so that both sides were more or less equally ornamental. The watches that accompany them have their backs enamelled and jewelled to match but have plain clear faces on which the time could be read without removing the chatelaine from the belt.

THE EIGHTEENTH CENTURY

If chatelaines were the most important kind of daytime jewellery in the eighteenth century, the next most important were undoubtedly buckles. They were made of diamond-set gold, of paste, of gilt metal, and of silver; they were worn on shoes, at the waist, and to fasten bands of velvet at throat and wrists (Fig. 33). In the eighteenth century a whole protocol of shoe buckles was codified and a man's social position as well as his taste could be guessed from them. The rich farmer or the small squire had silver for week-days and decent gilt for Sundays; the country dandy cut steel and paste; the courtier diamonds[1] (Plate 163). Some of the most elegant of buckles are those set not with paste but with crystals. An example (Plate 162a) is formed of interlaced ribbons, one of reeded gold and one set with faceted crystals, with four pear-shaped rose-cut crystals at the corners. It is as well designed and well finished as the sapphire and diamond buckles of the Emperor of Russia (Plate 163b). Shoe buckles varied greatly in size; about 1770 they were so large as to cover the whole instep.

The lesser buckles that fastened a velvet bracelet or throatlet, commonly worn 'in undress', as has already been said, figured in the diamond *parures* of the Court. They were often set with an official miniature, but they also are commonly represented in rather less precious materials. Madame de Pompadour, for instance, had a pair of bracelet clasps set with cameos by Jacques Guay of Henri IV and Louis XV in a crown of emeralds[2] that though sumptuous and elegant in every detail were evidently intended for daylight use.

Such clasps *de luxe* were imitated in an endless series in cheaper materials. Many were set with miniatures in a kind of grisaille colouring to give something the effect of a cameo. A pair of bracelet clasps, for instance,[3] bought in Stockholm and said to have come from Russia, but undoubtedly English in manufacture, are set with miniatures of Faith and Hope after the Reynolds window at New College, Oxford, in grisaille on a ground of warm blue, that is enhanced by the rim of leaves on a matted ground in gold of two colours. The elegance and finish of the clasps suggest that they were exported to Russia for court wear; and indeed miniatures and enamels for such clasps were taken so seriously as to be exhibited at the Royal Academy.[4]

---

[1] In 1773 Aubert, the King's jeweller, made shoe buckles for the Comte d'Artois of seventy-two brilliants weighing altogether more than 139 carats. See A. Marcel in *Mémoires de l'Académie de Vaucluse*, 2nd ser. XIX, 1919, p. 89.

[2] See Babelon, *Gravure*, p. 159. A bracelet clasp with a cameo of Clementina Sobieska, wife of the young Pretender, in the collection of Her Majesty the Queen, appears to be by the same hand.

[3] In the Victoria and Albert Museum.

[4] e.g., by Augustus Toussaint the Younger, in the Exhibitions of 1775–8. Similar grisaille paintings were enamelled on watches and chatelaines, for example on one by Robert Atkins in the Fitzwilliam Museum, in borders of white and orange, and on another in the same collection by Périgal with borders picked out in blue and green. Joan Evans, *English Jewellery*, Plate B, 3, 4.

The demand for grisaille bracelets was soon met in a cheaper guise by the manufacturers of Bilston enamels (Plate 164a) who produced oval medallions about an inch high that could either be mounted as clasps or linked with thin gold, painted with heads of Jupiter and Bacchus and appropriate goddesses, and such subjects as Cupid and Psyche, in grisaille on a ground of dark purple.

A similar classicism was also achieved in relief. James Tassie, who had acquired the art of casting gems from the Regius Professor of Physics at Dublin, came to London in 1766 and had an enormous success with his paste copies of antique gems: a complete set, running into several thousands, was ordered by the Empress of Russia. These were occasionally mounted in jewels; but the greatest success in imitation cameos was reserved for Wedgwood. The catalogue of his firm published in 1773 includes a great number of small fictile cameos for rings and bracelets, as well as larger ones for inlaying in cabinets and wall decoration. The small ones were sold unset at a shilling apiece, and set in gilt metal at from 3/6 to 5/-. He announced that he was prepared to take casts from antique gems in private collections and to reproduce them.

The most charming Wedgwood jewellery is that composed of plaques set, like the contemporary chatelaines, in varied chains of gold (Plate 165a). Those illustrated are set with octagonally oval plaques of Wedgwood ware with the signs of the Zodiac, the clasps set with classical subjects. They look simple enough, but the alternation of slender and larger chains, the design of the chains themselves, and the delicately beaded settings are in fact highly sophisticated.

Such delicacy was impossible in the other metal in which Wedgwood plaques were commonly set: faceted steel (Plate 164d). This had been used much earlier for sword-hilts and caneheads, and soon after the middle of the eighteenth century to set Bilston enamels. The finest work was considered to be that made at Woodstock. In 1762 Matthew Boulton went into partnership with John Fothergill and set up the Soho manufactory where they soon developed the manufacture of faceted steel jewellery. Boulton and Watt ran their Birmingham factory between 1775 and 1800, and others were established at Sheffield, Birmingham and Wolverhampton.[1] In France faceted steel was chiefly used for buttons and buckles;[2] but about 1780 Sykes, a Yorkshireman, was established in the Palais Royal and dealt in steel jewellery of every kind. Yet such jewellery remains the nadir to which the jeweller's art sank in the century that saw the dawn of the Industrial Revolution.

[1] A collection of these jewels may be seen in the Nottingham Museum. A chatelaine of polished steel was exhibited by Durham of New Oxford Street at the Great Exhibition of 1851.
[2] Dauffe was a specialist in such work. See Vever, I, p. 108, n. 3.

CHAPTER EIGHT

1789-1870

The nineteenth century began not in 1800 but with the French Revolution. Indeed the Gothic Revival, and with it the revival of sentiment, which were felt years before 1789, themselves showed a revulsion from the scholarly classicism and reasoned intellectualism of the eighteenth century. So, too, the style and finish of classicism had before 1791 begun to be watered down to meet the requirements of the Industrial Age.

As usual, the change of feeling was most quickly felt in jewellery that was less intrinsically valuable than the diamond *parures* of the court ladies. The popularity of Young's *Night Thoughts on Life, Death and Immortality,* published in 1742, had helped, perhaps, to revive the liking for wearing memorials of the dead which had been felt in seventeenth-century England. At all events in the second half of the century, an enormous quantity of memorial jewellery was made and worn in this country. At first memorial rings sufficed — and a small book might be written about them alone — but after about 1775 there was an immense vogue for memorial clasps and brooches and pendants. They are usually elliptical or shuttle shaped, and rimmed with pearls, diamonds, little amethysts or pastes. The central medallion is sometimes filled with plaited hair, with initials; or has a plaque of enamel or paste in blue or purple, on which initials of gold set with pearls or diamonds are fixed. Sometimes a smooth crystal covers a whole picture executed in hair, with the help of a little colour, sometimes the medallion is frankly a miniature (Plate 166). Their subjects are funereal enough; a tomb (under a weeping willow of hair) opens to let an angel lead a shrouded figure to the Heaven where a crown (in little diamonds) awaits it; disconsolate widows weep under more willows by a broken column, or sisters bring their children to mourn at their aunt's urn. Yet they have the innocent and sentimental charm of amateur verses in the *Lady's Magazine*; they perfectly reflect the quiet life of nursery and parlour and drawing-room, and the funeral sermons preached in country churches in the last three decades of the eighteenth century.[1]

---

[1] An excellent collection may be seen in the Victoria and Albert Museum. The Spencer George Perceval Collection in the Fitzwilliam should also be studied.

There is no kind of jewel which is more entirely English; it is a reflection of the 'Anglomanie' that preceded the Revolution that they were ever worn in France. In 1778, indeed, there was a great vogue for hair jewellery, though it seems to have been rather sentimental than memorial in intention. The Marquis de Castéja ordered from Drais 'un cordon en cheveux, garniture guillochée et gravée, avec une gerbe dont le corps soit en cheveux bruns, les épis des plus blonds, le noeud entre les deux et le cordon en lozange'.[1] In Switzerland, too, painted enamels with domestic and sentimental (but not memorial) subjects were produced for watch cases and other ornaments at the end of the century and for some forty years later. A remarkably massive *parure* in the Cory bequest has oblong medallions of the peasant dresses of all the Swiss cantons in settings of turquoises and other semi-precious stones. It must date from about 1835.

Jewellery enclosing hair-work remained very popular in France until *c.* 1850. Sentimental jewellery also took other forms. In 1783[2] the same jeweller provided Madame de Mattiau with a chain with the motto *La racine est dans le coeur* under roses on the clasp, and another jewel with a bow and arrow on a blue ground and the motto *Je n'en veux lancer qu'une.* Similar sentiments are wordlessly expressed in jewels of about 1790 with bows and quivers, hymeneal torches, flaming hearts and doves (Plate 167a), charmingly executed in thin slices of cornelian, pearls and gold. The English equivalents (Plate 167c) are padlocks in similar materials, with space for hair at the back; they begin to show the rather heavy-handed plainness of English style in the years when war separated her from French influences. Far more elegant are the Swiss watches with painted landscapes and seascapes against skies delicately engraved and enamelled in translucent pinks 'à l'aurore'.[3] No less delicate, and even more technically remarkable, are the French watches of slightly later date (Plate 167b) with a pavé setting of half pearls in different sizes exquisitely arranged to form whirling scrolls.[4] In these not only the ring and edge but even the face and figures of the watch are set with minute pearls.[5]

The Paris company of goldsmiths had been suppressed by Turgot in 1776, but was soon afterwards revived at the wish of the members of the trade. It was definitely abolished by the Constituent Assembly on March 17, 1791, and for a time the glory of French jewellery was eclipsed. The crown jewels were stolen by the Revolutionaries,[6] and many of those that were recovered were sold under the Directory when it was in

---

[1] *Art décoratif,* I, 1908, p. 174.   [2] *Art décoratif,* I, 1908, p. 174.

[3] There are good examples in the Nelthropp Collection in the Guildhall Museum.

[4] Designs for jewels pavés with pearls, apparently English of about 1800, will be found in the Victoria and Albert Museum Department of Drawings, D. 310.99.

[5] The English contemporary watches are much clumsier; see, for example, that with a blue enamel back, a pearl rim and the initials J.M., hanging at an elaborate fob, which was given by Lord Nelson to Sir Jonathan Miles, Sheriff of London, in 1806. Nelthropp Collection, No. 558.

[6] Bapst, *Couronne,* p. 447 *et seqq.*

great need of money about 1795. Such ornaments as were produced under the inspiration of the Revolution[1] are of so trumpery a quality that it seems that their makers had little faith in the permanence of the changes they celebrated. It was, indeed, not long before the realm of France was back on a less egalitarian basis, and then the change was reflected in jewellery. Even under the Directory some elegant chains were produced to meet the need for long necklaces to go with the new short-waisted styles in women's dress.[2] For the most part they exploit the rather complicated arrangements of chains that had already been worked out for bracelets and chatelaines and fobs; the chain illustrated (Plate 165b) is formed of plaques alternately lozenge-shaped and circular, linked by a central chain of flat shiny links joined by two rings of finely ribbed gold, and by side chains of fine Trichinopoly plaiting. The front of the plaques is enamelled in black, to enhance the pearls and the central diamond with which they are set. The pearls are whole, so that they show also on the reverse of burnished gold.

By the time the Consulate was set up in 1799 many jewellers who had worked for Louis XVI were once more at work to meet the needs of the new society.[3]

Such needs were at first for rather showy jewels of gold and semi-precious stones. In 1800 a fashion drawing shows a lady wearing a long snake necklace hanging to the waist.[4] Another[5] depicts a very heavy chain with alternate oblong and round links, worn bandolier-wise; the lady's toilet is completed by a pair of the very long earrings called *poissardes*,[6] a heavy bracelet, and an ornamental hair-pin. In the next year[7] a watch was worn at the end of the long chain, and the bracelet had moved up to the top of the fore-arm just below the elbow. The *Journal des Dames* for Nivôse of the year IX of the new era — otherwise 1801 — describes some long chains set with moss-agates, and says the most fashionable are of knitted gold, circular and hollow, like a snake; and says that earrings grow longer and longer, with two or three annular links. By August the fashionable *sautoirs* are of double tubes of knitted gold linked from time to time by slides of enamelled gold. In 1802 the *Journal* recommends as the latest fashion 'colliers à la romaine' of twisted branches with one or three oval, square or hexagonal plaques of cornelian or moss agate, often rimmed with pearls. In all ornaments serpent forms were the most usual, and the most fashionable stone was cornelian.[8]

By this year it was no longer an insult to democracy to wear diamonds. The *Journal des Modes* advises their mounting in 'aigrettes couchées', especially in branches of jasmine; the quality to be desired above everything is lightness, and the diamonds must

---

[1] There is a small collection of them in the Musée Carnavalet at Paris.
[2] The fashion reached London in 1806; see *Lady's Magazine* for April.
[3] Vever, I, p. 22; some of their names are — or were until 1939 — still borne by firms of Paris jewellers.
[4] Vever, I, p. 56.   [5] ibid., I, p. 8.   [6] ibid., I, p. 14, plate facing.   [7] ibid., I, p. 17.
[8] See *Journal des Modes*, 15 brumaire, an X.

be clear set. It seems as if news must have reached Paris of the superb coronal of two meeting sprays of diamond wheat and grass that was made in Petersburg — probably by a French émigré jeweller — for the Empress Marie Feodorovna before the assassination of her husband Paul I in 1801. It too is all clear set, and there is much use of briolettes, held only at their pointed bases.[1] Briolettes, again, are used as a kind of fringe on the diadem made for her successor Elizabeth Alexeievna, wife of the Emperor Alexander I. Her tiara is crested with huge pear-shaped stones; the great central diamond is in a setting of formal volutes.

By 1803 Napoleon had recovered all that he could of the French crown jewels[2] and Josephine had the usufruct of what had been saved. She began with a fine set of pearls, and *parures* of rubies and emeralds, and after Napoleon had become Emperor nothing was too good for her. In March 1807[3] she had a whole new *parure* of diamonds: tiara, comb, earrings, a pair of bracelets, a two-row *rivière* and a garland of the 'hortensia' or hydrangea that bore her daughter's name. A portrait of the Empress painted by Gérard in 1805[4] shows her wearing a laurel-wreath crown, long earrings and a necklace remarkable for the immense size of the jewels with which it is set. In the picture of the marriage of Jérôme Bonaparte and the Princess of Wurtemburg painted by J. B. Regnault in 1807[5] she wears a *parure* of pearls of immense size and beauty; and in her portrait by Gérard[6] (Plate 169) she wears a diadem, necklace and earrings of emeralds set in diamonds and hung with immense pear pearls. A Regency *parure* of little less magnificence is that of sapphires and diamonds recently bequeathed by Lady Cory to the Victoria and Albert Museum.

A Napoleonic classicism had brought cameos once more into fashion. A portrait of Marie Caroline Queen of Naples[7] by Madame Vigée Le Brun (Plate 170) shows her wearing them in full dress, combined with a splendid *parure* of enormous pearls. David's picture of the *Sacre de Napoléon* painted in 1808 shows the Duchesses de la Rochefoucauld and de la Valette wearing diadems set with cameos. More often they were worn with a demi-toilette, as they are by Pauline Princess Borghese, in her portrait of 1806 by Robert Lefebvre[8] (Plate 171). Her bandeau and belt are of diamonds set in a Greek fret, with diamond-rimmed cameos at intervals. More of these are set in her comb and earrings; she wears a double *rivière* of diamonds.

The *Journal des Dames* for the 25th day of Ventôse in 1805 declares:

'Une femme à la mode porte des camées à sa ceinture, des camées sur son collier, un camée sur chacun de ses bracelets, un camée sur son diadème . . . Les pierres antiques,

[1] Christie's Sale, March 16, 1927, lot 116. It is illustrated in the catalogue.
[2] Bapst, *Couronne*, pp. 447 *et seqq*, 579.   [3] ibid., p. 581.   [4] Vever I, p. 24.
[5] Musée de Versailles, Vever I, p. 47.
[6] Musée de Versailles.   [7] Musée de Versailles.   [8] Musée de Versailles.

et, à leur défaut, les coquilles gravées, sont plus en vogue que jamais. Pour les étaler avec plus de profusion, les élégantes de la classe opulente ont remis à la mode les grands colliers dit sautoirs. A chaque retrousse de leurs bouts de manches drapés, est fixée une antique; et dans leurs coiffures les bandeaux ou les diadèmes, les centres de peignes et les têtes d'épingles ne présentent que des antiques.'

A picture of Josephine painted by Gérard in 1807[1] shows her wearing a pair of cameo clasps and a tiara of cameos linked by chains. One of her diadems survives, cut out of a single piece of shell with applications of gold round the cameo medallions carved upon it.[2] A private collection in England includes a *parure* that is said to have belonged to her: a crown (Plate 172a) and a lesser coronal (Plate 172b), earrings, a bracelet, a slide and comb all set with cameos in gold, rather coarsely matted and decorated with enamel in a blue that is neither royal blue nor lilac but between the two.[3] The crown, comb and clasp are set with cornelians; the rest with onyx and shell. The *parure* is of Imperial magnificence, but even a modest bourgeoise might possess a shell cameo set in gold (Plate 175a). That illustrated is a little poem in yellows, from the shaded tints of the shell to the varied golds of the setting, which has a wreath of laurel leaves in pale gold on a matted ground of dark gold with delicately beaded rims. Others were less expensively set in steel. Their manufacture continued in Italy all through the nineteenth century.

Other relatively inexpensive ornaments were made from *jaseron*, a very fine Venetian gold chain in fashion for about seven years between 1804 and 1811. Ingres' portrait of Madame Philibert Rivère,[4] painted in 1805, depicts her as wearing a necklace of six rows of it with bracelets to match. It was sometimes combined with plaques of the minute pictorial mosaics manufactured in Florence and Rome. Ingres' *Belle Zélie*,[5] painted in the following year, wears long earrings, and a modest pearl necklace worn with the clasp to the front. In 1804 combs were in fashion with quiver tops filled with arrows, and earrings formed as bunches of currants of cornelian; and in 1805 short necklaces and bracelets above the elbow,[6] and earrings of coral cherries.[7] In that year, too, the Pope started a new fashion at Paris when in November, after he had come there for Napoleon's coronation, he gave rosaries to the ladies of the Court. Villeneuve's Journal records 'Toutes les marchandes du Palais-Royal, bijoutiers et autres . . . vendent les chapelets'.[8] Another fleeting fashion was launched when in 1806 Napoleon gave his

[1] Masson, *Joséphine*, Plate on p. 28.
[2] Vever I, p. 41; in 1906 it belonged to Monsieur Le Bargy.
[3] The *parure* is in two red leather cases, which have spaces for a short necklace, a longer necklace, and two pairs of clasps or earrings.
[4] In the Louvre.   [5] At Rouen.
[6] Vever, I, p. 16, plate facing.   [7] *Art décoratif*, I, 1908, p. 178.
[8] Quot. *Art décoratif*, I, 1908, p. 180.

sister Elisa Bacciochi a bracelet of semi-precious stones of which the initials formed a motto, to celebrate the birth of her daughter.

Jewellery with the imperial devices appears to have been produced on a commercial scale. A collection of engraved designs published by Vallardi[1] gives an undistinguished repertoire, and a pair of gold bracelets in the Bowes Museum at Barnard Castle displays the NN and eagles and laurels of the Napoleonic iconography.

One of the technically most interesting kinds of costume jewellery of the early nineteenth century was that made of cast iron, for which a foundry was first set up in Berlin in 1804.[2] The early necklaces produced by the factory were formed of very light openwork medallions of classical subjects that are miracles of sulphur casting (Plate 175b), usually set in reeded or beaded gold. The répertoire was small: eight or ten models sufficed, sometimes linked by medallions of smaller size, sometimes with rings copied from a Greek earring.[3] In 1813 the Berlin factory achieved a new fame, for it produced the iron jewels worn by those who had given their golden ornaments for the funds of the rising against the Napoleonic occupation.

When Napoleon married the Archduchess Marie Louise of Austria in 1810 he bought her fresh *parures*, since Josephine naturally kept all hers, and indeed acquired an immense ruby and diamond *parure* in 1811.[4] Marie Louise was given a great set of diamonds: diadem, necklace, comb, earrings, bracelets, belt and head-dress; another of pearls, another of emeralds and diamonds, another of rubies, another of sapphires, and another of opals and diamonds.[5] Pauline Borghese rivalled the last with a morning *parure* of opals including a flat bandeau of opals set in diamonds and opal shoulder brooches; she wears it in her portrait by Robert Lefebvre, with bracelets of many little gold chains.[6]

After 1812 Napoleon bought no more *parures*;[7] all the money he and his nation could lay their hands on went in campaigns. The Empress bought a *parure* in faceted steel,[8] and the French manufacturers of such jewels — notably Frichot, Henriet and Schey[9] — did better business than Nitot with his diamonds.

Then, in 1814, the Bourbons returned, with 'une noblesse désargentée mais authentique', and for a short time it was the fashion to wear no jewels at all.[10] Some of the great Napoleonic *parures* of crown jewels passed once more into the King's hands, and

[1] Bib. Nat. Estampes Le 56a.
[2] Clifford Smith, p. 330; H. Schmitz, *Die Berliner Eisenkunstguss*, 1917 and 1926.
[3] Example in the Victoria and Albert Museum.
[4] Necklace, comb, diadem, girandole earrings, belt and a pair of bracelets, all of large rubies surrounded by diamonds. Vever, I, p. 50.
[5] Bapst, *Couronne*, p. 582.
[6] In the Musée de Versailles.
[7] Bapst, *Couronne*, p. 594.
[8] Archives Nationales o²30.
[9] Vever, I, p. 108, 110.
[10] Vever, I, p. 89.

between 1815 and 1820 were remounted by Bapst in a deliberate pastiche of eighteenth-century style.[1] The portrait of the Duchess of Angoulême by the Baron Gros,[2] painted not long after the Restoration, depicts her wearing a very deep diadem and a large waist-buckle, both of diamonds.

The typical Restoration jewels, however, are those of relatively small intrinsic value. The Crown Jewels still existed, at least in part, but few people had money to buy diamonds; and when they did they had them set in spreading collets to increase their apparent size. When a Neapolitan Princess arrived to marry the Duc de Berry the wedding present of jewellery she received from the City of Paris was set with paste.[3] The ordinary wear, even at court, was gold set with semi-precious stones, especially topazes and amethysts. These jewels, however, were designed in the grand manner to give the maximum of effect. Industry was beginning to invade the domain of art; in 1815 the Paris jeweller Odiot sent his son to London to study the new industrial techniques for jewels.[4] It even seems as if the Restoration fashion for *cannetille* — matted gold adorned with rather coarse filigrees — and for such gems as amethysts, topazes and aquamarines originated in England. The very name of *cannetille* was derived from the gold embroideries of the Imperial era, and the term well expresses the facile rotundities of the gold jewellery. The *Lady's Magazine* for June, 1790, recommends necklaces of two rows of filigree, and the *Morning Post* for January 30th, 1800, declares topazes and amethysts to be the most fashionable stones for earrings and necklaces. Miss Mitford in 1806 tells of meeting the rich Mrs. Beaumont wearing a necklace, bandeau, tiara, cestus, armlets, bracelets, brooches and shoe-knots all set with large amethysts. 'All these she wore', wrote the nineteen-year-old novelist, 'and I must confess, for a small dinner party, appeared rather too gaily decorated.'[5]

In Paris the fashion for topazes, amethysts, and aquamarines set in gold came in after 1815. A *grande parure* now in the Metropolitan Museum of New York, set with large amethysts in gold of several colours, comprises a tiara-comb, earrings, necklace, brooch, and a pair of bracelets (Plate 174). The aim of the whole is not only to produce the maximum effect, but also to produce it with the minimum of work. The flowers and leaves of the elaborate gold settings are mechanically stamped out to save labour. A similar economy in man-hours strikes the authentic modern note in the contemporary gold jewellery (Plate 176); it is stamped out of sheet metal, and only finished by hand. There is of necessity something a little vulgar about it, as there is about the fashionable contrast between amethysts and turquoises.[6] It is not surprising that the well-bred

[1] ibid., I, p. 123.　　　　　　　　　　　[2] In the Musée de Versailles.
[3] Barrera, p. 109.　　　　　　　　　　　[4] Joan Evans, *English Jewellery*, p. 155.
[5] V. Watson, *Mary Russell Mitford*, 1949, p. 68. A few weeks later Miss Mitford herself borrowed a necklace of Scotch pebbles with brooches and ornaments to match to wear at a ball at Alnwick.
[6] See, for example, a *demi-parure* in the Cory Bequest in the Victoria and Albert Museum.

bourgeoises who were painted by David and Ingres about 1820 wear very little jewellery. David's portrait of Madame Morel de Tangry and her two daughters,[1] for instance, shows the older lady wearing a gold chain and a serpent waist clasp. One of her daughters wears a gold tiara-comb with coral knobs; the other a three-string garnet necklace, a belt-clasp to match, and a spy-glass on a chain. In 1821 a fashion-paper[2] says that pearl necklaces are for girls of twenty and diamond *rivières* for dowagers. For married women 'de bonne compagnie' emeralds and amethysts are suitable, though gold snake necklaces are even nicer. Garnets are for little girls, and amber is for *grisettes*. Steel may be worn at concerts, jet at formal dinner parties; and paste is suitable only for actresses. Jet, indeed, came into fashion — together with Berlin iron work — when in 1820 the assassination of the Duc de Berry plunged society into mourning.[3] Its manufacture at Whitby continued through the long decades of the century in which Queen Victoria's widowhood kept mourning in fashion in England.[4] Similar influences introduced the use of black enamel in religious jewels of a Protestant kind, with no direct commemorative intention. The Cory Bequest in the Victoria and Albert Museum, for instance, includes a bracelet of gold enamelled black, lightened with diamonds and pearls, with five hanging lockets, adorned with a star, an A, and a cross, anchor and heart, for Faith, Hope and Charity. It must date from about 1870.

By about 1820 the recurring miracle of France's recovery from the ravages of war had once more happened, and jewellers could turn as of old to the creation of new diamond jewels. These were strongly naturalistic in design, with flowers and ears of corn and butterflies, and the style remained in fashion with relatively slight modifications for fifty years and more (Plate 177). Little but the technique of setting was changed. A huge bouquet brooch of diamonds — partly brilliants and partly rose-cut — made by Bapst, was given to the Duchesse de Berry on the birth of the Duc de Bordeaux in 1820;[5] it was over eight inches long. About 1840 such naturalistic bunches were a little modified by the introduction of dripping cascades of diamonds, like the seeds of some unknown plant. This decoration 'en pampilles' remained in fashion for at least fifteen years, and ended in a fashion for diamond aigrettes of corn, barley, and feathers, worn in the hair very much to the side, and often completed with real feathers.[6]

About 1845 greater naturalism was given to these bouquets by the use of translucent green enamel for the leaves, but the fashion did not endure for long. Froment Meurice, in his designs of 1849,[7] succeeded in producing naturalistic roses, lilies and pinks in diamonds and coloured stones without the aid of enamel; and the naturalistic jewels in

---

[1] In the Louvre. [2] Quoted Vever, I, p. 136.
[3] See Vever, I, pp. 134 and 344. By 1827 several firms were manufacturing it in Paris.
[4] See Flower, p. 22. The fashion for jet was revived by Adelina Patti in 1867, ibid., p. 124.
[5] Vever, I, p. 125; Bloche, p. 53.
[6] Vever, II, p. 227. [7] ibid., I, 174.

diamonds and precious stones that were admired in the 1851 Exhibition had no such contrasting colours as enamel afforded. A bouquet in rubies and diamonds by Messrs. J. V. Morel and Co. of London[1] included a rose, a tulip and a morning glory, and was especially admired because it took to pieces and could be transformed into a stomacher, head-dress, brooches and bracelet. It was rivalled by the jewels exhibited by a Petersburg firm[2] which included a diadem of bryony leaves in diamonds with fruits of emerald, a *berthe* of diamond currant branches with ruby fruit,[3] a bouquet of wild roses and lily of the valley in diamonds and a branch of ipomea in diamonds and turquoises.

In 1855 Fontenay, in the same spirit, composed an elegant diadem of diamond blackberry leaves, blossoms and fruit, narrow at the front and spreading out more deeply at the back, with light sprays reaching to the nape of the neck. Some of its lightness was due to the use of a new metal, platinum, for some of the settings.[4] Eight years later Massin produced the first of his wild roses: a jewel that was so much admired that versions of it were produced for some twenty years.[5] The final expression of naturalism in diamonds was the spray of lilac shown in the Exhibition of 1867 and bought by the Empress (Plate 179); the workman had a spray of real lilac on the bench before him all the time he was working at it.[6]

Already, however, the style had become too far cheapened and stereotyped. Massin had written:[7] 'J'ai vu en 1851 — que dis-je, j'ai fait plus que voir, j'ai pratiqué comme ouvrier cette joaillerie détestable dont on ne mourait pas, mais dont on ne vivait pas non plus, et lorsque je m'étonnais devant mon patron Fester de ce délabrement de toutes choses, il me disait "Que voulez-vous faire? Pourvu que je fasse de feuillages pointus avec des fleurs rondes ou des feuillages ronds avec des fleurs pointues, beaucoup de chatons, le tout à trente sous la pierre, c'est tout ce qu'on me demande".'

The only rival style to naturalism was one based on the French royal tradition of the eighteenth century.[8] Most of the very considerable remains of the Crown Jewels were reset for the marriage of Napoleon III and Eugénie in 1853;[9] and a good many of the jewels were designed in the *style Marie Antoinette*. A typical example is a diamond and pearl brooch by Lemonnier, eighteenth century in its general design and only

---

[1] *Reports of Juries*, 1852, III, p. 1119.   [2] Kaemmerer and Zeftigen.

[3] It seems to have inspired the *berthe* of diamond gooseberry leaves made from the crown jewels exhibited at the Paris Exhibition of 1855 and accompanied after 1865 by a garland of sixteen brooches each set with a central diamond with gooseberry leaves round and hanging *pampilles*. They formed a favourite *parure* of the Empress Eugénie. Bloche, p. 45.

[4] Vever, II, p. 163. Two Paris jewellers had advertised mourning rings in platinum as early as 1828. ibid., I, p. 119.

[5] Vever, II, p. 220.   [6] ibid., II, p. 289.   [7] ibid., II, p. 220.

[8] In England a certain amount of diamond jewellery was produced on more geometrical lines, notably Maltese and Jerusalem crosses; one of the latter, for example, was bought from Garrards by William IV in 1839. See Garrard, p. 103.

[9] Bapst, *Couronne*, p. 654.

nineteenth century in the details of its leafage[1] (Plate 180). Some of the great rose diamonds from the royal *Toison d'Or* were reset as another brooch (Plate 181) in a yet more careful pastiche of eighteenth-century workmanship.[2] At the Paris Exhibition of 1855 a further series of ornaments made for her use from the diamonds of the Crown Jewels was exhibited, including a belt formed of knots of brilliants and a diadem of ribbons, a *parure* completed in 1863 by two shoulder knots joined by four diamond chains,[3] intended for the fixing of a court train.

After about 1855, however, a new element of pure dressmaker's display makes itself evident in the Empress's jewels. Soon after 1856 Bapst made her a great *berthe* of diamond net-work with seventy-three pear pearls hanging in the reticulations: and the pearls had to be false, for enough real ones of the right size could not be found.[4]

The sequence of style can be better studied in the nineteenth century in the ornaments set with less precious stones than in diamond jewellery. It was an age not of great movements in art, that might find fitting expression in the most precious materials, but rather of passing fashions that had their greatest influence on jewels that were frankly a part of dress. In 1822, for example, there was a fashion for belt and bracelet clasps formed of linked hands; in the next year a fashion-paper declares: 'On porte . . . de larges bracelets d'or mat tout unis, qui semblent un lingot d'or . . . et que l'on trouverait affreux s'ils n'étaient pas à la mode.'[5] In 1825 every *élégante* had to wear a pendant 'en ferronnière' in the middle of her forehead, and two years later there was a fashion for theatrically Gothic golden belts with a very long piece hanging down in front.[6] In 1827, again, men of elegance wore a heavy gold chain — *chaîne de forçat* — over their black velvet waistcoats, going round their necks and into a pocket, and securing a purse, monocle or watch.[7] The feminine equivalent was no less heavy but was Gothic in design and supported a cross.[8]

In 1828 the actress Mademoiselle Mars had the misfortune to have her jewels stolen, and the list of them[9] gives an idea of the proportion between really precious jewels and those of a lesser kind. Of the first order she had two rows of brilliants in raised collets; eight sprays of wheat set with brilliants; a garland for the hair in brilliants; girandole earrings and a diamond cross. Of the intermediate kind to be worn *en demi-toilette* was a *sévigné* in coloured gold with a burnt topaz in the centre surrounded by large brilliants, with three opal drops similarly set, the gold studded with rubies and pearls; and a very

---

[1] Vever, II, p. 16.

[2] In the Louvre; it is for some inexplicable reason commonly called the 'broche reliquaire'.

[3] Vever, II, p. 141; Bloche, p. 33.

[4] ibid., II, p. 135.   [5] Vever, I. p. 107.

[6] Vever, I, p. 97. A remarkable example is pictured in the portrait of the Duchesse de Berry by Dubois Drahonnet in the Museum of Amiens.

[7] Vever, I, p. 141.   [8] ibid., I, p. 102.   [9] Barrera, pp. 110, 112.

complete *parure* of opals set in gold studded with small emeralds. Fashion really comes into its own with her bracelets: a Gothic armlet of enamelled gold set with a topaz, emeralds and brilliants; a bracelet of cameos set in square gold plaques, linked by wrought links; a bracelet of the kind known as 'bonne-foi', made of serpents; another in Greek key pattern set with angels' heads carved in turquoise and a cameo of Augustus; another made like a dog-collar with a sardonyx cameo clasp; another 'à la Cléopâtre', a snake of gold enamelled black, the head set with turquoises; and a seventh made as a chain with a heart padlock and 'graven with Hebrew Characters'.

A little later bracelets were yet more closely integrated into the dress; one in the Cory Bequest is a frill of delicately spotted gold to be worn like a cuff at the wrist.

The deep décolletages of the time encouraged a certain elaboration in necklaces. Heavy festoons were in vogue, whether of pearls or chains of delicate design, hanging from medallions either jewelled, enamelled or set with cameos in malachite. Malachite, indeed, is a characteristic stone of the decades between 1820 and 1840, whether carved or sliced into thin plaques.

The description of jewels on sale at Fossin's shop in Paris in 1834[1] shows little change from those in Mademoiselle Mars' casket. It records diadems, clasps, *rivières*, shoulder knots, *sévignés*, bandeaux, ears of corn and long earrings set with diamonds; opals set in black enamel powdered with little diamonds; turquoises set in dark gold ornamented with hieroglyphs; cameos; long chains set with coloured stones; Gothic bracelets and brooches, and card-cases 'like the Book of Hours of a chatelaine'.

These general descriptions show two new factors at work in the design of jewellery — factors that in fact fuse and merge: Romanticism and the revival of long-dead styles. A false and romantic Gothicism, that is not without its charm, came into vogue about 1830,[2] influenced less by engraved designs made for jewels than by the frontispieces and vignettes of 'romantic' books. It was a facet of the 'style cathédrale', with ogival forms, saints and angels, knights and pages and all the attributes of chivalry (Plate 182). Its most learned exponent was Froment Meurice, who though a craftsman rarely carried out his own designs;[3] in his work there is in consequence a curious literary and graphic quality; his jewels are like vignettes in the round (Fig. 34). The more elaborate his designs the more evident is the quality: a notable instance is his Gothic bracelet adorned with a large plaque with scenes from the life of Saint Louis.[4] In England A. W. Pugin between 1844 and 1850 designed Gothic jewels for Hardman and Co. of Birmingham (Plates 188, 189a and 189b). A much less learned Romanticism brought Scottish jewels with cairngorms and fresh-water pearls into fashion on the other side of the Channel.

---

[1] *Protée*, July 1834, quoted Vever, I, p. 219.   [2] Vever, I, p. 152.
[3] ibid., I, p. 178.   [4] Vever, I, p. 154.

FIG. 34. Engraved design. Froment Meurice. c. 1840

A rival style was based — equally by way of contemporary engravings — on that of the Renaissance. As early as 1830 the Duchesse de Berry encouraged Fauconnier to revive this style,[1] but his efforts were only moderately successful. By 1838 Frédéric Philippi was finding a certain vogue for his jewels of centaurs and fabulous animals with bodies of baroque pearls,[2] and by 1847 Froment Meurice too was producing designs in Renaissance style.[3] It was exploited a little later by the firm of Schichtegroll of Vienna (Plate 190). Meanwhile Fortunrato Pio Castellani of Rome was producing versions of classical Roman jewellery in gold and filigree that were much more archaeologically accurate. He seems to have begun producing jewels in the style about 1826, and to have continued, with relatively little change, until his retirement in 1851[4] (Plate 192b).

The eighteen-forties were much less poverty-stricken in France than they were in England; indeed a considerable measure of industrial prosperity brought a comfortable sufficiency of wealth to the middle classes. In their service the Romantic styles of Gothic and Renaissance were exploited by lesser men than Froment Meurice. The Revolution of 1848 might leave France for a few years without Court or Queen or Empress,[5] but the steady quiet stream of bourgeois jewellery continued with little change. At the

[1] ibid., I, p. 111.   [2] ibid., II, p. 195.   [3] ibid., I, p. 158.
[4] His firm continued to produce jewels in the style until a much later date.
[5] It had a great effect on the luxury trade; Froment Meurice would have had to shut his workrooms but for some Church orders. Vever, I, p. 174.

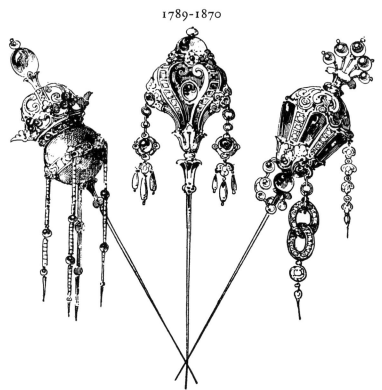

FIG. 35. Engraved design for hair-pins. Julienne. 1840

Exhibition of 1849 jewels of five kinds were exhibited:[1] filigree, with ornaments of metallic net, *cannetille*, coloured gold or small pearls; jewels of polished gold with stamped decoration, in the English style; 'le genre de Paris', fine both in materials and workmanship; diamond work; and 'le bijou d'art', in solid gold or silver, modelled or chased like a piece of miniature sculpture. Of these, filigree, polished gold and 'art jewellery' were all in essentials bourgeois. All are represented in any considerable collection of nineteenth-century jewels, whether in complete *parures* or in the *demi-parures* consisting only of brooch or necklace, and earrings. The filigree jewels are perhaps most charming when their lace-like fret of gold is enhanced by pearls and coloured stones (Plate 185); and the coarser *cannetille* is sometimes given an air of fairy delicacy by the use of enamel. A *demi-parure*, for instance (Plate 186) consists of a flexible necklace made like a ribbon in double knitting of fine gold wire, the upper surface studded with five rows of minute rosettes, those of the outer and middle rows enamelled alternately red with white centre, turquoise with black centre, black with white centre and green with red centre, with the intermediate rows in plain gold. The central pendant which

[1] *See* Rouvenat.

177

masks the clasp is set with a sea-green chrysoprase in a setting of filigree gold relieved by leaves enamelled alternately translucent red and green. Below it hang three chrysoprase drops in rosette settings to match the necklace; the drop earrings are similarly set. A number of jewels — bow and scroll brooches, bracelets (Plate 184) and lesser ornaments (Plate 187a) — were made of gold chased all over in scrolling patterns; a similar decoration in higher relief was used to give a vaguely shell-like ornament to watch cases.[1] Some jewels of the time are valueless but for their workmanship and design; a simple necklace, for example (Plate 187b), formed of small round plaques of matted gold enamelled in white, black and opaque lavender blue with petal-shaped designs in relief, and set with crystals and amethysts in shallow collets, is a miracle of taste on a minute scale. One feels that one has known the modest and exquisite gentlewoman for whom it was made.

The more ordinary jewels of the mid-nineteenth century followed a course of fashion that can be dated with some exactness. About 1835 the motive of a bird defending its nest against a snake came into fashion, and stayed in use as a jewel design for at least twenty years.[2] About 1840 the Algerian campaigns brought in a fashion for the elaborate knots and tassels of Algerian dress on pendants, brooches, earrings and the elaborate gold hair-pins then in fashion (Fig. 35). The final campaigns in Algeria brought in a fresh wave of similar influences in the years round 1860.[3] Similarly in 1852 Falize made a chatelaine in Moorish style enamelled with inscriptions in Arabic.[4] About 1848 there was a vogue for gold brooches and bracelets shaped like boughs of rotten wood; two years later tartans were in fashion, and Jacques Petit had some success with bracelets enamelled in plaided designs to match, made like flexible ribbons with a diamond buckle.[5] Mere prettiness was represented by jewels that were *pavé* all over with tiny turquoises: sometimes in flower designs, like the bouquet of convolvulus in the Cory bequest (Plate 178); more often in chains of heavy links, rosettes, hearts and padlocks.

The influence of the Empress Eugénie was against such petty trifles. Her wedding jewels naturally included some not intended for full-dress wear, but they were both simple and precious: a *parure*, for example, in pearls and rubies, and another in black pearls. It is typical that in the Winterhalter portrait of her and her ladies in morning dress, painted in 1854, she alone amongst them wears no jewels; they wear bracelets and pearl necklaces, but her beauty suffices unadorned. At other times she too wore pearls, sometimes in as many as five splendid rows; Princess Mathilde Bonaparte and Princess Metternich wore others no less splendid.

[1] Examples in the Nelthropp Collection in the Guildhall Museum are hall-marked 1823 and 1828.
[2] Vever, I, p. 153.   [3] Vever, II, pp. 184, 186.
[4] Rücklin, II, Plate 154. The Cory Bequest includes three plaques of black glasswork Arabic inscriptions in diamond sparks, set in pearled rims.
[5] Vever, II, pp. 180, 188.

A less important but parallel development may be followed in Victorian England,[1] with a time-lag of some ten years behind Paris. In France 'gothic' jewels came in about 1830; in England it is not until 1839 that the *World of Fashion* can declare:[2] 'The forms of our *bijoux* are now entirely borrowed from the style of the Middle Ages; massive great pins, with the heads richly chased, or composed of coloured gems set in small flowers ... all our ornaments, in short, are *moyen âge* ...'

The characteristic English trends were towards simplicity and sentiment. Queen Victoria wore classic *parures* on state occasions, but at other times favoured trifling sentimental jewels, such as a bracelet set with the first teeth of all her children. Every brooch and locket was apt to have a receptacle behind for a miniature or hair. As late as 1858, indeed, the English fashion paper *La Belle Assemblée*[3] recorded a revival of hair jewellery.

'The sentimental jewellery of Limonnier is of another character from what all the world is acquainted with, and which gives the locket, or brooch, or ring, in which some beloved tress or precious curl is enshrined, the appearance of having been designed from a mortuary tablet. Have we not all met ladies wearing as a brooch, by way of loving remembrance, a tomb between two willow trees formed of the hair of the individual for whom their crape was worn, and which from its very nature must be laid aside with it? Our artist converts the relic into an ornament for all times and places — expands it into a broad ribbon as a bracelet and fastens it with a forget-me-not in turquoises and brilliants, weaves it into chains for the neck, the *flacon*, or the fan; makes it into a medallion of leaves and flowers; and of these last the most beautiful specimens I have seen have been formed of the saintly white hair of age. This he converts into orange-flowers, white roses, chrysanthemums and most charming of all, clusters of lily-of-the-valley.'[4]

Another English fashion, that was considered the height of unobtrusive good taste, was to wear a velvet ribbon round the throat with the ends crossed in front and fastened by a brooch. The fashion was invented about 1838 and endured for twenty years.

The juries of the 1851 Exhibition seem to have been a little disappointed in its jewellery exhibits,[5] which indeed showed little novelty of style. Messrs. Garrard, besides handsome diamond *parures* of the usual kind, exhibited 'an elegant gold bracelet of Gothic design, on which are chased out, upon a trellis work of gold on blue enamel, carved in the style of the fifteenth century, two angels holding a pearl and ruby, and capable of being detached: the design by Mr. Smith'. Other exhibits included a

---

[1] For a general study see M. Flower, *Victorian Jewellery*, 1951.
[2] Quoted Flower, p. 16, n.1. [3] Quoted Flower, p. 21.
[4] Directions to the amateur for making hair jewellery will be found in Alexanna Speight, *The Lock of Hair*, 1871.
[5] *Reports of Juries*, 1852, III, p. 1119. There were four or five exhibits of imitation jewels by Paris makers and at least one of English manufacture.

pendant in Renaissance style, and a bracelet 'in imitation of the Sculptures of Nineveh' (See Plate 192c). The 'bijou d'art' was represented by a bracelet of oxidised silver by Rudolphe of Paris, with the figures of three children contending for some birds, and another enamelled with two cupids playing among vines and holding up a sapphire set in four claws of pearl.

After the Exhibition a fresh wave of Neo-Greek classicism came in to complicate the already eclectic design of jewels. In 1855 Froment Meurice exhibited a brooch combining the Greek subject of Arethusa with Renaissance elements,[1] and a little later Alexis Falize used a great deal of black enamel on gold in Greek anthemion designs. In 1860 the Campana Collection of some twelve hundred pieces of Greek, Etruscan and Roman jewellery was acquired by the Louvre and inspired the work of many jewellers, notably Fontenay and Castellani.[2] The portrait of the Empress Eugénie painted by Winterhalter in 1864[3] shows her wearing a great golden diadem of the classical lunette shape set with a single emerald. Cheap reproductions of ancient jewels of a heavy kind were made by the electrotype process, notably by Alexandre Gueyton,[4] chiefly for use as buckles and clasps.

In the years after 1860 pettiness and silliness invaded the design of jewels. Lizards, snakes, dragonflies and beetles were in fashion,[5] and gold earrings were designed for daytime wear with such subjects as sitting hens, stable lanterns, barrows, windmills, lamps and watering-cans. They were often as much as four inches long.[6] They were rivalled by monumental jewels, extremely plain, in the English taste; the gold was given a fine colour by an acid bath, and was often set with coral or ornamented with black enamel.[7] In 1861, for instance, Félix Duval produced massive and hideous jewels like harness or handcuffs, formed of chains and bolts and shackles and screws. Some of it was called 'chemin de fer' or 'machine à vapeur'.[8] Slightly less monumental, but hardly less ugly, were the jewels shaped as horseshoes and whips and bits and spurs and lucky nails; their vogue began about 1857 and reached its height in 1864.[9] In 1869 'a very coquettish suite, of dogs' heads cut in coloured coral and set in polished jet', was recommended for wear in a country house.[10]

Such sporting jewels were succeeded by immensely heavy lockets, intended for photographs, often set with half-pearl and turquoises: an English fashion that conquered Paris.[11]

---

[1] Vever, II, p. 121.   [2] ibid., II, p. 148.   [3] ibid., II, p. 260.

[4] Vever, II, p. 21. Similar reproductions of Celtic jewels had been shown by a Dublin firm at the 1851 Exhibition.

[5] Vever, II, p. 224. Fontenay made beetles and a grasshopper in jewelled jade looted from Pekin. In England there was a fashion for house-flies, under crystal or jewelled, about 1867. See Flower, p. 123.

[6] Vever, II, p. 96.

[7] ibid., II, p. 264. The use of 15, 12 and 9 carat gold in England had been authorised in 1854.

[8] ibid., II, p. 268.   [9] Vever, II, p. 269; Flower, p. 34.

[10] Flower, p. 123.   [11] Vever, III, p. 350.

The Universal Exhibition at Paris in 1867 was no less a success than the London Exhibition of 1851 had been, and gave a more important place to jewellery, in which section the most important exhibitors were all French. Design was eclectic: Louis XVI, Etruscan and Renaissance styles were all represented. Mariette Bey was excavating in the Nile Valley; the Suez Canal was nearing completion, and as a consequence many people were interested in Egypt: and the novelty in the jewellery exhibited was ornaments in Egyptian style.[1] Festoon and fringe necklaces and *berthes* were in fashion, to complete the very low *décolletages* that the Empress favoured, and humming-birds in diamonds a rage.[2] Long brooches for fastening cashmere shawls were in demand, often of gold ornamented with lines and anthemia in black enamel. It was, however, significantly in technique rather than in design that change was evident. Aluminium, then a rare metal, made a fleeting appearance in jewellery,[3] *pavé* settings were much in evidence,[4] and the same principle was developed in diamond setting in the *monture illusion* in which hardly any metal was visible.[5]

Such ornaments, in which the legendary techniques that had made jewellery a kind of sculpture in miniature were brought to nothing, were a prelude to a new and debased age of jewels. The years round 1870 mark fundamental changes in every aspect of the history of the craft. In England Queen Victoria had already retired into the seclusion of her widowhood; in France the fall of Napoleon III in 1870 left the country not only without a monarch to guide its destinies, but also without an Empress to lead its fashions.[6] South African diamonds first appeared on the Paris market — then, but not for long, the chief international exchange for the stones[7] — in 1869; by about 1872 they had become a real factor in the trade.[8] The consequent use of larger and poorer stones coincided with the invention of the *monture illusion* to substitute an ideal of mere glitter for the formal beauty of earlier diamond jewellery. The decline of the *genre* was accelerated by the use of mass-produced settings. As early as 1852 a jeweller named Beltête who suffered from rheumatism in his fingers had invented a mechanical process for cutting out and stamping settings.[9] The process, improved and developed, is still in use; and the manufacture of 'jeweller's findings' has become an active branch of the trade. The jewels produced by such processes have a curiously soulless quality; no person of sensibility can find in them the poetry that for centuries had been discoverable

[1] The vogue continued for a few years and in 1873 a Turin jeweller exhibited some portentous ornaments in Egyptian style at Vienna. Rücklin, II, Plate 155.

[2] Vever, II, p. 292.   [3] Vever, II, p. 271.

[4] An example of this year is a pendant in the Royal collection given to Princess Victoria Mary of Teck by her godmother Queen Victoria.

[5] Vever, II, p. 306. In 1863 the Empress had two diamond ball-headed hair-pins set in this fashion. Bloche, p. 31.

[6] After Napoleon's death in 1873 the exiled Empress sold many of her jewels.

[7] *See* A. Cerfberr de Médelsheim.   [8] Vever, II, p. 350.   [9] Vever, II, p. 231, n. 1.

in jewels. The aesthetes of Des Esseintes'[1] generation found diamonds common, rubies and emeralds depreciated, and turquoises vulgar; the old poetry was dead, though echoes of it lived on in the names of such gems as chrysoberyls and peridots and olivines and almandines and cymophanes and aquamarines. Beauty which has departed from things may live on in words: and so it was with jewels in the last third of the nineteenth century.

[1] J. K. Huysmans, *À Rebours*, chapter IV; written in 1884.

Envoi

It is not easy to see the future for the art of jewellery; it may even be considered that as an art it has not a future. For all the centuries of recorded time it has existed as an art in which style and fashion were set by the taste of an aristocracy; bourgeois jewellery, peasant jewellery and jewellery in less precious materials such as we now call costume jewellery, all imitated court fashions.

This source of inspiration has come to an end. Since 1918 comparatively few jewels have been designed for court wear in any country; since 1939 hardly any. In jewels, as in furniture, we have learned to appreciate the craftsmanship of the past, and enough jewels survive from more splendid ages to meet all the ceremonial needs of the present. Moreover the political and economic tendencies of the Western world do not now encourage the making of splendid jewels even for the *nouveaux riches* who have no ancestral caskets to draw on. Many countries recognize a purchase tax or a luxury tax as a fiscal weapon, and this, whatever else it falls on, is certain to fall on jewels. Indeed if people buy jewels nowadays, even antique ones, it is most often as an investment, unlikely to depreciate, on which a capital levy need not be paid.

The trade is now divided into categories of designers, craftsmen and salesmen, and they rarely overlap. It is significant that Fabergé, who to many people is the Cellini of the late nineteenth century, never made a jewel in his life and only gave the most general ideas for their design: he was a great salesman, and that in his day sufficed. In London now very few jewel-sellers have even a workroom of their own. Designers and craftsmen are more closely linked; a jewel designer who goes through the professional course at a school of art ends with a fair knowledge of its technique, though one not comparable with that of the apprentice who has served his five years. Yet for one as for the other, once qualified, there is hardly enough work to go round. Only a few very wealthy firms can afford to make jewels of the fine kind,[1] and an experienced diamond setter or designer of diamond jewellery may think himself lucky if he finds a job with a firm making costume jewellery in marcasite.

Costume jewellery is a more flourishing trade. Yet it is more and more of a trade and less and less of an art. Every year it grows more mechanized; the machines are still hand

[1] In Paris in 1950 there was an experimental 'Co-operative' of some twelve master craftsmen that held a germ of promise; but France had then no purchase tax.

operated, but production is already on a producer-belt system. Two to three weeks' training in a factory suffices, for skill lies not in style or finish but only in speed.

Design, to be worth anything, must be portentously serious. Even rocaille was designed with the whole heart and mind: it is light as comedy, but it is neither flippant nor cynical. Yet there is something in the ephemeral and meretricious quality of modern 'costume' jewellery which seems to invoke both these qualities in the designer. What the modern world needs in its jewels — as in all else — is the serious pursuit of beauty. Without it all is lost.

What future lies before costume jewellery with no fine jewels to emulate and an increasing trend towards mass production? A hundred years ago machine-made lace began to be produced at a price within the reach of all. In little more than fifty years it had killed the trade in hand-made lace. Will the development of cheap machine-made jewellery have the same effect in this levelling age? Already the American manufacturers are producing costume jewels that are intended to have no longer a life than that of the dress they adorn. It may be that the next century will see jewels being produced that are of no more value or account than a button or a tassel; and one of the oldest of human crafts will have been brought to an end.

Bibliography

M. Accàscina. 'Oreficeria siciliana: il tesoro di Enna', in *Dedalo*, XI, 1930, p. 151.

H. R. d'Allemagne. *Les accessoires du costume et du mobilier depuis le treizième jusqu'au milieu du dix-neuvième siècle*, Paris, 1928.

A. Andersson. 'Anna Reinholdsdotters guldkedja [with English summary]', in *Fornvännen*, Stockholm, 1958, p. 47.

S. Anjou and R. J. Charleston. 'Marc Gunter's designs for jewellers 1684 to 1733', in *Rosska Konstae. Mus.*, 1956, p. 43.

Anon. 'Jewels of Marie-Louise', in *Connoisseur*, CXXXII, 1953, p. 210.

Anon. 'Exhibition of Renaissance Jewels', in *Oberlin College, Allen Memorial Art Museum Bulletin*, XVII, no. 2, 1960, p. 39.

Anon. 'Lady and the marten: an elaborately ornamented mannerist jewel in the form of a marten's head', in *Art News*, LXVI, 1967, p. 40.

Antiquaries, Society of. *Liber Quotidianus Contrarotulatoris Garderobae . . . Edwardi Primi*, 1787.

J. von Arneth. *Monumente des K. K. Münz-und Antiken-Cabinettes in Wien*. Vienna, 1845, and other later eds.

B. Astrand. 'Heliga bokstäver i silver', in *Kulturen*, 1961, p. 92.

A. Babel. *Les métiers de l'ancien Genève. Horlogerie et Orfèvrerie*, Geneva, 1916.

E. Babelon. *Histoire de la gravure sur gemmes en France*, Paris, 1902.

E. Babelon. *Catalogue des camées antiques et modernes de la Bibliothèque Nationale*, Paris, 1897.

M. Baerwald and J. T. Mahoney. *The Story of Jewelry*, London and New York, 1960.

W. Paley Baildon. 'Three Inventories: (1) The Earl of Huntingdon, 1377; (2) Brother John Randolf, 1419; (3) Sir John de Boys, 1426', in *Archaeologia*, LXI, 1908–9, p. 163.

J. Banister. 'Changing fashions in memorial jewellery', in *Antique Dealer and Collectors Guide*, XXII, iv, 1967, p. 53.

G. Bapst. *Histoire des Joyaux de la Couronne de France*, Paris, 1889.

G. Bapst. *Inventaire de Marie-Josèphe de Saxe, Dauphine de France*, Paris, 1883.

G. Bapst. *Testament du roi Jean le Bon*, Paris, 1884.

BIBLIOGRAPHY

G. Bapst. *Du rôle économique des joyaux dans la vie politique et la vie privée pendant la seconde partie du XVIe siècle*, Paris, 1887.

H. Barbet de Jouy. *Musée Impérial du Louvre. Les gemmes et joyaux de la Couronne*, Paris, 1865.

Madame A. De Barrera. *Gems and Jewels*, London, 1860.

H. Barth. *Das Geschmeide, Schmuck- und Edelsteinkunde*, Berlin, 2 vols., 1903.

E. Bassermann-Jordan. *Der Schmuck*, Leipzig, 1909.

C. P. Beard. 'Cap-Brooches of the Renaissance', in *Connoisseur*, CIV, 1939, p. 287.

C. P. Beard. 'The "Lion" jewel, a work of Corvinianus Saur in the possession of Lord Fairhaven', in *Connoisseur*, CI, 1938, p. 72.

S. Beissel. *Kunstschätze des Aachener Kaiserdomes*, Münster Gladbach, 1904.

R. Berliner. *Italian Drawings for Jewellery, 1700–1785*, Cooper Union Museum for the Arts of Decoration, New York, 1940.

Berlin Königliche Museen *see* Königliche Museen zu Berlin

R. de Berquen. *Les Merveilles des Indes orientales et occidentales*, Paris, 1661.

Le Bijou. Revue artistique et industrielle de la bijouterie, 1874–90.

Birmingham City Museum and Art Gallery. *Exhibition of Gemstones & Jewellery*, 1960.

A. Blanchet. 'Une quittance délivrée en 1626 par deux orfèvres pour une chaîne d'or', in *Bull. Soc. Nat. Antiq. de France*, 1956, p. 100.

Y. L. Blanchot. *Les bijoux anciens*, Paris, 1929.

A. Bloche. *La vente des diamants de la Couronne*, Paris, 1888.

A. de Boislisle. 'Inventaire des bijoux . . . appartenant à la Comtesse de Montpensier (1874)', in *Annuaire-Bulletin de la Société de l'histoire de France*, XVII, 1880, p.269.

E. Bonnaffé. *Inventaire de la duchesse de Valentinois*, Paris, 1878.

A. De Boodt (Boethius). *Gemmarvm et Lapidvm Historia*, Hanover, 1609; other eds. 1636, 1647 etc. French trans., *Le parfaict Joaillier*, Lyon, 1644.

A. de la Borderie. 'Inventaire des meubles et bijoux de Marguerite de Bretagne', in *Bulletin de la Société Archéologique de Nantes*, IV, Nantes, 1864, p. 45.

H. Bösch. 'Ein märkischer Familienschmuck aus dem Anfange des 17 Jahrhunderts' in *Mittheilungen aus dem germanischen Nationalmuseum, 1894*, Nuremberg, 1894, p. 73.

E. G. G. Bos. 'Een renaissance-hanger met huwelijkssymbolen', in *Bulletin of the Rijksmuseum*, XIV, 1966, p. 65.

M. Bourbon. 'Inventaire du mobilier d'Yves de Vieux-Pont, 1416', in *Bulletin Archéologique*, 1884, p. 322.

A. Bourguet. 'Les bracelets de la Reine', in *Revue d'histoire diplomatique*, XIX, 1905, p. 441.

R. Boyvin. *Le livre de bijouterie*, Paris, 1876.

BIBLIOGRAPHY

E. D. S. Bradford. *English Victorian Jewellery*, London, 1959.

E. D. S. Bradford. *Four Centuries of European Jewellery*, London, 1953.

J. Braun, S. J. *Meisterwerke der deutschen Goldschmiedekunst der vorgotischen Zeit*, 2 vols., Munich, 1922.

J. S. Brewer. *Letters and Papers, Foreign and Domestic, of the reign of Henry VIII*, Public Record Office, London, 1867–.

P. Brewis. 'A gold Fede-Ring brooch, English of 15th century', in *Archaeologia Aeliana*, 4th series, VII, 1930, p. 184.

P. Brewis. 'Six silver ring brooches of the fourteenth century', in *ibid*, 4th series, IV, p. 105.

British Museum. *The Waddesdon bequest. The collection of jewels, plate and other works of art bequeathed . . . by Baron F. Rothschild M.P.*, C. H. Read. London, 1899.

F. J. Britten. *Old Clocks and Watches and their Makers* (1899), 6th ed., London, 1933.

F. L. Bruel. 'Deux inventaires de bagues, joyaux, pierreries et dorures de la reine Marie de Médicis' in *Archives de l'Art Français*, new series II, 1908, p. 186.

Budapest. Hungarian Museum of Decorative Arts. (*La collection d'orfèvrerie et de joaillerie du Musée . . . et un compte-rendu du trésor des Esterhazi*). A. Somogyi. Hungarian text with French summary, 1963.

C. G. Bulgari. *Argentieri Gemmari e Orafi d'Italia*, Rome, 1958–.

R. F. Burckhardt. 'Ueber vier Kleinodien Karls des Kühnen', in *Anzeiger fur Schweizerische Altertumskunde*, new series XXXIII, Zurich, 1931, p. 247.

J. T. Butler. 'Important acquisition by the Walters Art Gallery', in *Connoisseur*, CLXVII, 1968, p. 65.

J. Caley. 'Extract from the "Liber Memorandorum Cameriorum Receptae Scaccariae" concerning jewels pledged in the 17th of Henry VI to Cardinal Beaufort', in *Archaeologia*, XXI, 1827, p. 34.

J. G. Callander. 'Fourteenth Century Brooches and other Ornaments in the National Museum of Antiquities of Scotland', in *Proc. Soc. Ants. of Scotland*, 5th series, X, 1923–4, p. 160.

R. Cameron. 'Perles', in *L'Oeil*, no. 72, 1960, p. 66.

G. Campori. *Raccolta di cataloghi ed inventarii inediti*, Modena, 1870.

J. Camus. *La venue en France de Valentine Visconti, Duchesse d'Orléans et l'inventaire de ses joyaux apportés de Lombardie*, Turin, 1898.

A. Castellani. *Antique Jewellery and its Revival*, London, 1862.

A. Castellani. *Della Oreficeria Italiana*, Rome, 1872.

B. Cellini. *Trattati . . . dell' Oreficeria . . . della Scultura*, 1568.

B. Cellini. *The Treatises of Benvenuto Cellini on Goldsmithing and Sculpture*, trans. C. R. Ashbee, 1888, reprinted Dover Press, New York, 1967.

BIBLIOGRAPHY

M. C. A. de Cerfberr De Medelsheim. *Diamants, montres et bijoux (Exposition Universelle de 1868)*, Paris, n.d. (1868).

S. J. A. Churchill. 'The Goldsmiths of Rome under the Papal authority'. in *Papers of the British School at Rome*, IV, No. 2, 1907, p. 161.

S. J. A. Churchill. *The Goldsmiths of Italy: some accounts of their guilds, statutes and work, compiled* (by C. G. E. Bunt) *from the . . . material collected by the late Sidney J. A. Churchill*, London, 1926.

G. Claretta. 'Breve notizia sul vasellame e sulle gioie dei Duchi di Savoia alla metà del secolo XV', in *Atti della Società di Archeologia e belli arti per la provincia de Torino*, II, Turin, 1878, p. 227.

H. Clouzot. 'Les Toutin, orfèvres, graveurs et peintres sur émail', in *Revue de l'art ancien et moderne*, XXIV, 1908, p. 456, XXV, 1909, p. 39.

H. Clouzot. 'Les émaillistes de l'Ecole de Blois', in *Revue de l'art ancien et moderne*, XXVI, 1909, p. 101.

H. Clouzot. 'Les émaillistes français sous Louis XIV', in *Revue de l'art ancien et moderne*, XXX, 1911, pp. 119, 179.

A. J. Collins. *Jewels and plate of Queen Elizabeth I: the inventory of 1574*, London, 1955.

L. Courajod (ed). *Livre-journal de Lazare Duvaux, marchand bijoutier ordinaire du Roy, 1748–58*, 2 vols., Paris, 1873.

L. Coutil. 'Broches du Musée des Antiquités de Rouen', in *Bull. de la Soc. Préhistorique française*, II, 1938, p. 1.

J. D. Cowen. 'An English inscribed brooch of the fourteenth century', in *Proc. Soc. Ants. of Newcastle upon Tyne*, 4th series, VII, 1937, p. 203.

J. Cox. *A descriptive catalogue of the several superb. . . pieces of mechanism and jewellery exhibited in . . . the Museum at Spring Gardens, Charing Cross*, London, 1772. French trans., 1773.

J. Cox. *A descriptive inventory of the several exquisite and magnificent pieces of mechanism and jewellery* [etc.], London, 1773. Another ed., 1774.

L. Van Der Cruyen. *Nouveau livre de desseins, contenant les ouvrages de la joaillerie inventés et dessinés par L.v.d.C.*, 1770. Facsimile reproduction, 1912.

L. Cust. 'John of Antwerp, goldsmith, and Hans Holbein', in *Burlington Magazine*, VIII, 1905–6, p. 356.

O. M. Dalton. 'Early brooches of cloisonné enamel', in *Proc. Soc. Ants.*, XX, 1905, p. 64.

A. Darcel. 'Les arts industriels à l'exposition de Londres: la bijouterie et la joaillerie', in *Gazette des Beaux-Arts*, XIII, 1862, p. 437.

C. J. H. Davenport. *Jewellery*, London, 1905.

J. C. Davillier. *Recherches sur l'orfèvrerie en Espagne au moyen âge et à la Renaissance*, Paris, 1879.

BIBLIOGRAPHY

K. Degen. 'Der Mainzer Adlerfurspan im Darmstadter Landesmuseum', in *Mainzer Zeitschrift*, LII, 1937, p. 39.

Chanoine C. C. A. Dehaisnes. *Documents et extraits divers concernant l'histoire de l'art dans la Flandre, l'Artois et le Hainaut, avant le XVe siècle*, Lille, 2 vols., 1886.

P. Deschamps. 'L'orfèvrerie à Conques vers l'an mille', in *Bulletin monumental*, CVI, 1948, p. 75.

A. Détrez. 'Dessins de Bijoux du XVIIIe siècle', in *L'Art décoratif*, XII, 1910, p. 155.

A. Détrez. 'Joailliers aristocratiques sous la Révolution et l'Empire', in *L'Art décoratif*, X, 1908, p. 175.

F. Deuchler. *Die Burgunderbeute: Inventar der Beutestucke aus den Schlachten von Grandson, Murten und Nancy, 1476–77*. Bern, 1963.

H. W. Dickinson. *Matthew Boulton*, Cambridge, 1937.

L. Douet-D'Arcq. *Comptes de l'argenterie des rois de France au XIVe siècle*, Paris, 1851.

L. Douet-D'Arcq. *Nouveau recueil de comptes de l'argenterie des rois de France*, Paris, 1874.

L. Douet-D'Arcq. 'Inventaire des meubles de la reine Jeanne de Boulogne, 1360', in *Bibliothèque de l'Ecole des Chartes*, XL, 1879, p. 545.

Dresden. Grünes Gewölbe. *Schmuckanhänger. Katalog . . .*, Dresden, 1965.

A. Duflos. *Recueil de Dessins de Joaillerie*, Paris, 1767.

F. Dumont. 'Les bijoux romantiques', in *Connaissance des Arts*, no. 29, 1954, p. 46.

F. Dumont. 'Froment Meurice, le Victor Hugo de l'orfèvrerie', in *Connaissance des Arts*, no. 57, 1956, p. 42.

E. Dusenbury. 'Crosses in the collection of the [Newark] Museum', in *Museum*, XII, 1960, no. 2.

Th. M. Duyvené De Wit-Klinkhamer. 'Een vroeg XVIe eeuws medallion', in *Bulletin of the Rijksmuseum*, XIV, 1966, p. 29.

G. Egger. 'Stilverbindung und neue künstlerische Form. Zu einigen Goldschmiedarbeiten des Historismus', in *Alte und moderne Kunst*, no. 79, 1965, p.8.

L. Enault. *Les diamants de la Couronne*, Paris, 1884.

Joan Evans. *English Jewellery from the Fifth Century A.D. to 1800*, London, 1921.

Joan Evans. *English Posies and Posy Rings*, London, 1931.

Joan Evans. 'Wheel-shaped brooches', in *Art Bulletin*, Sept. 1933, p. 197.

Joan Evans. 'Gilles Légaré and his Work', in *Burlington Magazine*, XXX, 1917, p. 140.

Joan Evans. 'Un bijou magique dessiné par Hans Holbein', in *Gazette des Beaux-Arts*, XIV, 1926, p. 357.

Joan Evans. *Magical Jewels of the Middle Ages and the Renaissance*, Oxford, 1922.

John Evans. 'Pilgrims' signs', in *Proceedings of the Society of Antiquaries*, 2nd series, XXII, 1908, p. 102.

BIBLIOGRAPHY

G. Faider-Feytmans. 'Une fibule arquée provenant de Marchelepot', in *Revue du Louvre*, XI, no. I, 1961, p. 11.

F. W. Fairholt. 'On an inventory of the household goods of Sir Thomas Ramsay, Lord Mayor of London 1577, in *Archaeologia* XL, 1866, p. 311.

O. von Falke and H. Frauberger. *Deutsche Schmelzarbeiten des Mittelalters*, Frankfurt, 1904.

O. von Falke and H. Frauberger. *Der Mainzer Goldschmuck der Kaiserin Gisela*, Berlin, 1913.

U. Fischer. 'Ein Renaissanceanhänger im Grünen Gewölbe', *Dresdener Kunstblätter*, VI, 1962, p. 42.

M. Flower. *Victorian Jewellery*, London, 1951. Revised ed., 1967.

H. Focillon. *Benvenuto Cellini*, Paris (1911).

E. Fontenay. *Les bijoux anciens et modernes*, Paris, 1887.

A. Forgeais. 'Enseignes de Pèlerinages', in Vol. II of *Collection de Plombs historiés trouvés dans la Seine*, Paris, 1863.

R. Forrer. *Geschichte des Gold- und Silberschmuckes nach Originalen der Strassburger historischen Schmuck-Ausstellung von 1904*, Strasburg, 1905.

C. D. Fortnum. 'Notes on some of the Antique and Renaissance Gems and Jewels in Her Majesty's Collection at Windsor Castle', in *Archaeologia*, XLV, 1877, p. 1.

C. Fregnac. *Jewellery: from the Renaissance to Art Nouveau*, trans. D. L. de Lauriston, London, 1965.

E. de Fréville. 'Notice historique sur l'inventaire des biens meubles de Gabrielle d'Estrées', in *Bibliothèque de l'Ecole des Chartes*, III, 1841–2, p. 148.

Prince A. Galitzin. *Inventaire des Meubles, Bijoux et Livres estant à Chenonceaux le huit Janvier, 1603*, Paris, 1856.

Garrard and Co. *Garrard's 1721–1911: Crown Jewellers and Goldsmiths during six reigns and three centuries*, London [1912].

J. Gauthier. 'Le portrait de Béatrix de Cusance au Musée du Louvre et l'inventaire de ses joyaux en 1663', in *Académie des Sciences, Belles Lettres et Arts de Besançon; Procès Verbaux et Mémoires*, 1897, Besançon, p. 128.

V. Gay. *Glossaire Archéologique du Moyen âge et de la Renaissance*, 2 vols., Paris, 1882–1928.

P. Gerstner. *Die Entwicklung der Pforzheimer Bijouterie-Industrie von 1767–1907*, Tübingen, 1908.

R. Gilbert. 'American jewelry from the Gold Rush to Art Nouveau', in *Art in America*, LIII, 1965–6, no. 6, p. 80.

T. G. Goldberg, F. Mishukov, N. G. Platonova, M. M. Postnikova-Loseva. *Russkoe zolotoe ... L'orfèvrerie et la bijouterie russes aux XV–XX siècles*, Moscow, 1967.

BIBLIOGRAPHY

G. Gozzadini. *Di alcuni gioielli notati in un libro di ricordi del secolo XVI* [Bologna, c. 1865].

J. M. Graves. *Deux Inventaires de la Maison d'Orléans* (1389 and 1408), Paris, 1926.

G. Gross, 'Au pays des cristaux', in *Costumes et Coutumes*, XXXV, 1962, p. 35.

A. H. Grundy. 'Early XIXth century jewellery', in *Apollo*, LXX, 1959, p. 80.

A. H. Grundy. 'Victorian jewellery', in *Apollo*, LXXIII, 1961, p. 40.

J. J. Guiffrey. *Inventaires de Jean Duc de Berry, 1401–1416*, 2 vols., Paris, 1894–6.

M. Haberlandt. *Völkerschmuck*, Vienna and Leipzig, 1906.

Y. Hackenbroch. *Italienisches Email des frühen Mittelalters*, Bâle, 1938.

Y. Hackenbroch. 'A jewelled necklace in the British Museum', in *Antiquaries Journal*, XXI, 1941, p. 342.

Y. Hackenbroch. 'Commessi', in *Antichità Viva*, V, no. 3, May–June 1966, p. 13.

Y. Hackenbroch. 'Jewels by Giovanni Battista Scolari', in *Connoisseur*, CLIX, 1965, p. 200.

Y. Hackenbroch. 'Renaissance pendants after designs of Jost Amman', in *Connoisseur*, CLX, 1965, p. 58.

Y. Hackenbroch. 'New knowledge on jewels and designs after Etienne Delaune', in *Connoisseur*, CLXII, 1966, p. 82.

Y. Hackenbroch. 'Commessi', in *Metropolitan Museum of Art Bulletin*, new series, XXIV, 1966, no. 7, p. 212.

Y. Hackenbroch. 'Catherine de'Medici and her court jeweller François Dujardin', in *Connoisseur*, CLXIII, 1966, p. 28.

Y. Hackenbroch. 'Jewellery of the court of Albrecht V at Munich', in *Connoisseur*, CLXV, 1967, p. 74.

Y. Hackenbroch. 'Erasmus Hornick as a jeweller', in *Connoisseur*, CLXVI, 1967, p. 54.

Y. Hackenbroch. 'Un gioiello della corte di Monaco ora in Santa Barbara a Mantova', in *Antichità Viva*, VI, no. 3, 1967, p. 51.

A. Haeberle. *Die Goldschmiede zu Ulm*, Ulm, 1934.

W. Halford and C. Young. *The jewellers' book of patterns in hair work*, London, 1864.

Edward Hall. *Henry VIII* (introduction by C. Whibley), 2 vols., London, 1904.

W. J. Hardy. 'On a lawsuit concerning the Lady Elizabeth Stuart's jewels', in *Archaeologia*, LVI, 1898–9, p. 127.

A. Hartshorne. 'The gold chains, the pendants, the paternosters and the zones of the Middle Ages, the Renaissance and later times', in *Archaeological Journal*, LXVI, 1909, p. 77.

A. Hartshorne. 'Notes on collars of SS', in *Archaeological Journal*, XXXIX, 1882, p. 376.

H. Havard. *Dictionnaire de l'ameublement et de la décoration*. 5 vols., Paris, 1887–.

BIBLIOGRAPHY

H. Havard. *Histoire de l'orfèvrerie française*. Paris, 1896.

J. Hayward. 'Eighteenth-century jewelry', in *Antiques*, LXVII, 1955, p. 312.

J. Hayward. 'Nineteenth-century jewelry', in *Antiques*, LXVIII, 1955, p. 140.

J. Hayward. 'Jewellery', in *The Late Georgian Period 1760–1810* (Connoisseur Period Guides), 1956, p. 141.

J. Hayward. 'Jewellery', in *The Early Georgian Period, 1714–1760* (Connoisseur Period Guides, London), 1957. p. 149.

J. Hayward. 'Jewellery', in *The Regency Period* (Connoisseur Period Guides), 1958, p. 149.

J. Hayward. 'Jewellery', in *The Early Victorian Period 1830–1860* (Connoisseur Period Guides), 1958, p. 143.

J. H. von Hefner Alteneck. *Deutsche Goldschmiede-Werke des sechzehnten Jahrhunderts*, Frankfurt, 1890.

A. Héjj-Détári. *Old Hungarian Jewellery*, Budapest, 1965.

W. Herbert. *The History of the Twelve Great Livery Companies of London*, 2 vols., London, 1837 [1833] (Goldsmiths Company, II, p. 121).

J. Hernández Perera. 'Velázquez y las joyas', in *Archivo Español de Arte*, XXXIII, 1960, p. 251.

E. His. *Dessins d'ornements de Hans Holbein*, Paris, 1886.

W. Holzhausen. 'Meisterwerke der Juwelierkunst des 16. und 17. Jahrhunderts', in *Jahrbuch der Kunsthistorischen Sammlungen in Wien*, new series IX, 1935, p. 167.

W. Holzhausen. 'Deutsche Goldemailarbeiten am 1600 in Palazzo Pitti in Florenz', in *Pantheon*, II, 1928, p. 483.

H. Honour. 'Magazine of wonders: Wittelsbach treasure now on show at the recently restored Residenz Museum at Munich', in *Connoisseur*, CXLIV, 1959, p. 79.

W. H. St. John Hope, 'A mitre belonging to Lady Herries', in *Proc. Soc. Ants.*, XXIV, 1912, p. 127.

W. H. St. John Hope. *Heraldry for Craftsmen and Designers*, London, 1913.

Graham Hughes. *Jewelry*, London, 1966.

G. Humann. *Die Kunstwerke der Münsterkirche zu Essen*. 2 vols., Düsseldorf, 1904.

J. Hunt. 'Jewelled neck furs and "Flohpelze"', in *Pantheon*, XXI, 1963, p. 150.

H. Hymans. *Catalogue des Estampes d'ornement faisant partie des collections de la Bibliothèque royale de Belgique*, Brussels, 1907.

R. Jessup. *Anglo-Saxon Jewellery*, London, 1950.

'Joyaux et bijoux', in *Jardin des Arts*, no. 77, 1961, p. 2–39 [special issue devoted to jewellery].

Königliche Museen zu Berlin. *Katalog der Ornamenttisch-Sammlung des Kunstgewerbe-Museums*, Leipzig, 1894.

BIBLIOGRAPHY

L. Kunze. 'Das Kronenkreuz im Krakauer Domschatz: ein Arbeitsbericht', in *Forschungen und Forschriften*, XXXIV, 1960, p. 309.

J. Labarte. *Inventaire du mobilier de Charles V, roi de France*, Paris, 1879.

J. Labarte. *Histoire des Arts Industriels au Moyen Age et à l'époque de la Renaissance*, II, Paris, 1864, p. 551.

L. E. S. J. de Laborde. *Les Ducs de Bourgogne*, part II: *Preuves*. 3 vols., Paris 1849–52.

L. E. S. J. de Laborde. *Notice des Émaux . . . du Musée du Louvre*, part II, *Glossaire*, Paris, 1853.

P. Lacroix and F. Seré. (*Le Livre d'or des métiers.*) *Histoire de l'orfèvrerie-joaillerie et des anciennes communautés et confréries d'orfèvres-joailliers de la France et de la Belgique*, Paris, 1850.

P. Lacroix. 'Inventaire des Joyaux de la Couronne de France en 1560', in *Revue des Arts*, III, p. 334, IV, pp. 445, 518.

La Mode et le Bijou see *Revue de la bijouterie*, etc.

A. Lang. *Portraits and jewels of Mary Stuart*, Glasgow, 1906.

P. Lanza di Scalea. *Donne e gioielli in Sicilia nel medio evo e nel Rinascimento*, Palermo and Turin, 1892.

P. Laplagne-Barris. 'Les joyaux de Jean Ier, Comte d'Armagnac', in *Revue de Gascogne*, XV, 1874, Auch, p. 499.

J. de Laprade. 'Une inventaire des joyaux de la reine Catherine de Navarre (1517): richesses anciennes du château de Pau', in *Gazette des Beaux-Arts*, ser 6, LIX, 1962, p. 277.

G. Le Breton. 'Inventaire des bijoux et de l'orfèvrerie appartenant à Mme. la comtesse de Sault, confiés à l'amiral de Villars et trouvés après sa mort en 1595', in *Bulletin des Travaux Historiques*, II.

A. Lejard (ed.). *L'orfèvrerie, la joaillerie*, Paris, 1942.

R. Lemon. 'Warrant of Indemnity and Discharge to Lionel Earl of Middlesex . . . for having delivered certain jewels to King James the First', in *Archaeologia*, XXI, 1827, p. 148.

T. Lenk. 'Johan IIIs Salbator och Agnus Dei', in *Livrustkammaren*, VII, 1955, Stockholm, p. 25.

P. Lesley. *Handbook of the Lillian Thomas Pratt collection: Russian imperial jewels*, Richmond, Virginia, 1960 (Virginia Museum of Fine Arts).

M. D. S. Lewis. 'Antique garnet jewellery', in *Connoisseur Year Book*, 1957, p. 96.

R. W. Lightbown. 'An Islamic crystal mounted as a pendant in the West', in *Bulletin*, Victoria and Albert Museum, IV, 1968, p. 50.

R. W. Lightbown. 'Jean Petitot and Jacques Bordier at the English Court', in *Connoisseur*, CLXVIII, 1968, p. 82.

BIBLIOGRAPHY

Lisbon, Palacio Nacional Da Ajuda. *Catálogo das jóias e pratas da coroa*, Oporto, 1954.

London Museum. *The Cheapside Hoard of Elizabeth and Jacobean Jewellery* (Catalogues, No. 2) 1928.

F. Luthmer. *Goldschmuck der Renaissance*, Berlin, 1881.

F. Luthmer. *Gold und Silber*, Leipzig, 1888.

F. Luthmer. *Der Schatz des Freiherrn Karl von Rothschild. Meisterwerke alter Goldschmiedekunst*, 2 vols, Frankfurt, 1883–5.

R. van Lutterwelt. 'Een medaillon met het portret van Gustaf Adolf', in *Bulletin of the Rijksmuseum*, Amsterdam, II, 1954, p. 21.

R. van Lutterwelt. 'Een gouden ereketen van Christiaan IV van Denemarken', in *Bulletin k. nederl. Oudheidk. Bond.*, VII, 1954, p. 54.

E. Maclagan and C. C. Oman. 'An English gold rosary of about 1500', in *Archaeologia*, LXXXV, 1935, p. 1.

F. Madden. *Privy Purse expenses of the Princess Mary, daughter of King Henry the Eighth*. London, 1831.

A. de Maillé. 'Les bijoux en cheveux', in *Gazette des Beaux Arts*, LXI, 1963, p. 181.

F. Malaguzzi Valeri. *La corte di Lodovico il Moro*, 4 vols., Milan 1913–1923.

R. Manuel. 'Craft masonic jewels', in *Connoisseur*, IV, 1902, pp. 155, 263.

A. Marcel. 'Aubert d'Avignon, joaillier du roi et garde des diamants de la couronne, 1736–85', in *Mémoires de l'Académie de Vaucluse*, 2nd series., XIX, 1919, p. 89.

R. Marsham. 'On a manuscript book of prayers in a binding of gold enamelled, said to have been given by Queen Anne Boleyn to a lady of the Wyatt family', in *Archaeologia*, XLIV, 1873, p. 259.

S. Masferrer I Cantó. *La joia catalana*, Barcelona, 1930.

F. Masson. *L'Impératice Marie Louise*. Paris, 1902.

L. C. Ménabréa. 'Chroniques de Yolande de France, Duchesse de Savoie', in *Académie Royale de Savoie, Documents*, I, Chambéry. 1859.

M. Merlet. 'Inventaire des joyaux de Jeanne de Hochberg, duchesse de Longueville, 1514', in *Bulletin du Comité des Travaux historiques et scientifiques, Section d'archéologie*, 1884, pt. I, p. 371.

Metropolitan Museum of Art, New York, *Mediaeval Jewellery*, 1940. *Renaissance Jewellery*, 1940.

E. A. Meyer. 'Zur Geschichte des hochmittelalterlichen Schmuckes', in *Adolf Goldschmidt zu seinem siebenzigsten Geburtstag*, Berlin, 1935, p. 19.

U. Middeldorf. 'On the origins of émail sur ronde-bosse', in *Gazette-des Beaux-Arts*, series 6, LV, 1960, p. 233.

G. Migeon. *Musée du Louvre, Collection Paul Garnier; Horloges et Montres*, Paris, n.d. (c. 1918.)

BIBLIOGRAPHY

V. Miletic. *Nakit u Bosni i Heregovini od kasne antike do najnovigeg doba* (*Jewellery in Bosnia and Herzegovina from late antiquity to the present day*), Sarajevo, 1963.

E. Modigliani. *Catalogo della mostra degli oggetti d'arte e di storia restituiti dall'Austria-Ungheria*, Rome, 1923.

E. Molinier. *Dictionnaire des Émailleurs depuis le moyen âge jusqu'à la fin du XVIIIe siècle*, Paris, 1885.

A. de Montaiglon. 'Joyaux et pierreries . . . de la reine Jeanne d'Évreux', in *Archives de l'art français*, 2nd series, 1861, p. 448.

L. Montalto. *La corte de Alfonso I di Aragona. Vesti e gale*, Naples, 1922.

H. de Montégut. 'Inventaire des bijoux de Jeanne de Bourdeille, dame de Sainte-Aulaire et de Lanmary', in *Bulletin de la Société historique et archéologique du Périgord*, VIII, Périgueux, 1881, pp. 159, 232, and 334.

B. de Montesquiou-Fezensac. 'Le talisman de Charlemagne', in *Art de France*, II, Paris, 1962, p. 66.

H. Moranvillé. *Inventaire de l'orfèvrerie et des bijoux de Louis I, duc d'Anjou*, Paris, 1906.

P. Moreau. *Nouveau[x] et IV.e. [V.e.] cahiers concernant l'orphèvrerie bijouterie, etc. Compose[s] et grave[s] par P. M.*, 1771, facsimile ed., 1907.

L. Morelli. 'Gioelli antichi', in *Il Secolo XX*, XIII, 1914.

E. Moses. *Kunstgewerbe Museum der Stadt Köln. Der Schmuck der Sammlung W. Clemens*, 1925.

T. Müller and E. Steingräber. 'Die französische Goldemailplastik um 1400', in *Münchener Jahrbuch*, V, 1954, p. 29.

E. Müntz. 'L'Orfèvrerie romaine de la Renaissance, avec une étude spéciale sur Caradosso in *Gazette des Beaux Arts*, XXVII, 1883, pp. 411, 491.

A. R. Myers. 'The jewels of Queen Margaret of Anjou', in *Bulletin of the John Rylands Library*, Manchester, XLI, 1959, p. 113.

S. M. Newton. 'Pendant of an Order of St. Hubert', in *Apollo*, new series LXXXV, 1967, p. 126.

New York Metropolitan Museum of Art, *see* Metropolitan Museum of Art, New York.

J. Nichols. *The Progresses and Public Processions of Queen Elizabeth*, 3 vols., London, 1788–1821.

J. G. Nichols and J. E. Jackson. 'Inventory of the goods of Dame Agnes Hungerford, attainted of Murder 14 Hen. VIII', in *Archaeologia*, XXXVIII, 1860, p. 354.

N. H. Nicolas, Sir. *Testamenta Vetusta*, 2 vols., London, 1826.

S. de la Nicollière. 'Description du chapeau ducal, etc., . . . des ducs de Bretagne', in *Bulletin de la Société Archéologique de Nantes*, I, Nantes, 1859, p. 395.

J. J. Oeri. *Der Onyx von Schaffhausen*, Zurich [1882].

Oeuvres de bijouterie et joaillerie des XVIIe et XVIIIe siècles, Paris, 1911.

BIBLIOGRAPHY

C. C. Oman. 'The Goldsmiths of St. Alban's Abbey during the 12th and 13th centuries', in *The St. Albans and Hertfordshire Architectural and Archaeological Society Transactions*, 1932, p. 215.

C. C. Oman. 'A note on a design by Valentin Sezenius', in *Apollo*, VI, 1927, p. 149.

C. C. Oman. 'Relics of "Belted Will" Howard', in *Country Life*, CIII, 1948, p. 1076.

C. C. Oman. 'Jewels of Our Lady of the Pillar at Saragossa', in *Apollo*, new series LXXXV, 1967, p. 400.

C. C. Oman. 'A miniature triptych of about 1400', in *Burlington Magazine*, CX, 1968, p. 93.

M. L. D'Otrange (Otrange-Mastai). 'A collection of Renaissance jewels at the Art Institute of Chicago', in *Connoisseur*, CXXX, 1952, p. 66.

M. L. D'Otrange (Otrange-Mastai). 'Jewels of the XVth and XVIth centuries', in *Connoisseur*, CXXXII, 1953, p. 126.

M. L. D'Otrange (Otrange-Mastai). 'Collection of Renaissance jewels owned by M. J. Desmon' in *Connoisseur*, CXXXIX, 1957, p. 126.

M. L. D'Otrange (Otrange-Mastai). 'The exquisite art of Carlo Giuliano', in *Apollo*, LIX, 1954, p. 145.

S. Oved. *The Book of Necklaces*, London, 1953.

F. Palgrave. *The Antient Kalendars and Inventories of the Treasury of His Majesty's Exchequer*, 3 vols., 1836.

E. W. Palm. 'Renaissance secular jewellery in the cathedral at Ciudad Trujillo', in *Burlington Magazine*, XCIII, p. 316.

L. Pannier. 'Les joyaux des ducs de Guyenne', in *Revue Archéologique*, XXVI, 1873, pp. 158, 306, 384; XXVII, 1874, p. 37.

Paris. Musée des Arts Décoratifs. *Les nouvelles collections*, etc., 10. Bijoux 1907.

Paris. Musée du Louvre. *Dix siècles de joaillerie française*, exhibition catalogue, 1962.

C. Pasztory-Alcsuti. *Les anciens bijoux hongrois*, Budapest, 1941.

R. Payne-Gallwey. *A history of the George worn on the scaffold by Charles I*, London, 1908.

M. Percival. *Chats on old jewellery and trinkets*, London, 1912.

C. Piacenti Aschengreen. *Il Museo degli Argenti a Firenze*, 1967.

C. Piacenti Aschengreen. 'Two jewellers at the Grand Ducal Court of Florence around 1618', in *Mitteilungen des Kunsthistorischen Instituts in Florenz*, 1965, p. 106.

C. Piacenti Aschengreen. 'I Santi Protettori della Toscana 1718', in *Festschrift Ulrich Middeldorf*, 1968.

J. F. Pichon. (Sale Catalogue). *Collections de feu M. le Baron Jérôme Pichon. Objets antiques, du moyen-âge, de la Renaissance*, etc., Paris, 1897.

A. Pinchart. *Archives des Arts, Sciences et Lettres*, Ghent, 1860–81.

BIBLIOGRAPHY

A. Podlaha and E. Sittler. *Der Domschatz in Prag*, Prague, 1903.

V. Promis. 'Due inventari del secolo XVII', in *Miscellanea di storia italiana*, XIX, Turin, 1880, p. 212.

B. and H. Prost. *Inventaires mobiliers et extraits des comptes des ducs de Bourgogne*, 2 vols., Paris, 1902–14.

C. Pulszky, E. Radisics and E. Molinier. *Chefs d'oeuvre d'orfèvrerie ayant figuré à l'Exposition de Budapest*, Budapest, Paris, New York and London, 2 vols. [Paris], 1884–8.

A. P. Purey Cust. *The Collar of SS*, Leeds, 1910.

F. Rademacher. *Fränkische Goldscheibenfibeln*, Munich, 1940.

R. Ramírez de Arellano. *Estudio sobre la historia de la orfevrería toledana*, Toledo, 1915.

R. H. Randall. 'Walters Art Gallery: Jewellery through the ages', in *Apollo*, new series LXXXXIV, 1966, p. 495.

Revue de la bijouterie, joaillerie, orfèvrerie, 1900–4. Begun as *La Mode et le Bijou*.

J. M. Richard. *Mahaut, Comtesse d'Artois et de Bourgogne, 1302–29*, 1887.

J. Robertson. *Inventaires de la Royne Descosse Douairière de France*, Edinburgh (Bannatyne Club), 1863.

J. C. Roche. *The history, development and organisation of the Birmingham jewellery and allied trades*, Birmingham, 1927. Supplement to *The Dial*.

J. H. Roman. *Inventaires et documents relatifs aux joyaux et tapisseries des princes d'Orléans-Valois, 1389–1481*, Paris, 1894.

J. Rosas. *Joias Portuguesas: as 'lacas de Ouro'*, Oporto, 1942.

J. Rosas. 'The crown jewels and silver of Portugal', in *Apollo*, LXIV, 1956, p. 214.

M. Rosenberg. *Niello seit dem Jahre 1000 nach Chr.*, Frankfurt, 1925.

M. Rosenberg. *Studien über Goldschmiedekunst in der Sammlung Figdor*, Vienna, 1911.

F. Rossi. *Capolavori di oreficeria italiana dall' XI al XVIII secolo*, 1956. English trans., *Italian Jewelled Arts*, 1957.

B. H. Röttger. *Der Maler Hans Mielich*, Munich, 1925.

J. Rouchon. 'Inventaire des joyaux d'une bourgeoise de Puy en Velay, 1601', in *Bulletin Archéologique*, 1914, p. 556.

L. Rouvenat. *Exposition de 1849: fabrique de bijouterie et joaillerie fines*, Paris, 1849.

L. Rouvenat. *Album de joaillerie et de bijouterie*, Paris, 1855.

H. Roy. *La Vie, la Mode et le Costume au dix-septième siècle, Époque Louis XIII. Etude sur la Cour de Lorraine*, Paris, 1924.

R. Ruecklin. *Das Schmuckbuch*, 2 vols., Leipzig, 1901.

A. B. Ryley. *Old paste*, London, 1913.

T. Rymer. *Foedera*, ed. J. Caley and F. Holbrooke, London, 1830.

BIBLIOGRAPHY

San Francisco. M. H. de Young Memorial Museum. *Exhibition of Renaissance jewels selected from the collection of Martin J. Desmoni.* New York (privately printed), 1958.

G. Scharf. 'Note upon Collars', in *Archaeologia,* XXXIX, 1863, p. 265.

E. von Schauss. *Historischer und Geschreibender Catalog der Königlich Bayerischen Schatzkammer zu München,* Munich, 1879.

F. Schlunk. 'The Crosses of Oviedo', in *Art Bulletin,* XXXII, 1950, p. 90.

H. Schmitz. *Berliner Eisenkunstguss,* Munich, 1917.

H. Schnitzler. *Der Dom zu Aachen,* Düsseldorf, 1950.

E. Sènemand. 'Inventaire des meubles de Marguerite de Rohan, Comtesse d'Angoulême, 1497', in *Bulletin de la Société archéologique et historique de la Charente,* 3rd series., II, Angoulême, 1861, p. 48.

W. Seton. *The Penicuik Jewels of Mary Queen of Scots,* London, 1923.

A. Sharp. 'Notes on Stuart Jewellery', in *Proc. Soc. Ants. Scotland,* LVII, 1922–3, p. 226.

E. P. Shirley. 'An inventory of the effects of Henry Howard, K.G., Earl of Northampton, taken on his death in 1614,' in *Archaeologia,* XLII, 1869, p. 347.

R. H. Skaife. 'Register of the Guild of Corpus Christi of the City of York', *Surtees Society,* LVII, 1871.

H. Clifford Smith. 'The King's Gems and Jewels at Windsor Castle', in *Connoisseur,* IV, 1902, p. 221; V, 1903, pp. 77, 238.

H. Clifford Smith. *Jewellery,* London, 1908.

H. Clifford Smith. *The Danny Unicorn jewel,* London, 1914.

H. Clifford Smith. 'Jewellery of Tudor Times', in *Illustrated London News,* July 9, 1949, p. 44.

H. Clifford Smith, 'Renaissance jewellery in the Wernher Collection at Luton Hoo', in *Connoisseur,* May, 1950.

C. Roach Smith. 'Mediaeval Brooches', in *Collectanea Antiqua,* IV, 1857, p. 108.

F. Russell-Smith. 'Sleeve buttons of the seventeenth and eighteenth centuries', in *Connoisseur,* CXXXIX, 1957, p. 36.

J. A. Smith. 'Ancient Scottish silver chains with gilt ornaments', in *Proc. Soc. Ants. Scotland,* X, 1875, p. 321.

A. Speight. *The Lock of Hair,* London, 1871.

E. Steingräber. *Alter Schmuck: die Kunst des europäischen Schmuckes,* Munich, 1956. English Trans., *Antique jewellery; its history in Europe from 800 to 1900,* London, 1957.

E. Steingräber. 'Suddeutsche Goldemailplastik der Frührenaissance', in *Studien zur Geschichte der europäischen Plastik* (Festschrift Th. Müller), 1965, p. 223.

R. Stettiner. *Das Kleinodienbuch des Jakob Mores in der Hamburgischen Stadtbibliothek,* Hamburg, 1916.

BIBLIOGRAPHY

J. Stockbauer. *Der Metall-Schmuck in der Mustersammlung des Bayrischen Gewer-bemuseums zu Nurnberg*, Nuremberg, 1887.

P. Stone. 'Baroque pearls', in *Apollo*, LXVIII, 1958, p. 194; LXIX, 1959, pp. 33, 107.

R. C. Strong. 'Three Royal Jewels: the Three Brothers, the Mirror of Great Britain and the Feather', in *Burlington Magazine*, CVIII, 1966, p. 350.

J. Struthers. 'Note of a gold brooch of the 13th or 14th century, found in the Water of Ardoch, near Doune Castle', in *Proc. Soc. Ants. Scotland*, VIII, 1871, p. 330.

H. Tait. 'Tudor Hat Badges', in *British Museum Quarterly*, XX, 1955–6, p. 37.

H. Tait. 'A Tudor jewel; gold enamelled pendant', in *Museums Journal*, LVI, 1957, p. 233.

H. Tait. 'Historiated Tudor Jewellery', in *Antiquaries' Journal*, XLII, 1962, p. 226.

H. Tait. 'A Tudor gold enamelled buckle', in *British Museum Quarterly*, XXVI, 1962–3, p. 112.

H. Tait. 'Anonymous loan to the British Museum: Renaissance jewellery', in *Connoisseur*, CLIV, 1963, p. 147.

G. Tescione. *Il corallo nella storia e nell'arte*, Naples, 1965.

Abbé J. R. A. Texier. 'Dictionnaire d'Orfèvrerie, de gravure et de ciselure chrétiennes', in Migne, *Encyclopédie Théologique*, XXVII, 1856.

T. Thomson. *A collection of Inventories and other Records of the Royal Wardrobe and Jewelhouse*, Edinburgh, 1815.

E. Thornam. *Gamle smykker i Norge, 1550–1900*, Oslo, Kunstindustrimuseet, 1928.

G. Thury. *Die Vogelfibeln der Germanischen Völkerwanderungszeit*, Bonn, 1939.

U. Tibaldi. 'Benvenuto Cellini a Mantova', in *Vasari*, XVIII, 1960, p. 130.

A. B. Tonnochy. 'Jewels and Engraved Gems at Windsor Castle', in *Connoisseur*, XCV, 1935, p. 275.

L. de la Tremoïlle. *Guy de la Tremoïlle et Marie de Sully, Livre de Comptes, 1395–1406*, Nantes, 1887.

G. G. Trivulzio. 'Gioje di Ludovico il Moro', in *Archivio Storico Lombardo*, III, Milan, 1876, p. 530.

O. Tschumi. *Burgunder, Alamannen und Langobarden in der Schweiz*, Bern, 1945.

T. H. Turner. 'The Will of Humphrey de Bohun, Earl of Hereford and Essex, with extracts from the inventory of his effects,' in *Arch. Journ.*, II, 1846, p. 339.

P. Fraser Tytler. *Historical Notes on the Lennox or Darnley Jewel: the property of the Queen*, London, 1843.

G. Upmark. *Upsala Domkyrkas Silfver-Kammare*, Stockholm, 1910. Many subsequent eds.

L. Vayer. 'L'Imago Pietatis di Lorenzo Ghiberti', in *Acta Historiae Artium*, Budapest, VIII, 1962, p. 45.

BIBLIOGRAPHY

P. Verdier. 'An unknown masterpiece by Henri Toutin', in *Connoisseur*, CLXII, 1966, p. 2.

A. Verhaegen. 'Collier en or émaillé conservé dans le trésor de l'église collégiale d'Essen (Prusse rhénane)', in *Revue de l'Art Chrétien*, 3rd series., V, 1887, p. 275.

P. Verlet. 'Une plaque de l'Ordre du Saint-Esprit', in *Revue des Arts*, I, 1951, p. 176.

E. Veron. 'De quelques bijoux de deuil du XVI siècle', in *L'Art*, XXIX, 1882, p. 17.

H. Vever. *La bijouterie française au XIXe siècle*, vol. I, *1800–50*, Paris, 1906.

A. del Vita. 'Le antiche oreficerie de Castiglion Fiorentino,' in *Dedalo*, I, 1920–21, p. 423.

E. Wattai. 'Amargitszigeti korono [a late 13th century crown]', in *Budapest Regisegei*, XVIII, 1958, p. 191.

E. von Watzdorf, *J. M. Dinglinger*, Berlin, 1962.

E. von Watzdorf, 'Der Dresdner Goldschmied Abraham Schwedler und sein Kreis', in *Zeitschrift für Kunstwissenschaft*, XVI, 1962, p. 81.

E. von Watzdorf, 'Fürstlicher Schmuck der Renaissance aus dem Besitz der Kurfürstin Anna von Sachsen', in *Münchner Jahrbuch der Bildenden Kunst*, new series XI, 1934, p. 50.

F. P. Weber. *Aspects of Death and correlated aspects of Life in Art, Epigram and Poetry* (1910), 4th ed., London, 1922.

Wedgwood and Bentley. *A Catalogue of Cameos, Intaglios, Medals and Bas-reliefs . . . made by Wedgwood and Bentley and sold at their Rooms in Great Newport Street*, London, 1773.

Wellington, Duke of. 'The scaffold George of Charles I', in *Antiquaries Journal*, XXXIII, 1953, p. 159.

G. C. Williamson. *Catalogue of the Collection of Jewels and Precious Works of Art, the property of J. Pierpont Morgan*, London, 1910.

G. C. Williamson. *Catalogue of the Collection of Watches, the property of J. Pierpont Morgan*, London, 1912.

B. Young. 'A jewel of St. Catherine', in *Metropolitan Museum Bulletin*, XXIV, 1965–1966, p. 316.

Index

Note: References to precious stones are necessarily selective. In addition, references are made to Colour Plates, which are reproduced in black and white in this edition.

INDEX

architectural influence, on jewellery, 52, 69, 74, 80

armour, jewels for, 56

Arre, Sieur d', and false jewels, 151

'art jewellery', 180

Arte of Limning, by Nicholas Hilliard, 107 *and n* 5

Arthaud, Louis, of Lyons, watches by, 141 *n* 1

Artois, Count of, 51; buckles of, 163 *n* 1

  Mahaut, Countess of, jewels of, 48, 50, *and n* 10, 51 *and n* 7, 60 *n* 1

  Marguerite, Countess of, *see* Hainault

Arundel, Sussex, effigy at, 65 *n* 11

Arundel, Joan, effigy of, 65 *n* 11

  jewels of, 71

Ashmole, Elias, jewels of, 143 *n* 5

Astyll, Richard, portrait cameos by, 95

Atkins, Robert, watch by, 163 *n* 4

Atlantid figures, use of in jewellery, 91

Aubert, buckles by, 163 *n* 1

Augsburg, St. Ulrich of, cross of, 78

  jewellery design at, 104, 122

  jewels of, 110 *n* 9

Augustus, Emperor, cameo of, 49, Pl. 10b

d'Aulnoy, Madame, on Spanish jewellery, 145–6

Austria, Anne of, jewels of, 106, Pl. 73

  Archduchess Blanca of, necklace of, 158, *n* 3

  Eleanor of, Queen of France, portrait and jewels of, 87, 100, Pl. 56

  Elisabeth of, Queen of France, portrait and jewels of, 105, Pl. 74

  Isabella of, portrait and jewels of, 87, Pl. 55

  Don John of, jewel of, 85, Pl. 46a

  Margaret of, Duchess of Savoy, jewels and portrait of, 72, Pl. 32

  Maria of, Queen of Spain, jewel of, 142

  Archduchess Marie Louise of, jewels of, 170

  Princess Mary of, portrait of, 128

Aventurine paste, 159

Aylesbury, Bucks., Archaeological Museum, brooch in, 47 *and n* 3

Baccio Bandinelli, 82

Bacciocci, Elisa, bracelet of, 170

badges, leaden, 64

  development of, 64–7

'Bagshot diamonds', 152 *n* 1

balases, 51, 55, 62, 73, 99 *and n* 5

Baldwin, Emperor of Constantinople, 50

Bâle, Historisches Museum, drawings in, 73 *n* 1, Pl. 27

bandeaux, jewelled, 48, 170, 171

Bangor cathedral, effigy in, 77

Bapst, jeweller, 151 *n* 3, 157, 171, 172, 174

Bar, Yolande de, jewels of, 67

Barcelona, goldsmiths' guild of, 101

  reliquaries from, 134 *n* 1

Baret, John, of Bury, jewels of, 74 *and n* 3

Barnard Castle, Yorks, Bowes Museum, bracelets in, 170

Barnes, Mrs., of Redland Hall, jewels belonging to, 122 *n* 1

Baroque design in jewellery, 126

Barre, Pierre de la, 134 *n* 4

Bavaria, Duke Albert V of, jewels of, 106, Pl. 73

  Prince Albert of, jewels and portrait of, 94–5

  Isabella of, jewel of, 75

beads, 50, 77, 78

  of ambergris, 142

  pomander, 118

Beauchamp, Thomas, Earl of Warwick, brooches of, 64

Beaujeu, Anne de, jewels and portrait of, 71, Pl. 31

Beaumont, Mrs., jewels of, 171

Beauvoir, Richard, jeweller, 149

Bedford, Duke of, picture in collection of, 97, *n* 7

Belamy, Jean, diamond-cutter, 68

Belle Assemblée, La, 179

Belle Zélie, La, painting of, 169 *and n* 5

Bellini, Gentile, portrait by, 76, Pl. 53

Beltête, jeweller, 181

belts, jewelled, 46, 47, 51, 55, 56, 67, 74, 84, 106, 107, 118, 125, 129, *n* 2, 174, Pl. 94

  harness for, designs for, 86, 89, Figs. 2, 5

Berkeley Castle, Glos., jewels at, 101, 118

Berkhausen, Hieronymus, designer, 132 *n* 1

Berlin, cast-iron jewellery from, 170, 172

  Museum, jewels in, 43 *n* 3

  Royal Gallery, portrait in, 86 *and n* 3

Bernard, Nicholas, of Paris, watch-case by, Pl. 108c

Bernardi, Giovanni, cameo-cutter, 81

Berquen, Louis de, and diamond-cutting, 68 *n* 6

  Robert de, *Merveilles des Indes* by, 68 *n* 6

  advice to apprentices by, 144

INDEX

INDEX

INDEX

INDEX

INDEX

INDEX

INDEX

INDEX

INDEX

INDEX

INDEX

INDEX

INDEX

Pau, Château de, jewels from, 101

Pauwels, Noe, of Brussels, designs by, 152. Fig. 31

pavé settings, 166, 178, 181. Pl. 167b

pawn, jewels in, 103–4, 106, 130, 141

pax, 44

pea-pod form, jewels in, 134, 137. Figs. 22–4. Pls. 118, 119

pearls, 42–4, 49–60 ff, 99, 100, 103, 125, 141, 162, 166, 175, 177, 180 *and passim*
  baroque, 110, 112
  black, 178
  false, 69 *n 4*, 159, 174
  French, 159
  fresh-water, 53, 175

pebbles, Scotch, 171 *n 5*

Pemberton, Mrs., miniature of, 126 *n 1*

pendants, 50–1, 52 *n 2*, 71–3, 81–3, 87, 91 *and n 1*, 105, 110–16, 120, 129, 177, 178. Figs. 3, 4, 7–9, 13–18, 27. Col. Pls. VIb, VII, VIII. Pls. 6a, 19c, d, 26b, d, 36b, 37, 38a, 39, 41b, c, 42, 44d, 48b, 50, 59, 60–61, 63b, c, 65b, 66, 67, 70–2, 73, 79–89, 91, 92c, 95, 97a, 98b, 110, 112–14, 124a, b, 125b, f, 128, 135a, d, 137, 138, 140b, 151, 173a, 187a, 188, 191
  bird, 129. Pls. 84, 110, 140b
  coffin, 142–3. Pls. 124a, b, 125f
  cross, 143, 174. Pl. 188
  'en ferronnière', 174
  figured, 110–13
  reliquary, 60, 74, 75–76. Pls. 12c, d, 36b, 37, 38a, 42
  sea-horse, merman, etc., Pls. 78–93
  vinaigrette, Pl. 187a

Penicuik Locket, the, 119

Périgal, Francis, watches by, 161 *n*, 164 *n 4*

Perres, Alice, jewels of, 55

Perthes, Blanche de, crown of, 48 *n 4*

Perugia, Lantizio di, seal by, Pl. 49a

Peruzzi, Vicenzo, inventor of brilliant-cutting, 152

Petit, Jacques, jewels by, 178

pewter, use of in jewellery, 79

Philip le Hardi, *see* Burgundy

Philip, Marquis of Namur, 48

Philippe le Bon, Duke of Burgundy, *see* Burgundy

Philippi, Frédéric, jewels by, 176

Phillips, Messrs. S. J., Collection of, Col. Pl. XI. Pl. 176

Phoenix Jewel, the, 120

photographs, lockets for, 180

Pierpont Morgan Collection, the late, jewels from, 76 *and n 6*, 110 *n 1*, 112 *n 3*, 118, 120 *n 4*, 127 *and n 2*, 128 *and n 1*, 139, 140. Pls. 97b, 107a, 108c

pilgrims, jewels of, 73–80 (*see also* enseignes)

pinchbeck, 160 *and n 1*

Pinchbeck, Christopher, 160 *and n 1*

plaques, 62–3
  hinged, for girdles, 74

platinum, 173 *and n 4*

Ploumyer, Allart, jeweller, 86

Pointe de Bretagne Diamond, 100

pointillé engraving, 53, 75, 78

poissardes, 167

Poissy, Abbey at, ring-brooch from, 58 *and n 1*

Poitiers, Diane de, jewels borrowed by, 100 *n 8*

Poitou, ring-brooches from, 47 *n 1*

political significance of jewellery, 64–7

Pollaiuolo, Antonio, painting by, 82
  Piero, painting by, 83

Polo, Domenico del, cameo portraits by, 95

pomanders, 101, 118

Pompadour, Madame de, jewels of, 163

Pope, the, and fashion for rosaries, 169
  wax roundels blessed by, 50

Portinari, Tommaso, jewels of wife and daughter of, 71

Portland, Duke of, jewels in collection of, 119, 131 *n 3*

Portugal Diamond, the, 130

Portuguese jewellery, 130–1

Post-Roman jewellery, 40

Pouget, drawings by, 157 *n 2*

Pourbus, portrait by, 105 *and n 6*

Prague, centre of jewel design in, 104

pregnancy, jewels worn in, 50 *and n 9*

Primavera of Botticelli, jewels depicted in, 83

P.R.K., engraver, designs by, 127, 132 *n 1*

prophylactic jewels, 76

Pugin, A. W., designs by, 175

Puritanism, influence of on jewel design, 142

INDEX

INDEX

INDEX

Toledo, Eleanor, portrait and jewels of, 103
Toledo, Ohio, portrait at, 94 *n 1*
topazes, 148, 156, 171
Toplers Hill, Beds., brooches from, 60 *n 5*
Torre Abbey, Devon, jewel from, 143, Pl. 124a
Toussaint the Younger, Augustus, enamels by, 163 *n 4*
Toutin family, invention by, 139, Pls. 120a, b
Jean, of Chateaudun, designs by, 127, 132 *n 1*, 134 *n 4*, Pl. 106b
Town Eclogue, The, by Lady Mary Wortley Montagu, 160
Towneley Brooch, the, 43, Pl. 1b
trade, international, 105, 183–4
trade, modern conditions of, 183–4
tressons, 48
Trezzo, Jacopo di, cameo portrait by, 95
tribal jewellery, 40–3
Trichinopoly plaiting, 167
triptych pendant, 75
Tudor, Mary, *see* England
Tuke, Sir Brian, portrait of, 98
Turgot, 166
turquoises, 171, 175, 180, 182
Tuscany, Grand Duke of, jewels of, 106 *n 2*
Tutilo, goldsmith, 41
Tyldesley, Christopher, goldsmith, 65

Uffila, brooch of, 41
Ulrich of Augsburg, cross of, 78
Upsala Cathedral, pendant from tomb in, 96, Pl. 66
Urban VI, Pope, 51
Ursula, Saint, reliquary of, 54
U.S.A., costume jewellery from, 184
Utrecht, John of, 86

Valenciennes, Musée des Beaux Arts, Pl. 101
Valérie, Sainte, reliquary of, 63 *n 2*
Valette, Duchesse de la, jewels and portrait of, 168
Vallardi, designs by, 170 *and n 1*
Valois, Elisabeth of, jewels and portrait of, 106
Marguerite of, watch of, 108
Van der Goes, H., painting by, 70–1, Pl. 30
Vandyck, Sir Anthony, portraits by, 141, Pl. 122
Van Eyck, altar-piece by, 69 *n 5*

varicoloured jewels, 156
Vaughan, agent of Henry VIII, 87
Vauquer, Jean, *Livre de Fleurs propre pour Orfèvres et Graveurs* by, 137
Vautyer, of Blois, watch by, Pl. 119c
velvet ribbon and brooch, Victorian throat decoration, 81
Vendée, La, brooches in, 57 *n 2*
Veneto, Bartolommeo, portraits by, jewels depicted in, 84 *n 1*
Venice, jewels of, 117
Venturi, Girolamo, drawings by, 153 *and n 1*
Verdun, Nicholas of, clasp attributed to, 46, Pl. 4a
Verocchio, Andrea del, 82
Versailles, Museum of, paintings in, 125 *n 2*, Pls. 169–71
Vicentino, Valerio, cameo-cutter, 81
Victoria, Queen, *see* England; Victorian jewellery, 81, 172, 179
Vienna, Figdor Collection, pendants from, 106 *n 8*
Imperial Treasury, brooch in, 63 *n 6*, Col. Pl. I
Kunsthistorisches Museum, jewels in, 76 *n 6*, 84, 93, 97 *and n 7*, 115, 119, Pls. I, IV, Pls. 52b, 63a, 90c
portraits in, 97, *n 7*, 119 *n 7*, Pl. 54
paintings, in, 106 *and n 5*
Vigée Le Brun, Madame, portrait by, 168, Pl. 170
Villeneuve-lès-Avignon, Musée de l'Hospice, painting in, 70 *and n 4*
Villiers, *Journal d'un voyageur à Paris*, 151
Virgen de Pilar, shrine of, *see* Saragossa
Virtues, the, representation of in jewellery, 82, 114, 116, 118
Visby, Island of, buckle from, Pl. 4b
Viviano, Michelagnolo di, jeweller, 83
Vivot, designer, 134 *n 4*
Votive jewels, 41, 48–50, 56
Vovert, Jean, designer, 132 *n 1*, 137

W. A., monogrammist, 88
Waddesdon Bequest, *see* London, British Museum
Wall, John, goldsmith, 107
Walpole, Horace, jewel of, 116

223

INDEX

Walsingham Priory, Norfolk, forge at, 78

Warwick Castle, portraits in, 100 *and n 3*

    Countess of, jewels of, 137

    Thomas Beauchamp, Earl of, brooches of, 64

Watch-cases, 126, 128–9, 128 *n 1*, 134, 143, 145, 155, 159, 161–2, 166, *and n 5*, 178, Pls. 108, 109, 119, 120, 121a, b, d, 125c, 133a, b, 156, 157, 161, 167b

Watches, sham, 162

Watch-pendants, 108 *and n 6*

Weapons, jewelled, designs for, 94 *and n 5*

Wedgwood, Josiah, plaques by, 164, Pl. 165a

Weimar, Schloss Museum, portrait in, 99 *n 1*

Wellington, Duke of, Order of the Golden Fleece of, 154 *n 7*

Wenceslas of Ollmutz, 89

Wernher Collection, *see* Luton Hoo

Wertheimer, Charles, pendant from collection of, 115 *n 3*

Wessex, Ethelwulf, King of, ring of, 42

Whistles, jewelled, 86 *n 2*, 89, 91 *and n 3*

Whitby, jet from, 172

Whitehead, Mr., of Hambrook, Bristol, jewel of, 122 *n 1*

Wickes & Netherton, Messrs., jewellers, 151; Wickes, George, 150 *n 3*

Wild Jewel, the, 119

Willoughby, Lady, portrait and jewels of, 110 *and n 8*

Willow, John, watch by, 129

Wilton Diptych, the, jewels depicted in, 64, 66

Winterhalter, portraits by, 178, 180

Witt, Sir Robert, maquette in collection of, 114 *n 1*

Wittislingen, brooch fron, 41

Woeiriot, Pierre, designs by, 91, 142, Fig. 9

Wolverhampton, factory-made steel jewellery from, 164

women as principal wearers of jewels, 105, 107

wood, rotten, jewels in form of, 178

Woodstock, Oxfordshire, steel jewellery from, 164

World of Fashion, The, 179

Worms, Heyl zu Herrnsheim Collection at, brooches in, 51 *n 6*

Wortley Montagu, Lady Mary, *Town Eclogue* of, 160

Writtle, Essex, ring-brooches from, 46 *n 9*

Wurtemburg, Princess of, jewels and portraits of, 168

Wyatt, Thomas, jewel of, 101

Wykeham, William of, jewel of, 60, 61, Pl. 19a

Yeoman, Chaucer's, brooch of, 80

York, Guild of Corpus Christi at, jewels of, 73 *n 9*, 76 *n 4*, 77

    Margaret of, Duchess of Burgundy, jewels of, 70, 76, 79, Pl. 39

Young, *Night Thoughts,* influence of on jewellery, 165

Zodiac, use of signs of, 83

Zundt, Matthias, designs by, 91, Fig. 10

224

PLATE I
(a) Gold brooch, German, probably early eleventh century
(b) Brooch of enamelled gold. (The Towneley Brooch.)
German, late eleventh century

PLATE 2

(*a*) Eagle brooch of enamelled gold from the treasure of the Empress
Gisela, *c.* 1043

(*b*) Pair of brooches, perhaps from the same source

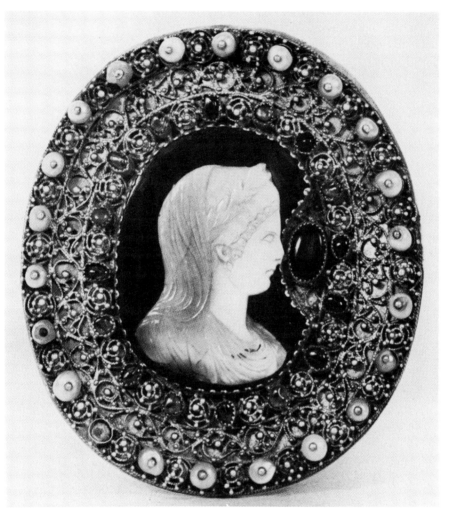

PLATE 3
Roman agate cameo in a setting of gold filigree and pearls. Twelfth century

PLATE 4

(a) Gilt bronze clasp, attributed to Nicholas of Verdun, c. 1200

(b) Silver buckle, perhaps Rhenish, found on the island of Visby, c. 1220

PLATE 5
Ring brooch and crown on the statue of a Queen from
Corbeil, *c.* 1150

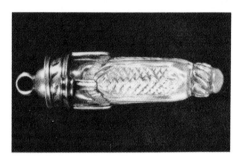

PLATE 6

(*a–c*) Pendant. An Islamic crystal fish set in a Western mount of silver, nielloed and gilt. Fish *c.* 1200 (?), mounts *c.* 1300. With screw stopper.
(*Slightly enlarged*)

(*d*) Brooch. Silver-gilt, ornamented with lions and eagles on foliage. Hungarian (?), thirteenth century

PLATE 7

(*a*) Buckle. Gold, nielloed with a battle scene. Hungarian, second half
of the thirteenth century. (*Slightly enlarged*).
Found with four gold buttons at Kiskunmajsa-Kúgyóspuszta

(*b*) Fragment of a crown. Four gold plaques decorated with gold
filigree and set with pearls, turquoises, garnets and sapphires.
Hungarian, second half of the thirteenth century. (*Reduced*)

(*c*) Fragment of a brooch matching the crown. Gold set with turquoises,
garnets and sapphires. Hungarian, second half of the thirteenth century. (*Reduced*)

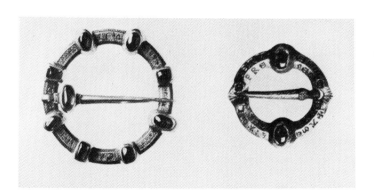

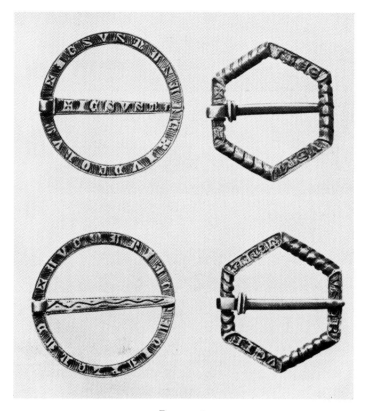

PLATE 8
Ring Brooches, thirteenth and fourteenth centuries
(*a–b*) Gold set with emeralds and rubies
(*c–d*) Silver, front and back

PLATE 9
(*a*) Crown holding relics sent from Constantinople in 1205
(*b*) Crown given by Saint Louis to the Dominicans of Liége before 1270
(*both slightly reduced*)

PLATE 10
(a) Crown worn by Richard Earl of Cornwall for his coronation as King
of the Romans in 1257 (*reduced*).
(b) The Jewel of St. Hilary, early thirteenth century

PLATE 11

The Schaffhausen Onyx, an antique cameo in a setting of gold and rubies
of the second half of the thirteenth century

PLATE 12

(*a*) Reliquary cross of jewelled gold, late thirteenth century. (*b*) Gold double cross, late thirteenth century. (*c*) Reliquary pendant of the Holy Thorn, of enamelled gold set with two large amethysts. Late thirteenth century

PLATE 13

(*a–b*) The Kames Brooch, gold, *c.* 1300

(*c*) Gold ring brooch set with rubies and sapphires, the back nielloed, *c.* 1300

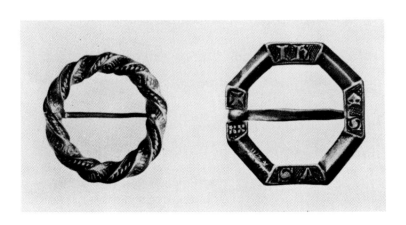

(a) Brooch found near Doune Castle, c. 1400. (b) Silver brooch inscribed
IHESVS NASERENE. Fourteenth or fifteenth century. (c) Gold brooch
with projecting setting for jewel, c. 1400. (d) Gold brooch with lobed ring.
Fourteenth century. (e) Gold brooch with cabalistic inscription. Fourteenth
century

PLATE 15
(*a*) Gold brooch set with rubies and sapphires. Fourteenth century
(*b*) Gold brooch set with pearls, emeralds and sapphires.
Early fourteenth century
(*c*) Silver brooch with gilded rosettes and collars, from Norham.
Fourteenth century

PLATE 16
The Glenlyon Brooch: silver gilt set with amethysts
and pearls inscribed. ? *c.* 1500. (*Reduced*)

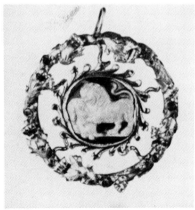

PLATE 17
(a) The Loch Buy Brooch; silver, set with crystals and pearls. Sixteenth century
(b) Gold brooch set with a cameo and rubies. Late fourteenth century

Plate 18

(a) Gold heart brooch, inscribed VOUS ESTES MA IOY MOVNDEINE. Late fourteenth century. (b) Gold brooch set with sapphires and pearls. Late fourteenth century. (c) Gold heart brooch once enamelled with peacock's feathers. Inscribed NOSTRE ET TOUTDIS A VOSTRE PLESIR. Fourteenth century. (d) Gold heart brooch with flowers in relief. Fourteenth century

PLATE 19

(*a*) The Founder's Jewel, left by William of Wykeham to New College, Oxford, in 1404. (*b*) Gold brooch in the form of a pelican. Fifteenth century. (*c*) Gold reliquary pendant engraved with figures of saints and the motto A MON DERREYNE

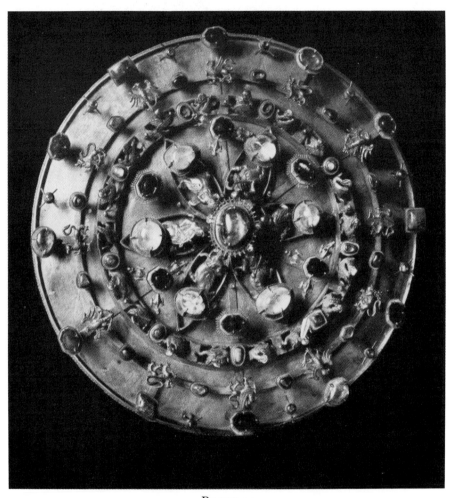

PLATE 20

Wheel-shaped fourteenth-century gold brooch, set with jewels and ornamented with grotesque figures, applied in the fifteenth century to a larger
plate of gold also jewelled and ornamented with eagles and lions of gold.
Found in the Motala River near Kumstad. (*Reduced*)

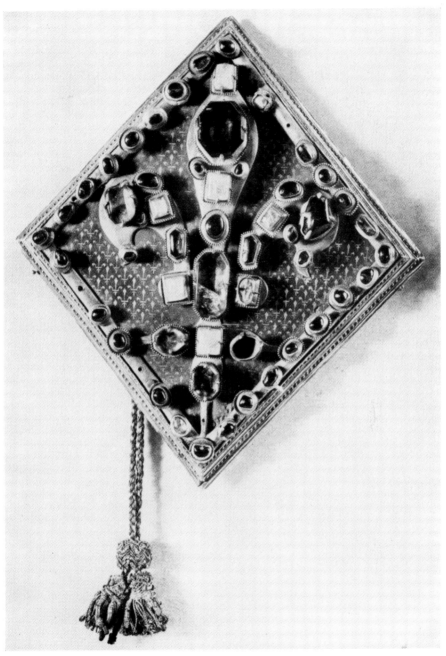

PLATE 21

The Fleur-de-Lys clasp of the French Regalia: enamelled gold set with
sapphires. (*Reduced*)

PLATE 22
Early fifteenth-century brooches
(a–e) Dedicated in the Cathedral of Essen
(f) From the river Meuse

PLATE 23
Brooches dedicated in the Cathedral of Essen. Early fifteenth century
(*a* and *c*) Lady in a garden
(*b*) Pelican in her piety
(*d*) Huntsman

PLATE 24
Reliquary brooch, silver gilt with gems and opaque enamels.
German *c.* 1375. (*Reduced*)

PLATE 25
The Bridal Crown worn by Princess Blanche, daughter of Henry IV of
England, at her marriage to the Elector Ludwig III in 1402. (*Reduced*)

PLATE 26
(a) Dress ornaments. Silver-gilt. From the 'Budapest Find'. Hungarian,
fifteenth century
(b–d) Pendant triptych. Gold, the doors set with crystal panels, enclosing
figures of the Virgin and Child and two angels in *émail en ronde bosse*.
French, c. 1400

PLATE 27
Miniatures of (a) the White Rose Jewel (1916.478), and (b) the
Three Brothers Jewel (1916.475) captured at Grandson in
in 1476 from Charles the Bold

PLATE 28
Detail from the *Virgin* by Gerard David, *c.* 1500

PLATE 29
Jewel Border from a Flemish Book of Hours, *c.* 1500

PLATE 30
Margaret of Denmark, Queen of Scotland. Detail from the picture by
Van der Goes, 1476

PLATE 31
Anne de Beaujeu
Detail from the triptych of the Maître de Moulins, *c.* 1498

PLATE 32
Margaret of Austria, Duchess of Savoy
Detail from a portrait, 1483

PLATE 33
Portrait of a Woman. French, *c.* 1500

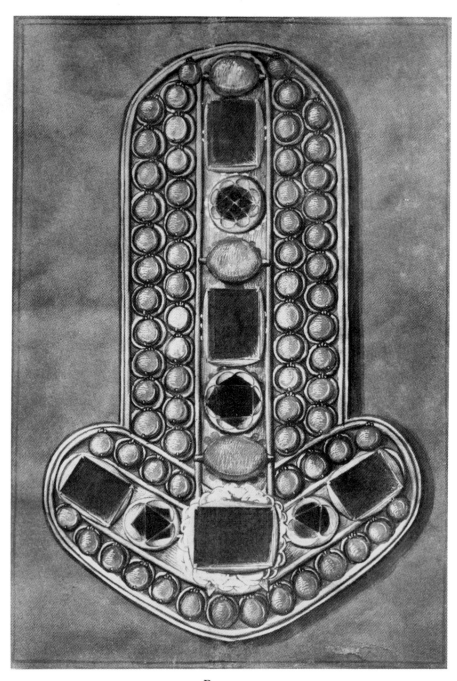

PLATE 34
Miniature painted about 1500 of the gold aigrette set with pearls and rubies
looted from the tent of the Duke of Burgundy at Grandson in 1476

PLATE 35
Buckle and mordant, inscribed VIRTVS VIN[*cit*]. Italian, fifteenth century

PLATE 36
(a) Buckle and belt end of nielloed silver, inscribed AMORE
(b) Reliquary pendant of silver nielloed and gilt;
on the obverse IHS. Italian, fifteenth century.

PLATE 37

(*a*) Pendant triptych, enamelled gold with a cameo of the Nativity. Burgundian, fifteenth century

(*b*) Silver gilt diptych with the Virgin and Child and the Crucifixion in relief on an enamelled ground. German, late fifteenth century

PLATE 38
(*a*) Pendant triptych reliquary. French, late fifteenth century
(*b*) Rosary of agate beads opening to show enamelled reliefs of the life of
Christ. Probably Italian. Early sixteenth century. (*Reduced*)

PLATE 39
Pendant mirror of Margaret, Duchess of Burgundy; silver gilt and gold
enamelled with Christ's entry into Jerusalem. *c.* 1470

PLATE 40
Cross found at Middlefart, Denmark. Early sixteenth century

PLATE 41

(*a*) Hat badge. Gold, with head of St. John the Baptist (enamelled white)
on a charger (enamelled red). Inscribed: INTER NATOS MVLIERVM NON
SVREXSIT. French, early sixteenth century. (*Enlarged*)

(*b–c*) Front and back of a reliquary pendant of enamelled gold. North
Italian, *c.* 1500

PLATE 42
The Reliquary Pendant of St. Thomas More. Enamelled
gold, sixteenth century

PLATE 43
Pilgrims' signs painted in a Flemish Book of Hours, *c.* 1500

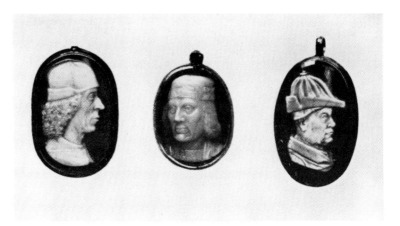

PLATE 44

(a) Cameo of Lorenzo de' Medici, c. 1490

(b) Cameo of Ludovico Sforza, c. 1500

(c) Cameo of Jean, duc de Berry. Early fifteenth century

(d) Drawing of a pendant with a table diamond held by a nymph and satyr, offered for sale to Henry VIII in 1546

PLATE 45
Portrait of Battista Sforza, *c.* 1480

PLATE 46

(a) Hat medallion, with the Conversion of St. Paul, once belonging to
Don John of Austria. (b) Hat medallion, with the Judgment of Paris.
(c) Hat medallion, gold, with a Battle Scene. (d) Hat medallion, with
Apollo driving the horses of the Sun.
Enamelled gold, probably Italian, middle of the sixteenth century

PLATE 47

(*a–b*) Hat medallion, with St. John and St. Mary Magdalene. The doors behind them open to reveal the veil of St. Veronica and the Annunciation.
(*c*) Hat medallion, with the Entombment and Angels holding the Robe of Christ and the Crown of Thorns. Enamelled gold, Italian, *c.* 1500

PLATE 48
(*a*) Brooch from a Florentine picture of the Virgin and Child, *c.* 1490
(*b*) Pendant from Lorenzo Lotto's *Lucrezia*, *c.* 1520

PLATE 49

(a) Back of a seal made for Cardinal Giovanni de'Medici.
Florentine c. 1500. (Reduced)

(b) Gold repoussé medallion for a cap-brooch. Italian, early
sixteenth century. (Twice actual size)

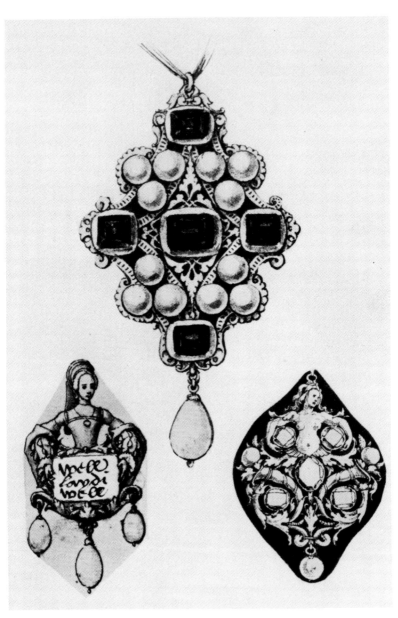

PLATE 50
Designs for pendants by Hans Holbein
c. 1530

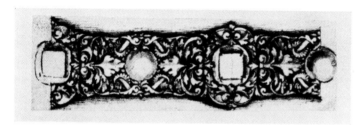

PLATE 51
Designs for chains by Hans Holbein
c. 1530

PLATE 52
(a) Hat medallion with St. John the Baptist in the Wilderness
(b) Hat medallion with St. John the Divine. Enamelled gold.
Italian, early sixteenth century

PLATE 53
Portrait of Caterina Cornaro (1454–1510),
Queen of Cyprus, *c.* 1500, by Gentile Bellini.

PLATE 54
Detail of the portrait of Bianca Maria Sforza, wife of the Emperor
Maximilian I, School of Bernardin Strigel, *c.* 1510

PLATE 55
Detail of the portrait of Isabella of Austria by Jan Gossaert, *c.* 1520

PLATE 56
Detail of the portrait of Eleanor of Austria, Spanish School, *c.* 1525

PLATE 57
Portrait of Henry VIII, *c.* 1536, by Hans Holbein

PLATE 58
Detail of the portrait of Anne of Cleves by Holbein, *c.* 1540

PLATE 59
Engraved designs for pendants by Virgil Solis of Nuremberg, *c.* 1540

PLATE 60
Designs for pendants by Etienne Delaune, *c.* 1560

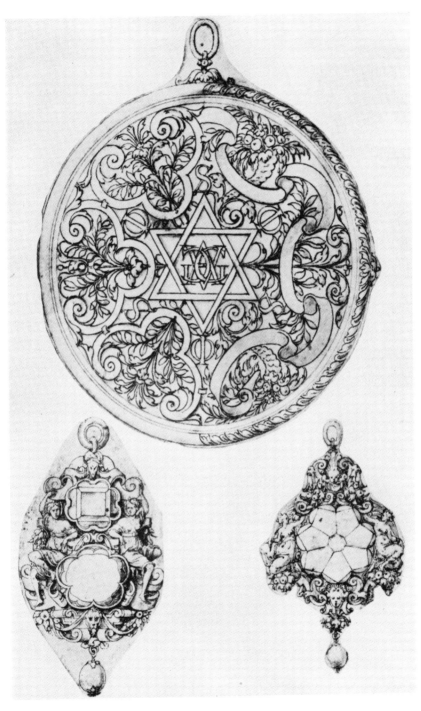

PLATE 61
Designs for Pendants by Etienne Delaune, *c.* 1560

PLATE 62

(a) Cap jewel with St. George and the Dragon. Probably German
(b) Cap jewel with David bearing the head of Goliath, the head
and body of chalcedony. Enamelled and jewelled gold. Middle of
the sixteenth century

PLATE 63

(a) Hat medallion of enamelled gold with Leda and the Swan, the head and body of chalcedony. The back bears the arms and devices of Francis I. Probably French, *c.* 1540

(b–c) Back and front of a pendant with the figure of Prudence, the head and arms of chalcedony. The back is enamelled with Diana after an engraved design by Etienne Delaune. Probably French, middle of the sixteenth century

PLATE 64

(*a*) Cameo of St. George and the Dragon with details and mount in
enamelled gold set with rubies and diamonds

(*b*) Cameo of Hercules in a mount of enamelled gold set with rubies

(*c*) Hat ornament of enamelled gold with the story of Judith and Holofernes

English, middle of the sixteenth century

PLATE 65

(a) Medallion from a hat ornament of enamelled gold, with the Adoration
of the Magi. German, c. 1540

(b) Portrait medallion of the Emperor Charles V; gold and enamel on a
bloodstone background in a rim of lapis lazuli, c. 1540

PLATE 66
Chain and pendant found in the tomb of Caterina Jagellonica, Queen of
Sweden, d. 1583; the pendant of enamelled gold with a crowned C in
rubies (*Reduced*)

PLATE 67
Pendant of enamelled gold with AA in table diamonds and a crown in
rubies made for Anna of Saxony, *c.* 1560

PLATE 69
Portrait of Henry VIII by Holbein, 1540

PLATE 70

Pendant book-cover of gold enamelled in black and white with the
Judgment of Solomon and the Worship of the Brazen Serpent.
English, middle of the sixteenth century

PLATE 71

Pendant book-cover of gold enamelled in many colours with the Creation
of Eve and a scene of nymphs surprised while bathing.
Middle of the sixteenth century

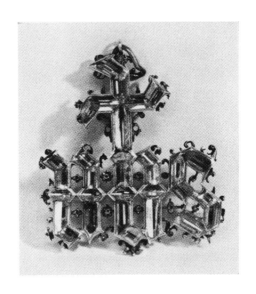

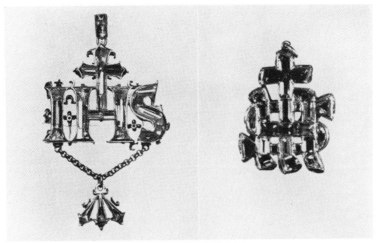

PLATE 72

IHS pendants of diamonds in settings of enamelled gold, *c.* 1600

PLATE 73
Drawings of a Carcanet, *Cotière* and Pendants by Hans Mielich, *c.* 1570

PLATE 74
Portrait of Elisabeth of Austria, wife of Charles IX of France. French
School, *c.* 1570

PLATE 75
Detail of the portrait of the Infanta Isabella Clara Eugenia, by Sanchez
Coello, *c.* 1570

PLATE 76
Portrait of Mary Tudor by Hans Eworth

PLATE 77
Portrait of Queen Elizabeth, *c.* 1575

PLATE 78
Headdress. Gold, set with pearls. Nuremberg, c. 1600. (*Reduced*)

PLATE 79

(a) Back of a sea-dragon pendant set with baroque pearls and emeralds. Probably German, c. 1575. (*Slightly reduced*)

(b) Front of the same pendant
(*Slightly reduced*)

PLATE 80

Back and front of a Sea-horse pendant of enamelled gold set with emeralds.
Probably German, *c.* 1575

PLATE 81
(a) The Canning Jewel, c. 1580
(b) Lizard pendant of enamelled gold set with a
baroque pearl. Probably Spanish, c. 1580

PLATE 82

(*a*) Mermaid pendant of enamelled gold set with emeralds. (*b*) Mermaid pendant of enamelled gold set with rubies. (*c*) Pendant of a Nereid and child of enamelled gold set with baroque pearls, emeralds and rubies. Probably German, *c.* 1580. (*All slightly reduced*)

PLATE 83
Back and front of a dragon pendant in enamelled gold and pearls
Spanish, *c.* 1570

PLATE 84
Spanish Bird pendants, *c.* 1580

PLATE 85

(*a*) Front of a pendant with the figure of Charity. German, *c.* 1590

(*b*) Back of the same pendant

PLATE 86
Front and back of a pendant with the Adoration of the Magi
German, c. 1610

PLATE 87
(a) Pendant with the figure of Justice
(b) Pendant with the Incredulity of St. Thomas
German, late sixteenth century

PLATE 88
(a) Pendant with the Annunciation
(b) Pendant with Hercules and the daughters of Atlas
Late sixteenth century

PLATE 89

Chain and pendant of gold enamelled with scenes of the Passion. German,
c. 1580, perhaps made for the Emperor Rudolf II

PLATE 90

(*a*) Cameo of Lucretia, mounted in enamelled gold. German, *c.* 1600.
(*b*) Cameo of a negress, mounted in enamelled gold. German, *c.* 1600.
(*c*) Cameo of Omphale in a rim of rubies. German, *c.* 1600. (*d*) Hat ornament of a cameo of a negro in a rim of rubies, *c.* 1580

PLATE 91
Sixteenth-century Ship Pendants
(a) Crystal hull and enamelled gold rigging
(b) Enamelled gold and pearls, probably Venetian (*Reduced*)
(c) Crystal hull in enamelled gold mount

PLATE 92
Portrait Cameos of Mary Queen of Scots
(*a*) In a pendant of enamelled gold, *c.* 1565. (*b*) In a cap brooch with a rim
of enamelled gold set with rubies, *c.* 1560. (*c*) In a heart-shaped locket of
enamelled gold set with rubies and emeralds, *c.* 1565. (*Slightly reduced*)

PLATE 93
The Heneage Jewel, given by Queen Elizabeth to Sir Thomas Heneage.
The miniature dated 158?, the jewel probably 1588; both by Nicholas
Hilliard

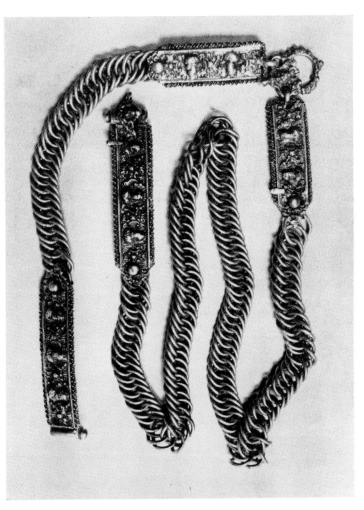

PLATE 94
Silver belt inscribed
MAREN KNVDSDATTER, 1608

PLATE 95

(a) Ovoid pendant of enamelled gold set with rubies and pearls. German, c. 1600

(b) Pendant of enamelled gold set with rubies and pearls, with a figure of David harping. ? Spanish, c. 1610

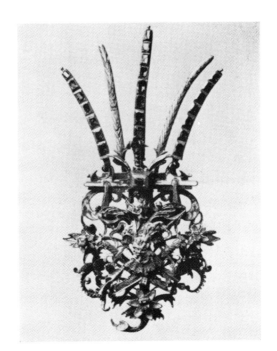

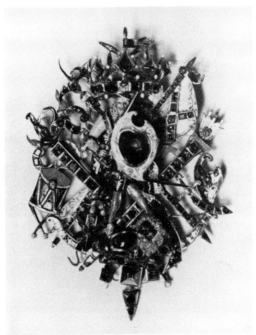

PLATE 96
Trophy Jewels. German, *c.* 1615
(*a*) Enamelled gold set with rubies and diamonds
(*b*) Enamelled gold set with rubies, said to have
been lost by Charles I on the field of Naseby

PLATE 97
(*a*) Pendant of Princess Maria Eleanora of Sweden. German, *c.* 1620
(*b*) Links from a necklace of enamelled gold set with pearls and diamonds.
German, *c.* 1620

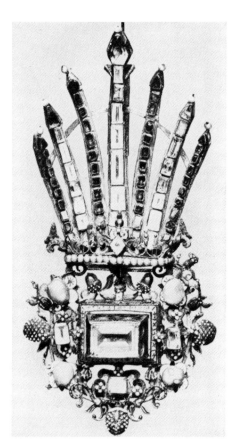

PLATE 98

(a) Aigrette of enamelled gold set with emeralds. ? Italian, c. 1600

(b) Pendant with Daniel in the Lion's Den, the back enamelled in
the style of Daniel Mignot, c. 1600

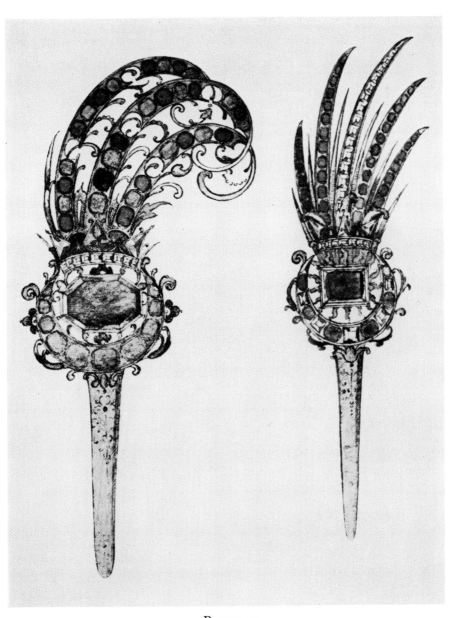

PLATE 99
Designs for Aigrettes set with rubies and emeralds by Arnold Lulls,
jeweller to Anne of Denmark, *c.* 1610

PLATE 100
Portrait of a Princess, by Alonzo Sanchez Coello, c. 1610

PLATE 101
Portrait of Dorothée de Croy,
Duchesse de Croy et d'Arschot (1575–1662),
painted in 1615, by Frans II Pourbus

PLATE 102
Portrait of Maria Capponi (1578–1656),
wife of Guido Pecori. Florentine, unknown painter, *c.* 1600

PLATE 103

Two Miniature Cases, c. 1610

(a–b) Enamelled in tawny red and set with table diamonds, containing a
miniature of Anne of Denmark

(c) Enamelled and set with rubies and diamonds, containing a miniature of
an unknown man by John Hoskins. The fretted lid is ornamented with a
knot end inscribed FAST THOVGH VNTIED

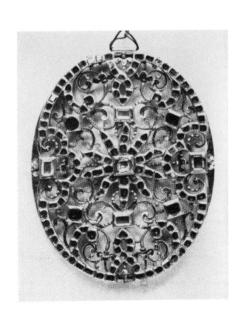

PLATE 104
Lid and Back of a miniature case containing a portrait of Queen Elizabeth,
the lid set with diamonds and the back enamelled in colours after a design
by Daniel Mignot. English, *c.* 1600

PLATE 105
Two gold miniature cases with champlevé enamel, *c.* 1610.
(*Both slightly reduced*)

PLATE 106
(a) Gold miniature case with champlevé enamel in white and black, c. 1620
(b) Design for a miniature case by Jean Toutin, 1619

PLATE 107
Email en résille sur verre, c. 1620
(*a*) Back of case containing an engraved silver portrait of Princess Mary of Austria, daughter of Philip II of Spain

(*b*) Oblong pendant with Apollo and Daphne

PLATE 108

(a) Watch case of pierced and engraved silver by Klotz of Augsburg.
End of the sixteenth century

(b) Watch case of pierced and enamelled gold in the style of Daniel
Mignot, c. 1620

(c) Watch case of enamelled gold. French, c. 1640

PLATE 109
Watch of enamelled gold set with cabochon sapphires. French, *c.* 1620

PLATE 110
Spanish Bird Pendants
c. 1620

PLATE III
Spanish devotional jewels
c. 1625

PLATE 112
Design for a diamond pendant, with three hanging pearls, by Arnold Lulls,
c. 1610

PLATE 113
Gold pendants set with amethysts,
c. 1630

PLATE 114
Pendant of diamonds set in gold with touches of black and white enamel
c. 1625

PLATE 115
Portrait of Claudia de' Medici by Sustermans, *c.* 1625

PLATE 116
Spanish Crosses, c. 1620

PLATE 117

(a) The Lyte jewel, of enamelled gold set with diamonds, containing a
miniature of James I given by him to Thomas Lyte of
Lyte's Cary, Somerset, c. 1620

(b) Plaque of *émail en résille sur verre*. French, c. 1620

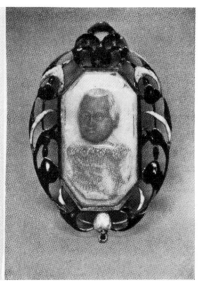

PLATE 118
Jewels in Pea-Pod Style
(a) Back of the case of a miniature by Peter Oliver, c. 1625, enamelled
after a design by Pierre Firens
(b) Cameo of Louis XIII as a child in an enamelled frame, c. 1610
(c–d) Cameo of Lucius Verus in a frame in the style of Pierre Marchand,
c. 1620

PLATE 119
Watches enamelled in Pea-Pod Style, c. 1620
(a–b) By Claude Pascal, The Hague
(c–d) By Vautyer, Blois

PLATE 120

(a–b) Watch by Daniel Bouquet set with rose diamonds and enamelled
with coloured flowers in low relief on black ground, c. 1665

(c) Watch of fretted and chased gold enamelled in pale colours. French,
c. 1650

PLATE 121

(*a–b*) Watch by Jacques Huon of Paris decorated in painted enamel with
flowers in pinkish grisaille on a black ground, *c.* 1660

(*c*) Cameo in a frame of enamelled flowers in the style of Gilles Légaré.
French, *c.* 1670

(*d*) Watch decorated with flowers in champlevé enamel, *c.* 1670

PLATE 122
Detail of the portrait of Lady Rich by Anthony van Dyck, *c.* 1635

PLATE 123
Portrait of the Duchesse de Longueville, *c.* 1640

PLATE 124
(*a–b*) Coffin pendant of enamelled gold inscribed 'Through the Resurrection of Christe we be all sanctified'. English, *c.* 1600
(*c*) Back of a badge of the Order of Malta enamelled with the Holy Family. French, *c.* 1670

PLATE 125

(*a*) Brooch with enamelled figures representing Jacob and Rachel at the Well on a ground of black. English, *c.* 1650. (*b*) Pendant enamelled with portraits of Charles I and Charles II. English, middle of the seventeenth century. (*c*) Watch case of gold filigree. English, *c.* 1640. (*d*) Slide for ribbon, enamelled with a death's head and cross-bones. English, *c.* 1640. (*e*) Buckle with hair under crystal, date 1728, English. (*f*) Coffin pendant of enamelled gold. English, *c.* 1640

PLATE 126

(*a*) Miniature case enamelled with flowers. English or Dutch, *c.* 1660.
(*b*) Back of miniature case set with emeralds. (*See Plate* 127a) (*c*) Back of
an enamelled miniature of a lady, with R.W.P. engraved on a matted
ground within a wreath of flowers in the style of Gilles Légaré. French,
c. 1670. (*d*) Back of memorial buckle. (*See Plate* 125e)

PLATE 127

(*a*) Miniature case set with emeralds between leaves of white enamel with touches of black. Probably French, *c.* 1670

(*b*) Necklace set with rose-cut crystals, the back enamelled in pale blue with touches of black. Probably Dutch. Middle of the seventeenth century

PLATE 128
Pendant and ear-rings set with topazes and diamonds. Spanish, middle of
the seventeenth century

PLATE 129
Portrait of Henrietta of England, Duchess of Orleans. French, *c.* 1665

PLATE 130
(a) Engraved designs for enamel by Gilles Légaré, 1663
(b) Watch case in pale blue enamel with touches of black and white, c. 1670

PLATE 131

(a) Jewel of gold set with diamonds and ornamented in white enamel, dedicated to the Shrine of the Virgen del Pilar at Saragossa in 1679

(b) Necklace of gold enamelled in black and white, the pendant set with diamonds, a pearl and a cabochon sapphire. French, c. 1670

PLATE 132

(a) Enamelled back of a miniature case formerly containing
a portrait of Louis XIV. French, c. 1680

(b) Enamelled back of a miniature case. French, c. 1680

PLATE 133
(*a–b*) Watch in black and white enamel. French, *c.* 1680
(*c*) Back of a miniature case in chased gold. English, *c.* 1710
(*d–e*) Miniature cases enamelled in the style of Louis Roupert of Metz,
c. 1680

PLATE 134

Breast ornament or *crochet* set with emeralds. Spanish early eighteenth century.
(*Slightly reduced*)

PLATE 135

(*a*) Pendant set with coloured topazes and emeralds. Spanish, *c.* 1680
(*b*) Arrow brooch set with diamonds and emeralds. French, *c.* 1670
(*c*) Slide for a ribbon set with table-cut diamonds. French, *c.* 1670
(*d*) Pendant set with rubies, emeralds and diamonds. Spanish, *c.* 1680

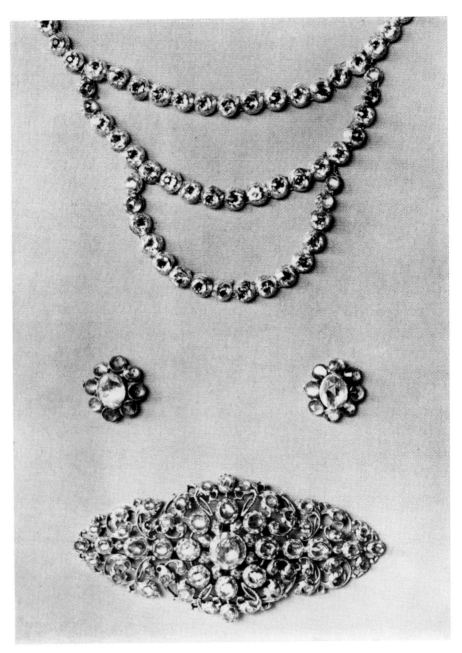

PLATE 136

Parure of crystals from the waxen funeral effigy of Frances Stuart, Duchess of Richmond. English, *c.* 1702. (*Slightly reduced*)

PLATE 137
(*a*) Pendant set with crystals.
English or Dutch, *c.* 1690.
H.M. The Queen.
(*Slightly reduced*)

(*b*) Back of the same pendant, enamelled and set with an enamelled portrait of William of Orange.

(*Slightly reduced*)

PLATE 138
Pendant of diamonds in scroll settings of gold. Spanish, early eighteenth
century

PLATE 139
Stomacher of rose-cut crystals. Probably English *c.* 1710. (*Slightly reduced*)

PLATE 140

(a) Bow brooch set with white topazes. Spanish, early eighteeenth century
(b) Bow and bird pendant set with crystals. Spanish, early eighteenth
century

PLATE 141
(a) Brooch in asymmetrical rocaille design set with rubies and diamonds.
Italian or German, c. 1740
(b) Brooch set with chrysolites. Portuguese, c. 1760

PLATE 142
Hat-clasp set with brilliants and a green diamond, made
for Augustus III of Saxony in 1740

PLATE 143
Order of the Golden Fleece in diamonds and rubies made
for Augustus III of Saxony, *c.* 1740

PLATE 144
Detail of the portrait of Maria Amalia Christina, Queen of Spain, by
Anton Raphael Mengs, c. 1760

PLATE 145
Detail of the portrait of Queen Charlotte from the studio of Allan Ramsay
c. 1762

PLATE 146
Flower Spray Brooches
(*a*) Set with chrysolites. Spanish or Portuguese, *c.* 1770
(*b*) Set with diamonds. Made by Duval at St. Petersburg for the
Empress Catherine the Great, *c.* 1760

PLATE 147
Bouquet of enamelled gold set with diamonds. Spanish, *c.* 1770

PLATE 148
Demi-parure of brooch and ear-rings set with chrysolites. Spanish, *c.* 1760

PLATE 149
Parure of diamonds and topazes. Spanish, middle of the eighteenth century

PLATE 150
Breast ornament set with foiled amethysts and topazes.
Spanish, *c.* 1770

PLATE 151
Necklace with alternative pendants in diamonds and topazes. French, *c.* 1760

PLATE 152
See Plate 153

PLATE 153
Parure of blue and white sapphires. French, *c.* 1760

PLATE 154
Two of a suite of three bow brooches set with diamonds. English, *c.* 1770

PLATE 155
(a) Necklace of crystals. English, c. 1790
(b) Pair of bracelet clasps with the initials of Marie Antoinette and her
device of doves in diamonds on a ground of blue paste. French, c. 1770

PLATE 156

Watch and chatelaine made by Thuilst for Queen Anne of engraved gold
with mother of pearl and garnets in rims of black and red enamel, *c.* 1705

PLATE 157
Gold watch and chatelaine by James Rowe of London, 1758

PLATE 158
Gold chatelaine and *étui*, the hook-plate chased with a seated Britannia
and the *étui* with Mars and Venus. English, *c.* 1740

PLATE 159
Chatelaines of base metal with designs in gilt on a silvered ground
English, c. 1760
(*Slightly reduced*)

PLATE 160
Chatelaine and *étui* of agate mounted in gold. English, *c.* 1770

PLATE 161

Gold watch and chatelaine, enamelled with figure subjects, the watch with
the French hall-mark for 1772–3. (*Slightly reduced*)

PLATE 162

(*a*) Buckle of gold set with rose-cut crystals. English, *c.* 1740

(*b*) Gold cross set with baguette and rose-cut crystals.
Perhaps Flemish, *c.* 1740

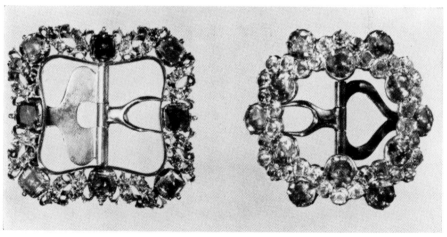

PLATE 163

(*a*) Waist buckle set with marcasites. French, *c.* 1770

(*b*) Shoe buckle, set with sapphires and diamonds. French, *c.* 1750

(*c*) Shoe buckle, set with blue and white pastes. Spanish, *c.* 1770

PLATE 164

(a) Detail of a bracelet formed of plaques of Bilston enamel. English,
c. 1775

(b–c) Buckles of cut steel. English, c. 1775

(d) Clasp of Wedgwood ware in a setting of cut steel. English, c. 1780

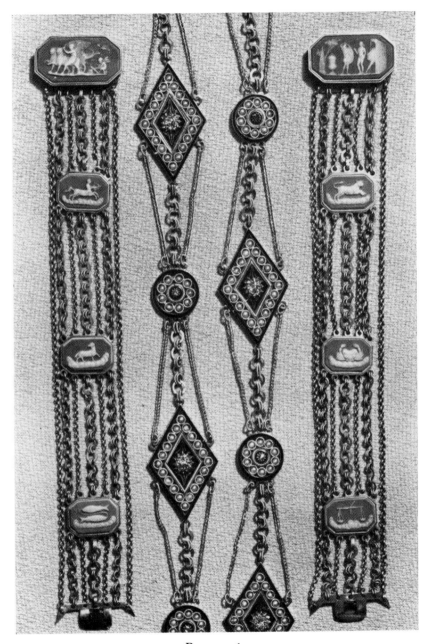

PLATE 165

(a–b) Pair of bracelets of gold chain set with Wedgwood plaques.
English, c. 1780

(c–d) Details of a *sautoir* of gold chains linked by plaques of
gold enamelled in black and set with diamonds and pearls. French, c. 1795

PLATE 166

English memorial jewellery, *c.* 1785, with miniatures partly executed in hair

PLATE 167

(a) Brooch of gold, partly enamelled, set with cornelians, emeralds and
pearls. French, c. 1790

(b) Watch and brooch *pavé*-set with pearls. Swiss, c. 1810

(c) Padlock of gold, set with cornelian and pearls. English, c. 1800

PLATE 168
Portrait of Katharina Barbara Freein von Liebert by Franz Josef Degle.
German, 1774

PLATE 169
Detail of the portrait of the Empress Josephine by Gérard, *c.* 1803

PLATE 170
Detail of the portrait of Marie Caroline, Queen of Naples, by Madame
Vigée Le Brun, *c.* 1806

PLATE 171
Detail of the portrait of Princess Borghese by Robert Lefebvre, 1806

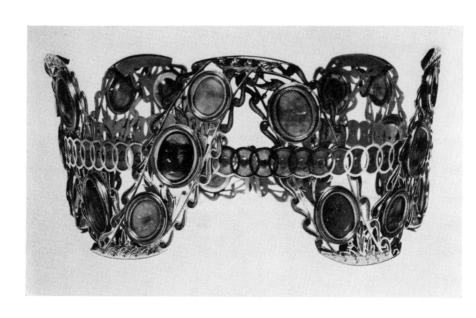

PLATE 172

Crown and diadem of gold enamelled in blue and set with cameos and intaglios, from a *parure* said to have belonged to the Empress Josephine, *c.* 1805 (*Reduced to three-quarter size*)

PLATE 173

(a) Pendant. Enamelled gold, set with a cornelian intaglio of Jove with
Venus and Cupid. Italian, c. 1820

(b) Earring (one of a pair).
Enamelled gold, set with a paste cameo. English, mid-nineteenth century

PLATE 174

Parure of amethysts set in gold. French, *c.* 1820

PLATE 175

(*a*) Shell cameo in a frame of gold in two colours. French, *c.* 1810

(*b*) Necklace of cast iron in settings of gold. Berlin, *c.* 1810

(*Slightly reduced*)

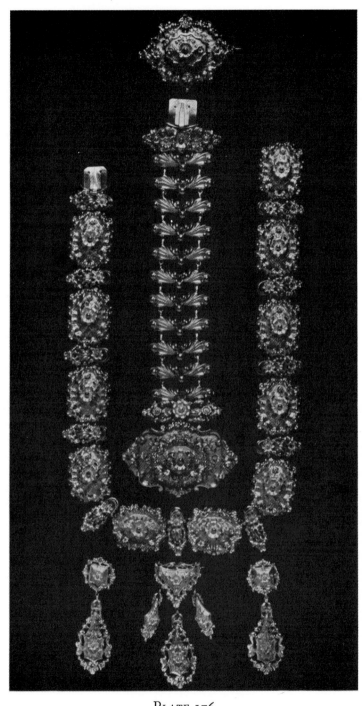

PLATE 176
Parure in stamped gold. French, *c.* 1825
(*Much reduced*)

PLATE 177
Brooch of diamonds and rubies designed as a bouquet of wild roses and a
butterfly. English, *c.* 1830

PLATE 178
Convolvulus brooch set with small turquoises. French, *c.* 1840

PLATE 179
Diamond spray of lilac, formerly belonging to
the Empress Eugénie. French, 1867

PLATE 180
Pearl and diamond brooch made by Lemonnier in 1853
for the marriage of the Empress Eugénie (*Reduced*)

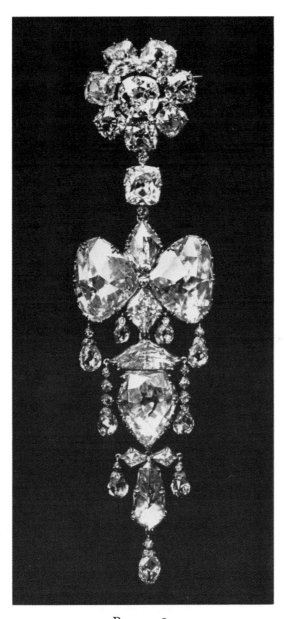

PLATE 181
Brooch set with diamonds from the Crown Jewels for
the Empress Eugénie. 1853

PLATE 182
'Gothic' Brooches
French, *c.* 1840

PLATE 183
Parure in coloured gold. French, *c.* 1830
(*Slightly reduced*)

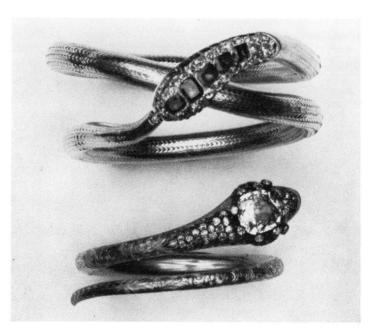

PLATE 184
Mid-nineteenth century Bracelets

PLATE 185

Demi-parure of gold filigree set with pearls and rubies, linked by strings
of small pearls. English, *c.* 1840

PLATE 186

Demi-parure of enamelled gold set with chrysoprases. French, *c.* 1830

PLATE 187
(a) Vinaigrette pendant in chased gold. English, c. 1840
(b) Necklace of gold, enamelled and set with pearls and amethysts. Perhaps
Swiss, c. 1835

PLATE 188

Necklace and pendant cross. Gold, enamelled black and green,
set with garnets and pearls. Designed by A. W. Pugin
and made for his third wife, Jane Knill. English, 1848

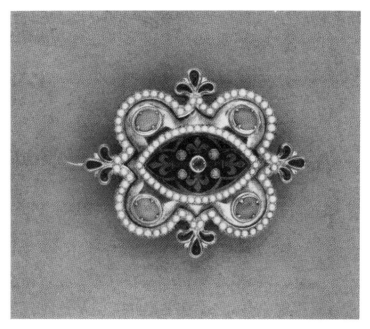

PLATE 189
(a) Neckband. Gold, enamelled green and white, set with a ruby,
diamonds, turquoises and pearls. Designed by A. W. Pugin for his third wife,
Jane Knill, and made by John Hardman and Co. Exhibited at the Great
Exhibition of 1851. English, 1848–50
(b) Brooch. Gold, enamelled green, set with turquoises, garnets
and pearls. Designed by A. W. Pugin and made for his third wife, Jane
Knill. English, 1848

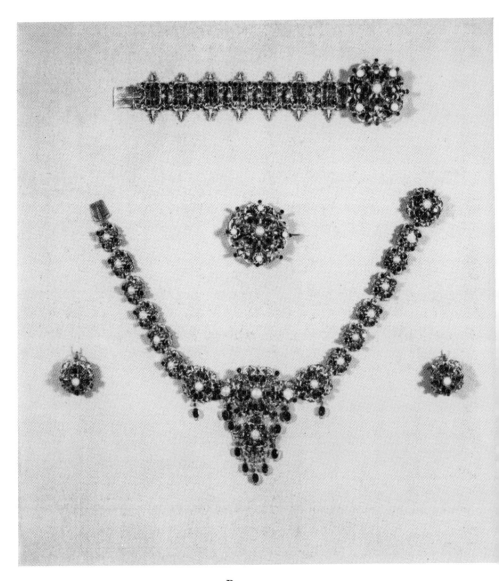

PLATE 190

Parure. Silver-gilt, enamelled (white with strokes of black),
and set with pearls, garnets and green garnets. Made by Schichtegroll,
Vienna, and shown at the Paris Exhibition in 1855

PLATE 191

Necklace of strands of small pearls mounted with gold enamelled in black and white, with a pendant set with an aquamarine and small rubies. By Giuliano, *c.* 1870

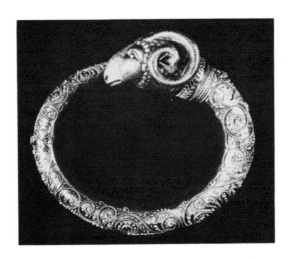

PLATE 192

(*a*) Bracelet. Gold, with filigree decoration in the Etruscan style.
Probably made by Pasquale Novissimo for Carlo Giuliano, *c.* 1880
(*b*) Bracelet. Gold, set with red agate scarabs. Made by Castellani of
Rome. Second half of the nineteenth century
(*c*) Bracelet. Gold, with applied decoration representing
Ashur-bani-pal, King of Assyria, sacrificing on his return from a lion
hunt, after Assyrian sculptures in the British Museum. By John Brogden,
London. English, *c.* 1851. Shown at the Great Exhibition, 1851

A CATALOG OF SELECTED
DOVER BOOKS
IN ALL FIELDS OF INTEREST

A CATALOG OF SELECTED DOVER
BOOKS IN ALL FIELDS OF INTEREST

DRAWINGS OF REMBRANDT, edited by Seymour Slive. Updated Lippmann, Hofstede de Groot edition, with definitive scholarly apparatus. All portraits, biblical sketches, landscapes, nudes. Oriental figures, classical studies, together with selection of work by followers. 550 illustrations. Total of 630pp. 9⅛ × 12¼.
21485-0, 21486-9 Pa., Two-vol. set $25.00

GHOST AND HORROR STORIES OF AMBROSE BIERCE, Ambrose Bierce. 24 tales vividly imagined, strangely prophetic, and decades ahead of their time in technical skill: "The Damned Thing," "An Inhabitant of Carcosa," "The Eyes of the Panther," "Moxon's Master," and 20 more. 199pp. 5⅜ × 8½. 20767-6 Pa. $3.95

ETHICAL WRITINGS OF MAIMONIDES, Maimonides. Most significant ethical works of great medieval sage, newly translated for utmost precision, readability. Laws Concerning Character Traits, Eight Chapters, more. 192pp. 5⅜ × 8½.
24522-5 Pa. $4.50

THE EXPLORATION OF THE COLORADO RIVER AND ITS CANYONS, J. W. Powell. Full text of Powell's 1,000-mile expedition down the fabled Colorado in 1869. Superb account of terrain, geology, vegetation, Indians, famine, mutiny, treacherous rapids, mighty canyons, during exploration of last unknown part of continental U.S. 400pp. 5⅜ × 8½. 20094-9 Pa. $6.95

HISTORY OF PHILOSOPHY, Julián Marías. Clearest one-volume history on the market. Every major philosopher and dozens of others, to Existentialism and later. 505pp. 5⅜ × 8½. 21739-6 Pa. $8.50

ALL ABOUT LIGHTNING, Martin A. Uman. Highly readable non-technical survey of nature and causes of lightning, thunderstorms, ball lightning, St. Elmo's Fire, much more. Illustrated. 192pp. 5⅜ × 8½. 25237-X Pa. $5.95

SAILING ALONE AROUND THE WORLD, Captain Joshua Slocum. First man to sail around the world, alone, in small boat. One of great feats of seamanship told in delightful manner. 67 illustrations. 294pp. 5⅜ × 8½. 20326-3 Pa. $4.95

LETTERS AND NOTES ON THE MANNERS, CUSTOMS AND CONDITIONS OF THE NORTH AMERICAN INDIANS, George Catlin. Classic account of life among Plains Indians: ceremonies, hunt, warfare, etc. 312 plates. 572pp. of text. 6⅛ × 9¼. 22118-0, 22119-9 Pa. Two-vol. set $15.90

ALASKA: The Harriman Expedition, 1899, John Burroughs, John Muir, et al. Informative, engrossing accounts of two-month, 9,000-mile expedition. Native peoples, wildlife, forests, geography, salmon industry, glaciers, more. Profusely illustrated. 240 black-and-white line drawings. 124 black-and-white photographs. 3 maps. Index. 576pp. 5⅜ × 8½. 25109-8 Pa. $11.95

ILLUSTRATED DICTIONARY OF HISTORIC ARCHITECTURE, edited by Cyril M. Harris. Extraordinary compendium of clear, concise definitions for over 5,000 important architectural terms complemented by over 2,000 line drawings. Covers full spectrum of architecture from ancient ruins to 20th-century Modernism. Preface. 592pp. 7½ × 9⅝. 24444-X Pa. $14.95

THE NIGHT BEFORE CHRISTMAS, Clement Moore. Full text, and woodcuts from original 1848 book. Also critical, historical material. 19 illustrations. 40pp. 4⅝ × 6. 22797-9 Pa. $2.50

THE LESSON OF JAPANESE ARCHITECTURE: 165 Photographs, Jiro Harada. Memorable gallery of 165 photographs taken in the 1930's of exquisite Japanese homes of the well-to-do and historic buildings. 13 line diagrams. 192pp. 8⅜ × 11¼. 24778-3 Pa. $8.95

THE AUTOBIOGRAPHY OF CHARLES DARWIN AND SELECTED LETTERS, edited by Francis Darwin. The fascinating life of eccentric genius composed of an intimate memoir by Darwin (intended for his children); commentary by his son, Francis; hundreds of fragments from notebooks, journals, papers; and letters to and from Lyell, Hooker, Huxley, Wallace and Henslow. xi + 365pp. 5⅜ × 8. 20479-0 Pa. $5.95

WONDERS OF THE SKY: Observing Rainbows, Comets, Eclipses, the Stars and Other Phenomena, Fred Schaaf. Charming, easy-to-read poetic guide to all manner of celestial events visible to the naked eye. Mock suns, glories, Belt of Venus, more. Illustrated. 299pp. 5¼ × 8¼. 24402-4 Pa. $7.95

BURNHAM'S CELESTIAL HANDBOOK, Robert Burnham, Jr. Thorough guide to the stars beyond our solar system. Exhaustive treatment. Alphabetical by constellation: Andromeda to Cetus in Vol. 1; Chamaeleon to Orion in Vol. 2; and Pavo to Vulpecula in Vol. 3. Hundreds of illustrations. Index in Vol. 3. 2,000pp. 6⅛ × 9¼. 23567-X, 23568-8, 23673-0 Pa., Three-vol. set $37.85

STAR NAMES: Their Lore and Meaning, Richard Hinckley Allen. Fascinating history of names various cultures have given to constellations and literary and folkloristic uses that have been made of stars. Indexes to subjects. Arabic and Greek names. Biblical references. Bibliography. 563pp. 5⅜ × 8½. 21079-0 Pa. $7.95

THIRTY YEARS THAT SHOOK PHYSICS: The Story of Quantum Theory, George Gamow. Lucid, accessible introduction to influential theory of energy and matter. Careful explanations of Dirac's anti-particles, Bohr's model of the atom, much more. 12 plates. Numerous drawings. 240pp. 5⅜ × 8½. 24895-X Pa. $4.95

CHINESE DOMESTIC FURNITURE IN PHOTOGRAPHS AND MEASURED DRAWINGS, Gustav Ecke. A rare volume, now affordably priced for antique collectors, furniture buffs and art historians. Detailed review of styles ranging from early Shang to late Ming. Unabridged republication. 161 black-and-white drawings, photos. Total of 224pp. 8⅜ × 11¼. (Available in U.S. only) 25171-3 Pa. $12.95

VINCENT VAN GOGH: A Biography, Julius Meier-Graefe. Dynamic, penetrating study of artist's life, relationship with brother, Theo, painting techniques, travels, more. Readable, engrossing. 160pp. 5⅜ × 8½. (Available in U.S. only) 25253-1 Pa. $3.95

CATALOG OF DOVER BOOKS

THE BOOK OF BEASTS: Being a Translation from a Latin Bestiary of the Twelfth Century, T. H. White. Wonderful catalog real and fanciful beasts: manticore, griffin, phoenix, amphivius, jaculus, many more. White's witty erudite commentary on scientific, historical aspects. Fascinating glimpse of medieval mind. Illustrated. 296pp. 5⅝ × 8¼. (Available in U.S. only) 24609-4 Pa. $5.95

FRANK LLOYD WRIGHT: ARCHITECTURE AND NATURE With 160 Illustrations, Donald Hoffmann. Profusely illustrated study of influence of nature—especially prairie—on Wright's designs for Fallingwater, Robie House, Guggenheim Museum, other masterpieces. 96pp. 9¼ × 10¾. 25098-9 Pa. $7.95

FRANK LLOYD WRIGHT'S FALLINGWATER, Donald Hoffmann. Wright's famous waterfall house: planning and construction of organic idea. History of site, owners, Wright's personal involvement. Photographs of various stages of building. Preface by Edgar Kaufmann, Jr. 100 illustrations. 112pp. 9¼ × 10. 23671-4 Pa. $7.95

YEARS WITH FRANK LLOYD WRIGHT: Apprentice to Genius, Edgar Tafel. Insightful memoir by a former apprentice presents a revealing portrait of Wright the man, the inspired teacher, the greatest American architect. 372 black-and-white illustrations. Preface. Index. vi + 228pp. 8¼ × 11. 24801-1 Pa. $9.95

THE STORY OF KING ARTHUR AND HIS KNIGHTS, Howard Pyle. Enchanting version of King Arthur fable has delighted generations with imaginative narratives of exciting adventures and unforgettable illustrations by the author. 41 illustrations. xviii + 313pp. 6⅛ × 9¼. 21445-1 Pa. $5.95

THE GODS OF THE EGYPTIANS, E. A. Wallis Budge. Thorough coverage of numerous gods of ancient Egypt by foremost Egyptologist. Information on evolution of cults, rites and gods; the cult of Osiris; the Book of the Dead and its rites; the sacred animals and birds; Heaven and Hell; and more. 956pp. 6⅛ × 9¼. 22055-9, 22056-7 Pa., Two-vol. set $21.90

A THEOLOGICO-POLITICAL TREATISE, Benedict Spinoza. Also contains unfinished *Political Treatise*. Great classic on religious liberty, theory of government on common consent. R. Elwes translation. Total of 421pp. 5⅜ × 8½. 20249-6 Pa. $6.95

INCIDENTS OF TRAVEL IN CENTRAL AMERICA, CHIAPAS, AND YUCATAN, John L. Stephens. Almost single-handed discovery of Maya culture; exploration of ruined cities, monuments, temples; customs of Indians. 115 drawings. 892pp. 5⅜ × 8½. 22404-X, 22405-8 Pa., Two-vol. set $15.90

LOS CAPRICHOS, Francisco Goya. 80 plates of wild, grotesque monsters and caricatures. Prado manuscript included. 183pp. 6⅜ × 9⅜. 22384-1 Pa. $4.95

AUTOBIOGRAPHY: The Story of My Experiments with Truth, Mohandas K. Gandhi. Not hagiography, but Gandhi in his own words. Boyhood, legal studies, purification, the growth of the Satyagraha (nonviolent protest) movement. Critical, inspiring work of the man who freed India. 480pp. 5⅜ × 8½. (Available in U.S. only) 24593-4 Pa. $6.95

HOW TO WRITE, Gertrude Stein. Gertrude Stein claimed anyone could understand her unconventional writing—here are clues to help. Fascinating improvisations, language experiments, explanations illuminate Stein's craft and the art of writing. Total of 414pp. 4⅝ × 6⅜. 23144-5 Pa. $5.95

ADVENTURES AT SEA IN THE GREAT AGE OF SAIL: Five Firsthand Narratives, edited by Elliot Snow. Rare true accounts of exploration, whaling, shipwreck, fierce natives, trade, shipboard life, more. 33 illustrations. Introduction. 353pp. 5⅜ × 8½. 25177-2 Pa. $7.95

THE HERBAL OR GENERAL HISTORY OF PLANTS, John Gerard. Classic descriptions of about 2,850 plants—with over 2,700 illustrations—includes Latin and English names, physical descriptions, varieties, time and place of growth, more. 2,706 illustrations. xlv + 1,678pp. 8½ × 12¼. 23147-X Cloth. $75.00

DOROTHY AND THE WIZARD IN OZ, L. Frank Baum. Dorothy and the Wizard visit the center of the Earth, where people are vegetables, glass houses grow and Oz characters reappear. Classic sequel to *Wizard of Oz.* 256pp. 5⅜ × 8. 24714-7 Pa. $4.95

SONGS OF EXPERIENCE: Facsimile Reproduction with 26 Plates in Full Color, William Blake. This facsimile of Blake's original "Illuminated Book" reproduces 26 full-color plates from a rare 1826 edition. Includes "The Tyger," "London," "Holy Thursday," and other immortal poems. 26 color plates. Printed text of poems. 48pp. 5¼ × 7. 24636-1 Pa. $3.50

SONGS OF INNOCENCE, William Blake. The first and most popular of Blake's famous "Illuminated Books," in a facsimile edition reproducing all 31 brightly colored plates. Additional printed text of each poem. 64pp. 5¼ × 7. 22764-2 Pa. $3.50

PRECIOUS STONES, Max Bauer. Classic, thorough study of diamonds, rubies, emeralds, garnets, etc.: physical character, occurrence, properties, use, similar topics. 20 plates, 8 in color. 94 figures. 659pp. 6⅛ × 9¼. 21910-0, 21911-9 Pa., Two-vol. set $15.90

ENCYCLOPEDIA OF VICTORIAN NEEDLEWORK, S. F. A. Caulfeild and Blanche Saward. Full, precise descriptions of stitches, techniques for dozens of needlecrafts—most exhaustive reference of its kind. Over 800 figures. Total of 679pp. 8⅛ × 11. Two volumes. Vol. 1 22800-2 Pa. $11.95
Vol. 2 22801-0 Pa. $11.95

THE MARVELOUS LAND OF OZ, L. Frank Baum. Second Oz book, the Scarecrow and Tin Woodman are back with hero named Tip, Oz magic. 136 illustrations. 287pp. 5⅜ × 8½. 20692-0 Pa. $5.95

WILD FOWL DECOYS, Joel Barber. Basic book on the subject, by foremost authority and collector. Reveals history of decoy making and rigging, place in American culture, different kinds of decoys, how to make them, and how to use them. 140 plates. 156pp. 7⅞ × 10¾. 20011-6 Pa. $8.95

HISTORY OF LACE, Mrs. Bury Palliser. Definitive, profusely illustrated chronicle of lace from earliest times to late 19th century. Laces of Italy, Greece, England, France, Belgium, etc. Landmark of needlework scholarship. 266 illustrations. 672pp. 6⅛ × 9¼. 24742-2 Pa. $14.95

ILLUSTRATED GUIDE TO SHAKER FURNITURE, Robert Meader. All furniture and appurtenances, with much on unknown local styles. 235 photos. 146pp. 9 × 12. 22819-3 Pa. $7.95

WHALE SHIPS AND WHALING: A Pictorial Survey, George Francis Dow. Over 200 vintage engravings, drawings, photographs of barks, brigs, cutters, other vessels. Also harpoons, lances, whaling guns, many other artifacts. Comprehensive text by foremost authority. 207 black-and-white illustrations. 288pp. 6 × 9.
24808-9 Pa. $8.95

THE BERTRAMS, Anthony Trollope. Powerful portrayal of blind self-will and thwarted ambition includes one of Trollope's most heartrending love stories. 497pp. 5⅜ × 8½. 25119-5 Pa. $8.95

ADVENTURES WITH A HAND LENS, Richard Headstrom. Clearly written guide to observing and studying flowers and grasses, fish scales, moth and insect wings, egg cases, buds, feathers, seeds, leaf scars, moss, molds, ferns, common crystals, etc.—all with an ordinary, inexpensive magnifying glass. 209 exact line drawings aid in your discoveries. 220pp. 5⅜ × 8½. 23330-8 Pa. $4.50

RODIN ON ART AND ARTISTS, Auguste Rodin. Great sculptor's candid, wide-ranging comments on meaning of art; great artists; relation of sculpture to poetry, painting, music; philosophy of life, more. 76 superb black-and-white illustrations of Rodin's sculpture, drawings and prints. 119pp. 8⅜ × 11¼. 24487-3 Pa. $6.95

FIFTY CLASSIC FRENCH FILMS, 1912–1982: A Pictorial Record, Anthony Slide. Memorable stills from Grand Illusion, Beauty and the Beast, Hiroshima, Mon Amour, many more. Credits, plot synopses, reviews, etc. 160pp. 8¼ × 11.
25256-6 Pa. $11.95

THE PRINCIPLES OF PSYCHOLOGY, William James. Famous long course complete, unabridged. Stream of thought, time perception, memory, experimental methods; great work decades ahead of its time. 94 figures. 1,391pp. 5⅜ × 8½.
20381-6, 20382-4 Pa., Two-vol. set $19.90

BODIES IN A BOOKSHOP, R. T. Campbell. Challenging mystery of blackmail and murder with ingenious plot and superbly drawn characters. In the best tradition of British suspense fiction. 192pp. 5⅜ × 8½. 24720-1 Pa. $3.95

CALLAS: PORTRAIT OF A PRIMA DONNA, George Jellinek. Renowned commentator on the musical scene chronicles incredible career and life of the most controversial, fascinating, influential operatic personality of our time. 64 black-and-white photographs. 416pp. 5⅜ × 8¼. 25047-4 Pa. $7.95

GEOMETRY, RELATIVITY AND THE FOURTH DIMENSION, Rudolph Rucker. Exposition of fourth dimension, concepts of relativity as Flatland characters continue adventures. Popular, easily followed yet accurate, profound. 141 illustrations. 133pp. 5⅜ × 8½. 23400-2 Pa. $3.50

HOUSEHOLD STORIES BY THE BROTHERS GRIMM, with pictures by Walter Crane. 53 classic stories—Rumpelstiltskin, Rapunzel, Hansel and Gretel, the Fisherman and his Wife, Snow White, Tom Thumb, Sleeping Beauty, Cinderella, and so much more—lavishly illustrated with original 19th century drawings. 114 illustrations. x + 269pp. 5⅜ × 8½. 21080-4 Pa. $4.50

SUNDIALS, Albert Waugh. Far and away the best, most thorough coverage of ideas, mathematics concerned, types, construction, adjusting anywhere. Over 100 illustrations. 230pp. 5⅜ × 8½. 22947-5 Pa. $4.50

PICTURE HISTORY OF THE NORMANDIE: With 190 Illustrations, Frank O. Braynard. Full story of legendary French ocean liner: Art Deco interiors, design innovations, furnishings, celebrities, maiden voyage, tragic fire, much more. Extensive text. 144pp. 8⅞ × 11¼. 25257-4 Pa. $9.95

THE FIRST AMERICAN COOKBOOK: A Facsimile of "American Cookery," 1796, Amelia Simmons. Facsimile of the first American-written cookbook published in the United States contains authentic recipes for colonial favorites—pumpkin pudding, winter squash pudding, spruce beer, Indian slapjacks, and more. Introductory Essay and Glossary of colonial cooking terms. 80pp. 5⅜ × 8½. 24710-4 Pa. $3.50

101 PUZZLES IN THOUGHT AND LOGIC, C. R. Wylie, Jr. Solve murders and robberies, find out which fishermen are liars, how a blind man could possibly identify a color—purely by your own reasoning! 107pp. 5⅜ × 8½. 20367-0 Pa. $2.50

THE BOOK OF WORLD-FAMOUS MUSIC—CLASSICAL, POPULAR AND FOLK, James J. Fuld. Revised and enlarged republication of landmark work in musico-bibliography. Full information about nearly 1,000 songs and compositions including first lines of music and lyrics. New supplement. Index. 800pp. 5⅜ × 8¼. 24857-7 Pa. $14.95

ANTHROPOLOGY AND MODERN LIFE, Franz Boas. Great anthropologist's classic treatise on race and culture. Introduction by Ruth Bunzel. Only inexpensive paperback edition. 255pp. 5⅜ × 8½. 25245-0 Pa. $5.95

THE TALE OF PETER RABBIT, Beatrix Potter. The inimitable Peter's terrifying adventure in Mr. McGregor's garden, with all 27 wonderful, full-color Potter illustrations. 55pp. 4¼ × 5½. (Available in U.S. only) 22827-4 Pa. $1.75

THREE PROPHETIC SCIENCE FICTION NOVELS, H. G. Wells. *When the Sleeper Wakes, A Story of the Days to Come* and *The Time Machine* (full version). 335pp. 5⅜ × 8½. (Available in U.S. only) 20605-X Pa. $5.95

APICIUS COOKERY AND DINING IN IMPERIAL ROME, edited and translated by Joseph Dommers Vehling. Oldest known cookbook in existence offers readers a clear picture of what foods Romans ate, how they prepared them, etc. 49 illustrations. 301pp. 6⅛ × 9¼. 23563-7 Pa. $6.50

SHAKESPEARE LEXICON AND QUOTATION DICTIONARY, Alexander Schmidt. Full definitions, locations, shades of meaning of every word in plays and poems. More than 50,000 exact quotations. 1,485pp. 6½ × 9¼. 22726-X, 22727-8 Pa., Two-vol. set $27.90

THE WORLD'S GREAT SPEECHES, edited by Lewis Copeland and Lawrence W. Lamm. Vast collection of 278 speeches from Greeks to 1970. Powerful and effective models; unique look at history. 842pp. 5⅜ × 8½. 20468-5 Pa. $11.95

THE BLUE FAIRY BOOK, Andrew Lang. The first, most famous collection, with many familiar tales: Little Red Riding Hood, Aladdin and the Wonderful Lamp, Puss in Boots, Sleeping Beauty, Hansel and Gretel, Rumpelstiltskin; 37 in all. 138 illustrations. 390pp. 5⅜ × 8½. 21437-0 Pa. $5.95

THE STORY OF THE CHAMPIONS OF THE ROUND TABLE, Howard Pyle. Sir Launcelot, Sir Tristram and Sir Percival in spirited adventures of love and triumph retold in Pyle's inimitable style. 50 drawings, 31 full-page. xviii + 329pp. 6½ × 9¼. 21883-X Pa. $6.95

AUDUBON AND HIS JOURNALS, Maria Audubon. Unmatched two-volume portrait of the great artist, naturalist and author contains his journals, an excellent biography by his granddaughter, expert annotations by the noted ornithologist, Dr. Elliott Coues, and 37 superb illustrations. Total of 1,200pp. 5⅜ × 8.
Vol. I 25143-8 Pa. $8.95
Vol. II 25144-6 Pa. $8.95

GREAT DINOSAUR HUNTERS AND THEIR DISCOVERIES, Edwin H. Colbert. Fascinating, lavishly illustrated chronicle of dinosaur research, 1820's to 1960. Achievements of Cope, Marsh, Brown, Buckland, Mantell, Huxley, many others. 384pp. 5¼ × 8¼. 24701-5 Pa. $6.95

THE TASTEMAKERS, Russell Lynes. Informal, illustrated social history of American taste 1850's-1950's. First popularized categories Highbrow, Lowbrow, Middlebrow. 129 illustrations. New (1979) afterword. 384pp. 6 × 9.
23993-4 Pa. $6.95

DOUBLE CROSS PURPOSES, Ronald A. Knox. A treasure hunt in the Scottish Highlands, an old map, unidentified corpse, surprise discoveries keep reader guessing in this cleverly intricate tale of financial skullduggery. 2 black-and-white maps. 320pp. 5⅜ × 8½. (Available in U.S. only) 25032-6 Pa. $5.95

AUTHENTIC VICTORIAN DECORATION AND ORNAMENTATION IN FULL COLOR: 46 Plates from "Studies in Design," Christopher Dresser. Superb full-color lithographs reproduced from rare original portfolio of a major Victorian designer. 48pp. 9¼ × 12¼. 25083-0 Pa. $7.95

PRIMITIVE ART, Franz Boas. Remains the best text ever prepared on subject, thoroughly discussing Indian, African, Asian, Australian, and, especially, Northern American primitive art. Over 950 illustrations show ceramics, masks, totem poles, weapons, textiles, paintings, much more. 376pp. 5⅜ × 8. 20025-6 Pa. $6.95

SIDELIGHTS ON RELATIVITY, Albert Einstein. Unabridged republication of two lectures delivered by the great physicist in 1920-21. *Ether and Relativity* and *Geometry and Experience*. Elegant ideas in non-mathematical form, accessible to intelligent layman. vi + 56pp. 5⅜ × 8½. 24511-X Pa. $2.95

THE WIT AND HUMOR OF OSCAR WILDE, edited by Alvin Redman. More than 1,000 ripostes, paradoxes, wisecracks: Work is the curse of the drinking classes, I can resist everything except temptation, etc. 258pp. 5⅜ × 8½. 20602-5 Pa. $4.50

ADVENTURES WITH A MICROSCOPE, Richard Headstrom. 59 adventures with clothing fibers, protozoa, ferns and lichens, roots and leaves, much more. 142 illustrations. 232pp. 5⅜ × 8½. 23471-1 Pa. $3.95

PLANTS OF THE BIBLE, Harold N. Moldenke and Alma L. Moldenke. Standard reference to all 230 plants mentioned in Scriptures. Latin name, biblical reference, uses, modern identity, much more. Unsurpassed encyclopedic resource for scholars, botanists, nature lovers, students of Bible. Bibliography. Indexes. 123 black-and-white illustrations. 384pp. 6 × 9. 25069-5 Pa. $8.95

FAMOUS AMERICAN WOMEN: A Biographical Dictionary from Colonial Times to the Present, Robert McHenry, ed. From Pocahontas to Rosa Parks, 1,035 distinguished American women documented in separate biographical entries. Accurate, up-to-date data, numerous categories, spans 400 years. Indices. 493pp. 6½ × 9¼. 24523-3 Pa. $9.95

THE FABULOUS INTERIORS OF THE GREAT OCEAN LINERS IN HISTORIC PHOTOGRAPHS, William H. Miller, Jr. Some 200 superb photographs capture exquisite interiors of world's great "floating palaces"—1890's to 1980's: *Titanic, Ile de France, Queen Elizabeth, United States, Europa,* more. Approx. 200 black-and-white photographs. Captions. Text. Introduction. 160pp. 8⅞ × 11¾. 24756-2 Pa. $9.95

THE GREAT LUXURY LINERS, 1927–1954: A Photographic Record, William H. Miller, Jr. Nostalgic tribute to heyday of ocean liners. 186 photos of Ile de France, Normandie, Leviathan, Queen Elizabeth, United States, many others. Interior and exterior views. Introduction. Captions. 160pp. 9 × 12. 24056-8 Pa. $9.95

A NATURAL HISTORY OF THE DUCKS, John Charles Phillips. Great landmark of ornithology offers complete detailed coverage of nearly 200 species and subspecies of ducks: gadwall, sheldrake, merganser, pintail, many more. 74 full-color plates, 102 black-and-white. Bibliography. Total of 1,920pp. 8⅝ × 11¼. 25141-1, 25142-X Cloth. Two-vol. set $100.00

THE SEAWEED HANDBOOK: An Illustrated Guide to Seaweeds from North Carolina to Canada, Thomas F. Lee. Concise reference covers 78 species. Scientific and common names, habitat, distribution, more. Finding keys for easy identification. 224pp. 5⅜ × 8½. 25215-9 Pa. $5.95

THE TEN BOOKS OF ARCHITECTURE: The 1755 Leoni Edition, Leon Battista Alberti. Rare classic helped introduce the glories of ancient architecture to the Renaissance. 68 black-and-white plates. 336pp. 8⅜ × 11¼. 25239-6 Pa. $14.95

MISS MACKENZIE, Anthony Trollope. Minor masterpieces by Victorian master unmasks many truths about life in 19th-century England. First inexpensive edition in years. 392pp. 5⅜ × 8½. 25201-9 Pa. $7.95

THE RIME OF THE ANCIENT MARINER, Gustave Doré, Samuel Taylor Coleridge. Dramatic engravings considered by many to be his greatest work. The terrifying space of the open sea, the storms and whirlpools of an unknown ocean, the ice of Antarctica, more—all rendered in a powerful, chilling manner. Full text. 38 plates. 77pp. 9¼ × 12. 22305-1 Pa. $4.95

THE EXPEDITIONS OF ZEBULON MONTGOMERY PIKE, Zebulon Montgomery Pike. Fascinating first-hand accounts (1805–6) of exploration of Mississippi River, Indian wars, capture by Spanish dragoons, much more. 1,088pp. 5⅜ × 8½. 25254-X, 25255-8 Pa. Two-vol. set $23.90

A CONCISE HISTORY OF PHOTOGRAPHY: Third Revised Edition, Helmut Gernsheim. Best one-volume history—camera obscura, photochemistry, daguerreotypes, evolution of cameras, film, more. Also artistic aspects—landscape, portraits, fine art, etc. 281 black-and-white photographs. 26 in color. 176pp. 8⅜ × 11¼. 25128-4 Pa. $12.95

THE DORÉ BIBLE ILLUSTRATIONS, Gustave Doré. 241 detailed plates from the Bible: the Creation scenes, Adam and Eve, Flood, Babylon, battle sequences, life of Jesus, etc. Each plate is accompanied by the verses from the King James version of the Bible. 241pp. 9 × 12. 23004-X Pa. $8.95

HUGGER-MUGGER IN THE LOUVRE, Elliot Paul. Second Homer Evans mystery-comedy. Theft at the Louvre involves sleuth in hilarious, madcap caper. "A knockout."—Books. 336pp. 5⅜ × 8½. 25185-3 Pa. $5.95

FLATLAND, E. A. Abbott. Intriguing and enormously popular science-fiction classic explores the complexities of trying to survive as a two-dimensional being in a three-dimensional world. Amusingly illustrated by the author. 16 illustrations. 103pp. 5⅜ × 8½. 20001-9 Pa. $2.25

THE HISTORY OF THE LEWIS AND CLARK EXPEDITION, Meriwether Lewis and William Clark, edited by Elliott Coues. Classic edition of Lewis and Clark's day-by-day journals that later became the basis for U.S. claims to Oregon and the West. Accurate and invaluable geographical, botanical, biological, meteorological and anthropological material. Total of 1,508pp. 5⅜ × 8½. 21268-8, 21269-6, 21270-X Pa. Three-vol. set $25.50

LANGUAGE, TRUTH AND LOGIC, Alfred J. Ayer. Famous, clear introduction to Vienna, Cambridge schools of Logical Positivism. Role of philosophy, elimination of metaphysics, nature of analysis, etc. 160pp. 5⅜ × 8½. (Available in U.S. and Canada only) 20010-8 Pa. $2.95

MATHEMATICS FOR THE NONMATHEMATICIAN, Morris Kline. Detailed, college-level treatment of mathematics in cultural and historical context, with numerous exercises. For liberal arts students. Preface. Recommended Reading Lists. Tables. Index. Numerous black-and-white figures. xvi + 641pp. 5⅜ × 8½. 24823-2 Pa. $11.95

28 SCIENCE FICTION STORIES, H. G. Wells. Novels, *Star Begotten* and *Men Like Gods*, plus 26 short stories: "Empire of the Ants," "A Story of the Stone Age," "The Stolen Bacillus," "In the Abyss," etc. 915pp. 5⅜ × 8½. (Available in U.S. only) 20265-8 Cloth. $10.95

HANDBOOK OF PICTORIAL SYMBOLS, Rudolph Modley. 3,250 signs and symbols, many systems in full; official or heavy commercial use. Arranged by subject. Most in Pictorial Archive series. 143pp. 8⅛ × 11. 23357-X Pa. $5.95

INCIDENTS OF TRAVEL IN YUCATAN, John L. Stephens. Classic (1843) exploration of jungles of Yucatan, looking for evidences of Maya civilization. Travel adventures, Mexican and Indian culture, etc. Total of 669pp. 5⅜ × 8½. 20926-1, 20927-X Pa., Two-vol. set $9.90

DEGAS: An Intimate Portrait, Ambroise Vollard. Charming, anecdotal memoir by famous art dealer of one of the greatest 19th-century French painters. 14 black-and-white illustrations. Introduction by Harold L. Van Doren. 96pp. 5⅜ × 8½.
25131-4 Pa. $3.95

PERSONAL NARRATIVE OF A PILGRIMAGE TO ALMANDINAH AND MECCAH, Richard Burton. Great travel classic by remarkably colorful personality. Burton, disguised as a Moroccan, visited sacred shrines of Islam, narrowly escaping death. 47 illustrations. 959pp. 5⅜ × 8½. 21217-3, 21218-1 Pa., Two-vol. set $17.90

PHRASE AND WORD ORIGINS, A. H. Holt. Entertaining, reliable, modern study of more than 1,200 colorful words, phrases, origins and histories. Much unexpected information. 254pp. 5⅜ × 8½. 20758-7 Pa. $5.95

THE RED THUMB MARK, R. Austin Freeman. In this first Dr. Thorndyke case, the great scientific detective draws fascinating conclusions from the nature of a single fingerprint. Exciting story, authentic science. 320pp. 5⅜ × 8½. (Available in U.S. only) 25210-8 Pa. $5.95

AN EGYPTIAN HIEROGLYPHIC DICTIONARY, E. A. Wallis Budge. Monumental work containing about 25,000 words or terms that occur in texts ranging from 3000 B.C. to 600 A.D. Each entry consists of a transliteration of the word, the word in hieroglyphs, and the meaning in English. 1,314pp. 6⅝ × 10.
23615-3, 23616-1 Pa., Two-vol. set $27.90

THE COMPLEAT STRATEGYST: Being a Primer on the Theory of Games of Strategy, J. D. Williams. Highly entertaining classic describes, with many illustrated examples, how to select best strategies in conflict situations. Prefaces. Appendices. xvi + 268pp. 5⅜ × 8½. 25101-2 Pa. $5.95

THE ROAD TO OZ, L. Frank Baum. Dorothy meets the Shaggy Man, little Button-Bright and the Rainbow's beautiful daughter in this delightful trip to the magical Land of Oz. 272pp. 5⅜ × 8. 25208-6 Pa. $4.95

POINT AND LINE TO PLANE, Wassily Kandinsky. Seminal exposition of role of point, line, other elements in non-objective painting. Essential to understanding 20th-century art. 127 illustrations. 192pp. 6½ × 9¼. 23808-3 Pa. $4.50

LADY ANNA, Anthony Trollope. Moving chronicle of Countess Lovel's bitter struggle to win for herself and daughter Anna their rightful rank and fortune—perhaps at cost of sanity itself. 384pp. 5⅜ × 8½. 24669-8 Pa. $6.95

EGYPTIAN MAGIC, E. A. Wallis Budge. Sums up all that is known about magic in Ancient Egypt: the role of magic in controlling the gods, powerful amulets that warded off evil spirits, scarabs of immortality, use of wax images, formulas and spells, the secret name, much more. 253pp. 5⅜ × 8½. 22681-6 Pa. $4.50

THE DANCE OF SIVA, Ananda Coomaraswamy. Preeminent authority unfolds the vast metaphysic of India: the revelation of her art, conception of the universe, social organization, etc. 27 reproductions of art masterpieces. 192pp. 5⅜ × 8½.
24817-8 Pa. $5.95

CHRISTMAS CUSTOMS AND TRADITIONS, Clement A. Miles. Origin, evolution, significance of religious, secular practices. Caroling, gifts, yule logs, much more. Full, scholarly yet fascinating; non-sectarian. 400pp. 5⅜ × 8½.
23354-5 Pa. $6.50

THE HUMAN FIGURE IN MOTION, Eadweard Muybridge. More than 4,500 stopped-action photos, in action series, showing undraped men, women, children jumping, lying down, throwing, sitting, wrestling, carrying, etc. 390pp. 7⅞ × 10⅝.
20204-6 Cloth. $19.95

THE MAN WHO WAS THURSDAY, Gilbert Keith Chesterton. Witty, fast-paced novel about a club of anarchists in turn-of-the-century London. Brilliant social, religious, philosophical speculations. 128pp. 5⅜ × 8½. 25121-7 Pa. $3.95

A CEZANNE SKETCHBOOK: Figures, Portraits, Landscapes and Still Lifes, Paul Cezanne. Great artist experiments with tonal effects, light, mass, other qualities in over 100 drawings. A revealing view of developing master painter, precursor of Cubism. 102 black-and-white illustrations. 144pp. 8¾ × 6⅝. 24790-2 Pa. $5.95

AN ENCYCLOPEDIA OF BATTLES: Accounts of Over 1,560 Battles from 1479 B.C. to the Present, David Eggenberger. Presents essential details of every major battle in recorded history, from the first battle of Megiddo in 1479 B.C. to Grenada in 1984. List of Battle Maps. New Appendix covering the years 1967–1984. Index. 99 illustrations. 544pp. 6½ × 9¼. 24913-1 Pa. $14.95

AN ETYMOLOGICAL DICTIONARY OF MODERN ENGLISH, Ernest Weekley. Richest, fullest work, by foremost British lexicographer. Detailed word histories. Inexhaustible. Total of 856pp. 6½ × 9¼.
21873-2, 21874-0 Pa., Two-vol. set $17.00

WEBSTER'S AMERICAN MILITARY BIOGRAPHIES, edited by Robert McHenry. Over 1,000 figures who shaped 3 centuries of American military history. Detailed biographies of Nathan Hale, Douglas MacArthur, Mary Hallaren, others. Chronologies of engagements, more. Introduction. Addenda. 1,033 entries in alphabetical order. xi + 548pp. 6½ × 9¼. (Available in U.S. only)
24758-9 Pa. $11.95

LIFE IN ANCIENT EGYPT, Adolf Erman. Detailed older account, with much not in more recent books: domestic life, religion, magic, medicine, commerce, and whatever else needed for complete picture. Many illustrations. 597pp. 5⅜ × 8½.
22632-8 Pa. $8.95

HISTORIC COSTUME IN PICTURES, Braun & Schneider. Over 1,450 costumed figures shown, covering a wide variety of peoples: kings, emperors, nobles, priests, servants, soldiers, scholars, townsfolk, peasants, merchants, courtiers, cavaliers, and more. 256pp. 8⅜ × 11¼. 23150-X Pa. $7.95

THE NOTEBOOKS OF LEONARDO DA VINCI, edited by J. P. Richter. Extracts from manuscripts reveal great genius; on painting, sculpture, anatomy, sciences, geography, etc. Both Italian and English. 186 ms. pages reproduced, plus 500 additional drawings, including studies for *Last Supper, Sforza* monument, etc. 860pp. 7⅞ × 10¾. (Available in U.S. only) 22572-0, 22573-9 Pa., Two-vol. set $25.90

THE ART NOUVEAU STYLE BOOK OF ALPHONSE MUCHA: All 72 Plates from "Documents Decoratifs" in Original Color, Alphonse Mucha. Rare copyright-free design portfolio by high priest of Art Nouveau. Jewelry, wallpaper, stained glass, furniture, figure studies, plant and animal motifs, etc. Only complete one-volume edition. 80pp. 9⅜ × 12¼. 24044-4 Pa. $8.95

ANIMALS: 1,419 COPYRIGHT-FREE ILLUSTRATIONS OF MAMMALS, BIRDS, FISH, INSECTS, ETC., edited by Jim Harter. Clear wood engravings present, in extremely lifelike poses, over 1,000 species of animals. One of the most extensive pictorial sourcebooks of its kind. Captions. Index. 284pp. 9 × 12. 23766-4 Pa. $9.95

OBELISTS FLY HIGH, C. Daly King. Masterpiece of American detective fiction, long out of print, involves murder on a 1935 transcontinental flight—"a very thrilling story"—NY Times. Unabridged and unaltered republication of the edition published by William Collins Sons & Co. Ltd., London, 1935. 288pp. 5⅜ × 8½. (Available in U.S. only) 25036-9 Pa. $4.95

VICTORIAN AND EDWARDIAN FASHION: A Photographic Survey, Alison Gernsheim. First fashion history completely illustrated by contemporary photographs. Full text plus 235 photos, 1840–1914, in which many celebrities appear. 240pp. 6½ × 9¼. 24205-6 Pa. $6.00

THE ART OF THE FRENCH ILLUSTRATED BOOK, 1700–1914, Gordon N. Ray. Over 630 superb book illustrations by Fragonard, Delacroix, Daumier, Doré, Grandville, Manet, Mucha, Steinlen, Toulouse-Lautrec and many others. Preface. Introduction. 633 halftones. Indices of artists, authors & titles, binders and provenances. Appendices. Bibliography. 608pp. 8⅜ × 11¼. 25086-5 Pa. $24.95

THE WONDERFUL WIZARD OF OZ, L. Frank Baum. Facsimile in full color of America's finest children's classic. 143 illustrations by W. W. Denslow. 267pp. 5⅜ × 8½. 20691-2 Pa. $5.95

FRONTIERS OF MODERN PHYSICS: New Perspectives on Cosmology, Relativity, Black Holes and Extraterrestrial Intelligence, Tony Rothman, et al. For the intelligent layman. Subjects include: cosmological models of the universe; black holes; the neutrino; the search for extraterrestrial intelligence. Introduction. 46 black-and-white illustrations. 192pp. 5⅜ × 8½. 24587-X Pa. $6.95

THE FRIENDLY STARS, Martha Evans Martin & Donald Howard Menzel. Classic text marshalls the stars together in an engaging, non-technical survey, presenting them as sources of beauty in night sky. 23 illustrations. Foreword. 2 star charts. Index. 147pp. 5⅜ × 8½. 21099-5 Pa. $3.50

FADS AND FALLACIES IN THE NAME OF SCIENCE, Martin Gardner. Fair, witty appraisal of cranks, quacks, and quackeries of science and pseudoscience: hollow earth, Velikovsky, orgone energy, Dianetics, flying saucers, Bridey Murphy, food and medical fads, etc. Revised, expanded In the Name of Science. "A very able and even-tempered presentation."—The New Yorker. 363pp. 5⅜ × 8. 20394-8 Pa. $6.50

ANCIENT EGYPT: ITS CULTURE AND HISTORY, J. E Manchip White. From pre-dynastics through Ptolemies: society, history, political structure, religion, daily life, literature, cultural heritage. 48 plates. 217pp. 5⅜ × 8½. 22548-8 Pa. $4.95

SIR HARRY HOTSPUR OF HUMBLETHWAITE, Anthony Trollope. Incisive, unconventional psychological study of a conflict between a wealthy baronet, his idealistic daughter, and their scapegrace cousin. The 1870 novel in its first inexpensive edition in years. 250pp. 5⅜ × 8½. 24953-0 Pa. $5.95

LASERS AND HOLOGRAPHY, Winston E. Kock. Sound introduction to burgeoning field, expanded (1981) for second edition. Wave patterns, coherence, lasers, diffraction, zone plates, properties of holograms, recent advances. 84 illustrations. 160pp. 5⅜ × 8¼. (Except in United Kingdom) 24041-X Pa. $3.50

INTRODUCTION TO ARTIFICIAL INTELLIGENCE: SECOND, EN-LARGED EDITION, Philip C. Jackson, Jr. Comprehensive survey of artificial intelligence—the study of how machines (computers) can be made to act intelligently. Includes introductory and advanced material. Extensive notes updating the main text. 132 black-and-white illustrations. 512pp. 5⅜ × 8½. 24864-X Pa. $8.95

HISTORY OF INDIAN AND INDONESIAN ART, Ananda K. Coomaraswamy. Over 400 illustrations illuminate classic study of Indian art from earliest Harappa finds to early 20th century. Provides philosophical, religious and social insights. 304pp. 6⅜ × 9⅜. 25005-9 Pa. $8.95

THE GOLEM, Gustav Meyrink. Most famous supernatural novel in modern European literature, set in Ghetto of Old Prague around 1890. Compelling story of mystical experiences, strange transformations, profound terror. 13 black-and-white illustrations. 224pp. 5⅜ × 8½. (Available in U.S. only) 25025-3 Pa. $5.95

ARMADALE, Wilkie Collins. Third great mystery novel by the author of *The Woman in White* and *The Moonstone*. Original magazine version with 40 illustrations. 597pp. 5⅜ × 8½. 23429-0 Pa. $9.95

PICTORIAL ENCYCLOPEDIA OF HISTORIC ARCHITECTURAL PLANS, DETAILS AND ELEMENTS: With 1,880 Line Drawings of Arches, Domes, Doorways, Facades, Gables, Windows, etc., John Theodore Haneman. Sourcebook of inspiration for architects, designers, others. Bibliography. Captions. 141pp. 9 × 12. 24605-1 Pa. $6.95

BENCHLEY LOST AND FOUND, Robert Benchley. Finest humor from early 30's, about pet peeves, child psychologists, post office and others. Mostly unavailable elsewhere. 73 illustrations by Peter Arno and others. 183pp. 5⅜ × 8½. 22410-4 Pa. $3.95

ERTÉ GRAPHICS, Erté. Collection of striking color graphics: *Seasons, Alphabet, Numerals, Aces* and *Precious Stones*. 50 plates, including 4 on covers. 48pp. 9⅜ × 12¼. 23580-7 Pa. $6.95

THE JOURNAL OF HENRY D. THOREAU, edited by Bradford Torrey, F. H. Allen. Complete reprinting of 14 volumes, 1837–61, over two million words; the sourcebooks for *Walden*, etc. Definitive. All original sketches, plus 75 photographs. 1,804pp. 8½ × 12¼. 20312-3, 20313-1 Cloth., Two-vol. set $80.00

CASTLES: THEIR CONSTRUCTION AND HISTORY, Sidney Toy. Traces castle development from ancient roots. Nearly 200 photographs and drawings illustrate moats, keeps, baileys, many other features. Caernarvon, Dover Castles, Hadrian's Wall, Tower of London, dozens more. 256pp. 5⅜ × 8¼. 24898-4 Pa. $5.95

CATALOG OF DOVER BOOKS

AMERICAN CLIPPER SHIPS: 1833–1858, Octavius T. Howe & Frederick C. Matthews. Fully-illustrated, encyclopedic review of 352 clipper ships from the period of America's greatest maritime supremacy. Introduction. 109 halftones. 5 black-and-white line illustrations. Index. Total of 928pp. 5⅜ × 8½.
25115-2, 25116-0 Pa., Two-vol. set $17.90

TOWARDS A NEW ARCHITECTURE, Le Corbusier. Pioneering manifesto by great architect, near legendary founder of "International School." Technical and aesthetic theories, views on industry, economics, relation of form to function, "mass-production spirit," much more. Profusely illustrated. Unabridged translation of 13th French edition. Introduction by Frederick Etchells. 320pp. 6⅛ × 9¼. (Available in U.S. only)
25023-7 Pa. $8.95

THE BOOK OF KELLS, edited by Blanche Cirker. Inexpensive collection of 32 full-color, full-page plates from the greatest illuminated manuscript of the Middle Ages, painstakingly reproduced from rare facsimile edition. Publisher's Note. Captions. 32pp. 9⅜ × 12¼.
24345-1 Pa. $4.95

BEST SCIENCE FICTION STORIES OF H. G. WELLS, H. G. Wells. Full novel *The Invisible Man*, plus 17 short stories: "The Crystal Egg," "Aepyornis Island," "The Strange Orchid," etc. 303pp. 5⅜ × 8½. (Available in U.S. only)
21531-8 Pa. $4.95

AMERICAN SAILING SHIPS: Their Plans and History, Charles G. Davis. Photos, construction details of schooners, frigates, clippers, other sailcraft of 18th to early 20th centuries—plus entertaining discourse on design, rigging, nautical lore, much more. 137 black-and-white illustrations. 240pp. 6⅛ × 9¼.
24658-2 Pa. $5.95

ENTERTAINING MATHEMATICAL PUZZLES, Martin Gardner. Selection of author's favorite conundrums involving arithmetic, money, speed, etc., with lively commentary. Complete solutions. 112pp. 5⅜ × 8½.
25211-6 Pa. $2.95

THE WILL TO BELIEVE, HUMAN IMMORTALITY, William James. Two books bound together. Effect of irrational on logical, and arguments for human immortality. 402pp. 5⅜ × 8½.
20291-7 Pa. $7.50

THE HAUNTED MONASTERY and THE CHINESE MAZE MURDERS. Robert Van Gulik. 2 full novels by Van Gulik continue adventures of Judge Dee and his companions. An evil Taoist monastery, seemingly supernatural events; overgrown topiary maze that hides strange crimes. Set in 7th-century China. 27 illustrations. 328pp. 5⅜ × 8½.
23502-5 Pa. $5.95

CELEBRATED CASES OF JUDGE DEE (DEE GOONG AN), translated by Robert Van Gulik. Authentic 18th-century Chinese detective novel; Dee and associates solve three interlocked cases. Led to Van Gulik's own stories with same characters. Extensive introduction. 9 illustrations. 237pp. 5⅜ × 8½.
23337-5 Pa. $4.95

Prices subject to change without notice.
Available at your book dealer or write for free catalog to Dept. GI, Dover Publications, Inc., 31 East 2nd St., Mineola, N.Y. 11501. Dover publishes more than 175 books each year on science, elementary and advanced mathematics, biology, music, art, literary history, social sciences and other areas.